HOW TO
SUCCEED
IN THE
INCREDIBLE ICE
CREAM
BUSINESS

D1250501

HOW TO SUCCEED
IN THE INCREDIBLE ICE CREAM
BUSINESS

MALCOLM STOGO

MALCOLM STOGO ASSOCIATES
12 RIVERPOINTE ROAD

HASTINGS-ON-HUDSON, NEW YORK 10706
TEL:1-914-478-0610 - FAX: 1-914-231-5623
E-MAIL: MSTOGO@AOL.COM
WEBSITE: www.malcolmstogo.com - www.icecreamuniversity.org

Library of Congress Cataloging-in-Publication Data:
Stogo, Malcolm
    HOW TO SUCCEED IN THE INCREDIBLE ICE CREAM BUSINESS / Malcolm Stogo

    Includes bibliographical references and index. 276 pages

ISBN 0-9712703-0-9 (spiral bound)
Printed in the United States of America, 2001

CONTENTS

PREFACE

Being in the ice cream business is all about passion. It's an incredible, fun way to spend one's professional life. Because it is such a fun business, it can turn the most uncreative person into one who spends almost every waking moment thinking about ways to make the business a blast. Becoming successful at it is a matter of both common sense and always putting yourself into the customers' shoes. So if you keep these two synergies always on your mind, I can assure you, you will do well.

The idea for this book comes out of what I have learned and written about in my newsletters, *Batch Freezer News* and *Ice Cream Store News*. Simply put, the newsletters have inspired me to really dwell on what I think is important about succeeding in this business and how to get there. This book is also about how to keep improving on all the ways to produce, present and sell high quality, freshly made ice cream to the consuming public. The book has been exclusively written as an everyday tool for anyone who is actively trying to get an ice cream concept off the ground and for those who really want to improve their current operation. The first part of this book deals with getting started, answers to questions on how to write a business plan and find a location- probably the three most important aspects one must concentrate on in the beginning as one develops the concept from one's mind to a piece of paper. The second part is a series of 200 new recipes that have not appeared in any of my other books.

This book is also an outgrowth of my third book, ICE CREAM and Frozen Desserts, *A Commercial Guide to Production and Marketing.* It is, in a sense, an addendum, but it is also an entirely new text that includes new chapters that emphasize the retail store part of this business. As I have said in all of my previous books, if there is one message I can offer you on how to achieve success in this industry, it is that it takes hard work, good common sense, passion for what you are doing, and finally, you must be willing to listen and learn from others. Luck does play a part, but it finds you, you can't seek it out.

This book is intended for only those individuals who have passion for getting into this business. If you don't have it now, stop the process and look elsewhere. It is simply the best advice I could ever offer you.

ACKNOWLEDGMENTS

This book has been a labor of love. It's been fun to write, fun because I have seen and learned so much during the last three years writing my two newsletters, *Batch Freezer News* and *Ice Cream Store News* as well as conducting successful ice cream seminars. Yes, it's truly amazing that there is always so much to learn.

While I have written this book, the book is really a combination of many thoughts from many different people in this incredible business.

So, let's start from the beginning. My parents, Philip and Rose Stogo taught me early on about cooking beginning at age eight. Watching my mom throw in a little of this and a little of that has been my trademark. In other words, don't be afraid to experiment.

For anyone who knows me, you know that Bill and Sally Lambert are a big part of my life. Bill is my partner, mentor and friend. He is also the most knowledgeable ice cream person I know, so when I say thank you, Bill and Sally, it's really deep down from the bottom of my heart.

In every one of my books I have thanked my daughter, Emily, who at the age of six cracked the eggs that were used in the first ice cream I ever produced and sold. She is now a grown woman with a daughter of her own.

I thank my seminar team leaders, Marc Boccaccio and Robert Ellinger for being such terrific teachers and keeping me informed on what's really happening in our retail ice cream industry. Lisa Tanner, my co-author of ICE CREAM CAKES and our seminar cake instructor. Thank you Lisa, you are the best!

My pal, Tony Lana. He is my secret weapon. We talk almost every week about ice cream and when I need an answer fast, it's an easy telephone call to Long Island.

Steve Thompson of Emery Thompson has been my one man booster for many years.

A very special thank you to Umberto and Nicola Fabbri of Fabbri, Bologna, Italy and their representatives in the USA, Bob Bruno and John Yodice of Belizio Fine Foods and Gino Cocchi of Carpigiani Group, Bologna, Italy for their wonderful support in sponsoring our successful

Gelato Trips To Italy and making them an incredible learning experience for everyone.

Thank you Moe Berman and Dan Culhane for designing the wonderful cover for this book. You really take the fun aspect of ice cream to new heights!

A special thanks goes to all of my consulting clients like Ben Silloway who gave me my first consulting contract at Haagen-Dazs, Fahad Dawaish of Mafad Trading Company (Cone Zone) of Saudi Arabia who was my first international client, and Jerry Siegel of Haagen-Daz who has accepted my advice for over 15 years even though he had doubts about some of my suggestions some of the time. To these three clients and many more, I thank you for adding to my growth and success in this incredible ice cream business.

But the best thanks of all goes to Carole Gordon. Frankly speaking, I didn't intend to write this book, but meeting, falling in love and marrying her has brought incredible happiness into my life. This happiness gave me the spark to write this book and that's just the beginning. She single-handedly edited every page at some of the strangest hours of the day and night. This great love with Carole doesn't stop there. Early on, I knew I had a winner when I asked her during our first trip to Italy what Nocciola was. When she said "hazelnut," I simply smiled and said to myself, "Malcolm, you finally did it. You have found happiness. You now have the fun back in your life." So, it's now my turn to tell you all: Have fun in this business. Life is too short. Enjoy it and good luck!

CHAPTER 1
THE IDEA & THE PASSION FOR IT
Emerson said "Nothing great was ever achieved without enthusiasm."

STARTING A NEW BUSINESS

It's like taking a roller coaster ride and not knowing when it will stop. It's like getting married, what a ride. Opening a new business is exhilarating, exciting and exhausting, so if you are not ready for some rocky bumps along the way, you should simply not get involved.

I am constantly being called upon to give advice from many that have wanted to start their own ice cream business. In many cases, I've discovered incredible enthusiasm and an equally naive approach to what it takes to really get into it.

Are all these people wrong in their behavior? Not really, unless they have been through the experience before and should know better. I know because I have been one of the biggest culprits of this "being in one's own business mentality." I've been there more than once, so I speak from experience, but since I am now much older and hopefully, wiser, I now know better. But if I know one thing, having an idea is one thing, but having the passion for that idea is something else all together. So let's connect the two: the idea and the passion for it.

IDEA

All of us go through life having ideas of doing this or doing that. When it comes to the ice cream retail business, the original idea usually comes from simply the love of eating ice cream. While it might be love, the idea of actually wanting to be in the business must come with passion. And I mean plenty of passion. Ideas evolve, so if you are not exactly sure, you do have time to get your ideas down pat. And simply, the best way is to write a business plan. It will help you think out your ideas.

My First Ice Cream Idea

In 1976, my original idea for getting into this business basically came through the back door. While in the restaurant business in Philadelphia, the ice cream store next to my restaurant went out of business leaving a huge vacuum in the neighborhood for anyone wanting to buy an ice cream cone. Since the restaurant was unique in its own, I simply said to myself, "why don't we start making our own ice cream and sell it in the restaurant?" And that's exactly what we did. In 24 hours, we purchased a White Mountain ice cream machine using rock salt and ice, bought a couple of ice cream recipe books, and started experimenting. Within one week, we created our French custard ice cream mix recipe. The next step was creating flavors. We were clueless on how to get ingredients so we simply went to the supermarket and bought right off the shelf. I am proud to say if we weren't the first, we came very close to being the originators of Cookies and Cream, Milky Way, and Snickers ice cream. My ice cream was called <u>Malcolm's Natural</u>. Within two months we sold our first ice cream in pints to local gourmet shops using white paperboard containers with hand written labels (just like what Chinese restaurants use today for take-out orders).

PASSION

What is passion? Webster's Dictionary defines passion as "intense desire or being emotional about something." Well, both definitions are right, but to me passion is simply loving what I am doing and doing it all the time. While passion is the desire, carrying out that passion is hard work, thinking and creating, and when all is said and done, looking back and feeling very proud.

GETTING THE IDEA OFF THE GROUND

While one must have passion, getting the idea off the ground requires a lot more. So let's talk about what it takes to get your idea off the ground and the reasons for doing your idea in the first place.

- ***Making money***: In most cases, the driving force behind any idea is making money. We all want to make money and if you start your business right, believe me, you will. Think long term and it will come to you naturally. If you think for one minute that you will be rich the first year, you are going down the wrong road here. It simply won't happen! But, I will tell you one thing: the first winter after your first selling season is over is always the hardest. While you might have thought you made money that first season, it's the outstanding invoices to be paid to suppliers, the IRS and your landlord in the fall and winter that is the biggest surprise to most people starting out. Another reason many don't make money the first few years is the low prices beginners in this business charge for their products versus the <u>real</u> cost of those products.

- **Sense of accomplishment:** In all the years I have been in this business, I think "being proud of what I have accomplished" is the driving force behind my success, and it will make you successful. Standing outside your shop looking up at your sign and shop entrance two or three years down the line will absolutely bring a smile to your face. Believe me, I have seen it myself and with others like Maraline Olson of Screamin Mimi's*, in California, who spent two years researching her way through the SBA funding process; Gary Hunter of Lemon Quench*, North Carolina, who spent seven years working 12 hours a day, six days a week getting his frozen lemon slush into the theme parks around Charlotte; Chris Farrel of The Inside Scoop* in Trumbull, Connecticut, who, in three years, went from knowing nothing about ice cream creating to two stores, a growing wholesale business, and in the year 2000 was voted one of the top three ice creams in the state, Sloan Kamenstein of Sloan's* in West Palm Beach, Florida; who had an idea that being outrageous in the quality of product and selling non ice cream related items would make his store the rage of Florida, and Marc Boccaccio of Fresco Famous Italian Ices*, East Northport, New York who, along with his dad Tony, slaved away for 15 years growing a water ice business that is now the benchmark of every water ice business in New York.

- **Being your own boss:** Everyone wants to be his/her own boss when first starting out but rarely does anyone talk about it once in business. They just do what they have to do without asking anyone for permission. You simply have to make sure you have the cash to back up whatever you want to do because remember, the buck starts and stops with you! Just ask Mike and Erin Shindell of Durango Creamery*, Durango, Colorado, who left a high paying technology career in New York to move the whole family to Durango; David Spatafore of Mootime Creamery* of Coronado Beach, California, who got tired of flying 30 weeks a year all over the country; or Stan and Denise Zafran of Denise's Ice Cream* in Somerville, Massachusetts, both of whom worked for large corporations and hated every minute of it.

- **The challenge:** One challenge is getting up the nerve to even think about opening a business. But the real challenge starts the day you sign the lease and make some decisions on your own. There is no question about it, almost everyone I know who has opened for business was nervous doing it. And the closer one gets to opening the store, the higher the stress level gets. One word of advice here is to seek out a mentor to hold your hand. He/she has the experience to give you solid advice. And once you are open, rely on that mentor even more. Anyone who thinks he/she knows everything after six months is a fool. But strangely, I must admit many of my clients over the years thought they were experts in six months until they hit their first winter. As in any business, a little bit of knowledge is dangerous. So be honest with yourself and never stop learning.

BECOMING AN ENTREPRENEUR

What does it take to become an entrepreneur? Or more important, what must one do to make the transition from an idea of today to a success story of tomorrow? And how do you weather the ups and downs of developing the next concept of tomorrow?

While nothing is set in stone, there are a number of things we all do. We all talk to everyone we know about the idea. We go on and on about it to family, friends, and others, even strangers. We end up talking about it until we have pushed everyone we know to the point of exasperation.

Once we get there everyone congratulates us and tells us how smart we are. What they don't know is what it really took inside us mentally to get there. They don't know what it's like to wake up in the middle of the night realizing that we are no longer receiving the security of a paycheck. Panic sets in. That's when we know we have officially jumped onto the entrepreneurial seesaw. Here are a few tips to help you make the ride a little easier:

- Don't lose your balance. Stay focused on your vision.
- Remember that you are not alone. Establish a rapport with someone you trust who you can talk to frequently and will be objective with you.
- Schedule time away and renew your thought process, especially in

4

times when stress is hitting you the most.

- Turn "downs" into "ups" early on. Don't let problems linger.
- Maintain a healthy sense of humor.
- Attitude is everything.

Malcolm's Rules

Here are some simple common sense **"Malcolm Rules"** that will greatly increase your chances for success:

- *Enthusiasm:* If you don't have it now, you will never have it. It's also called "passion." It's a simple yes or no. If you don't have it, start looking elsewhere. Also, a word of advice: don't try to oversell your enthusiasm to your family, associates or friends. In many cases, they won't get it, but if you believe in it, stick to your guns. And use the writing of your business plan to prove yourself right or wrong.

- *Sense of concept or mental image before you spend one cent:* That's right, don't spend a cent until you have agreed on two things- passion and location.

- *You need to have money:* If you don't have the capitalization to properly launch your concept and <u>survive the first winter</u>, you should put off your idea now! Don't think for one second that you can depend on your capitalization from the receipts of your first selling season. Another fatal mistake is underestimating the cost of construction. So when you do your business plan, plug in an extra 25% both for leasehold improvements and equipment.

- *Run as fast as you can from a cheap location rent:* This is one of the most fatal mistakes new people make in launching their idea. A lot of it has to do with how much capital they have to spend. The greatest advice I can give is that a cheap secondary location is the single biggest reason for "business failure."

- *Write a business plan to sell yourself on the idea:* This is one smart idea. Doing it yourself will sell you on the merits of the idea and make you think real hard whether your idea is a good one. Believe me, writing a business plan takes time and if you do it right you will have to answer a zillion questions and it will force you to go and ask outsiders for many of the answers regarding the ice cream business. The plan will also increase or decrease your passion for this idea because every question will test your resolve especially when you find out how much money you really need to get into this business with your idea.

- ***Never open in the dead of winter:*** Yes, you will get the wrinkles out of the concept, but the flip side is that it's depressing trying to sell ice cream when it's 10 degrees outside. Even worse, the cash drain of paying rent, utilities, labor, and ingredients, is too severe for most. So, trust me, the best time to open is March or April for most of the country and October in Florida.

- ***Once in business, pay your taxes on time:*** The problem here is that once the summer is over, there is a tendency to use tax money for other things. It's a bad habit that will doom you.

- ***Cheaply made products usually result in customer complaints:*** Customers understand quality, so putting your best foot forward when you open for business is an absolute **"Malcolm Rule."** It's hard to explain but over the years I have learned that the difference between using high quality ingredients and cheaper ones is not that great, no more then 10%. So, if you are making your own ice cream and selling it yourself, this increase in cost is not that great when figuring out the cost of an ice cream cone.

- ***Build your business as a "repeat business":*** If you keep the word "repeat" on your brain, you will get your customers coming back to you over and over again. If you have a business in a residential location, besides location and product quality, there is nothing more important then working on ideas to get customers to come back again and again. And the best way to get them back is excellent customer service.

- ***Don't spend all your money on designing and building a Taj Mahal:*** Simple reasoning here. Don't get carried away or worse, don't let your architect have an open checkbook. You need some cash to buy ingredients, pay your employees, etc. If you do a clean build-out, you will make it easy for your customers to understand your concept. Being fancy is totally unnecessary.

- ***Don't sell your ice cream by weight:*** Remember, you are in the entertainment business, not the food business. Your shop should be a fun place, and the best way to be outrageous is to offer large size ice cream cones. Customers probably won't eat all the ice cream in the cone, but they love to look at the size of it, and they will tell everyone they know about it. So, if you make your own ice cream, you have the flexibility in profit margins to offer a large size cone.

CHAPTER 2
THE BUSINESS PLAN: GETTING THE MONEY
"Nine to five ain't taking me where I'm bound."
--Neil Diamond, from "Thank the Lord for the Nighttime"

That's right, going into business is not a nine-to-five job, believe me! And if you think you can go into business without researching and writing a business plan, you should have your head examined. Simply put, a business plan is essential to success. Without a well thought-out plan, you will be doomed to failure.

KNOW YOUR POTENTIAL BUSINESS
Too many people enter the ice cream business knowing little or nothing about the creative and business-side of the business. Why? Because in their hurry to get into business, they simply think they can learn everything from an equipment salesman, ingredient manufacturer, or tidbits from people already in business. Even worse, they purchase a book like one of mine and think just reading it will get them into business. Don't get me wrong, my book, **ICE CREAM and Frozen Desserts,** is a fabulous resource, but it's not an end-all to learning everything; it's just the beginning.

Learning everything means exploring many different paths. In short, these include:

- ***Don't start your business until you know it from the ground up:*** I mean this literally. Planning to go into the ice cream retail business should take no less then 18 months of research, writing a business plan, signing a lease and constructing a store.
- ***Work in an ice cream store for a few months, ask a million questions and learn to do everything:*** This is especially good for young people. It is an easy thing to do because while going to school, working during the summer months in the height of the season will expose you to everything about the business.
- ***Visiting as many ice cream stores as you can will illustrate to you the plus side and minus side of each:*** This is where good common sense comes into play and your love of the idea will really

stand out. During this exercise, you will taste good as well as bad products. You will see stores with outstanding design features and ones that look very tacky, employees who offer great customer service and ones who are rude and sloppy. After each visit, if possible, take a picture of the store inside and out and write down everything you observed. These notes will become invaluable when writing your business plan.

- *Go to a seminar that will teach you the ropes:* Seminars are the best way to learn hands-on how to operate an ice cream store and produce great ice cream products. Because they are short in length, the intensity of each will make you keenly aware of whether you think you have a good idea or not.
- *Reading as many books on the subject:* A book is a resource that you should use as you advance through the process of deciding to go into business. It is not an end-all. It will help you immensely when writing a business plan.

When you have done all of the above, you are now ready to start thinking about the next step: writing the business plan. But before you start, I have a fundamental question to ask you:

Does the location in which you want to open your store need an ice cream store and will the people pay for the ice cream products you want to sell?

THE BUSINESS PLAN

Everyone writes a business plan, but frankly for the wrong reasons. In most cases, the reason is to borrow money from a bank. How naive we are! Banks don't lend money to new businesses, and even if they were slightly willing to do so, the requirements are such that you will have to mortgage your life to get the loan, unless you can get a Small Business Administration (SBA) loan.

What your business plan should really be about is pouring out your heart and soul about why you want to open this business.

In reality, most of the money will come from your pocket, from your family and/or friends, or from a business partner, not from a bank. So the business plan is defining the following:

- What you want to accomplish
- How you are going to get there
- What it will cost

Before you even begin to write your business plan, go to a bookstore and purchase a book on business plans. That book plus everything you read here will help you immensely in the actual writing of your business plan.

A business plan that makes any kind of sense must be your thoughts, your words, and your findings of the following:

- *A resume that will demonstrate your business sense:* Let's be frank. If you are going to write a resume for your business plan, it better be one that shows you have the skills and experience to interest others like a bank or outside investors in investing in your idea. Keep the resume short, concise, with lots of bullet points of your accomplishments. When it comes right down to it, few people will part with their money unless they have a positive feeling about you as a person. In short, they want to like you and feel they can trust you. Open up the resume with a mission statement of who you are, what you have done, and what you want to do in the future. The future of course is your idea "right now."

- *A detailed personal financial statement:* It should be up-to-date and accurate. Remember that once you give someone your social security number, any credit check that is done on you will show everything. So be truthful and concise.

- *An honest and convincing description of your proposed business or idea:* Some of you will say, Why bother to write it down? I know how to operate. And besides, I am in no hurry to prepare my loan application to the bank or SBA. Let me tell you from hard, personal experience that you need a foundation document to refer to. If you don't have one, you are too likely to forget your good plans in the heat of getting your business underway. Take your time writing this. <u>Make sure the first and last paragraph of this description is one that will interest others in your idea immediately</u>.

- *A profit and loss projection and cash flow estimate for your new business in a form understandable to banks:* To a bank, besides the initial written introduction of your business plan, this is the most important element they will consider. They understand numbers. Let's face it, doing a projection and cash flow statement can be a stab in the dark because frankly for a newcomer knowing nothing, how can you know whether your business idea will be profitable before you do it? The honest answer is, you can't. This essential fact makes business scary. It also makes it fun. Just because you can't be sure you will make money, doesn't mean you should throw up your hands and ignore the whole problem. You can and should make some educated guesses. You can and should make some SWAGS ("Scientific Wild A-s Guesses"). The fun part is making these guesses come true.

The best way to make a SWAG about your business profitability is to divide it into the following three components:

Sales volume component: Based on the industry average throughout the United States, the average yearly sales numbers are as follows:

- Neighborhood ice cream stores do approximately $200,000 a year in business.
- Stores in suburban indoor shopping centers in a food court do approximately $250,000-350,000 a year.
- Stores in high-traffic urban, indoor malls, in a food court, do approximately $350,000-750,000 a year.
- Stores in urban high-traffic street locations do approximately $450,000-750,000 a year.

If your sales projection is not at least $200,000-250,000 a year and your bottom line is not at least 20-25% cash flow positive, you should forget about this idea immediately.

In your business plan, it is important to break down your sales projection for a given year. Following is an example of a neighborhood store doing $250,000 in annual sales ($20,833 per month):

Jan.	75% off the average monthly sales projection	$5,208
Feb.	50% off the average monthly sales projection	10,417
March	20% off the average monthly sales projection	16,666
April	5% above average monthly sales projection	22,136
May	25% above the average monthly sales projection	26,041
June	75% above the average monthly sales projection	36,457
July	100% above the average monthly sales projection	41,666
Aug.	75% above the average monthly sales projection	36,457
Sept.	10% above the average monthly sales projection	22,916
Oct.	35% off the average monthly sales projection	13,414
Nov.	35% off the average monthly sales projection	13,414
Dec.	75% off the average monthly sales projection	5,208
TOTAL		$250,000

Variable costs component: The variable cost component is the cost of your ingredients or products that are directly related to a sale to a customer. The following example breaks down the cost of making a batch of ice cream and how it translates to a specific customer's sale.

Costing an Ice Cream Batch

Very few operators really know what their ice cream costs are for setting a retail price for a cone or a 2 1/2 tub, wholesale. In many respects, it's a guessing game of setting a price that is on par or below the competition, resulting in a false sense of whether their business is going to be profitable or not. In my opinion, following this route is going down a road to disaster. If you want to be really smart about pricing your ice cream, use the below example as a gauge and substitute your costs in its place. You will be amazed at what you will find.

VANILLA ICE CREAM

2 1/2 Gals.	ice cream mix at $6.92 per gal.	= $17.30
4 Ozs.	2x vanilla extract at $47.40 gal.	= 1.48
10 Ozs.	pasteurized egg yolks at $45.93 for 30 lbs. =	.96
TOTAL		$19.74

Note: The above pricing example is done by weight, not fluid ounces.
Total production-376 ozs. - 5% Loss factor- 357 ozs. - $19.74
Divided by 376 ozs. = 5.25 cents

5.25 cents per ounce x 5 ounce serving =	26.25 cents
Cone and Napkin (per serving)-	6 cents
Total Cost Per Serving-	31.25 cents
Food Cost = 63 servings per batch x 31.25 =	$19.74
Cone and Napkin	3.78
TOTAL FOOD COST=	$23.52

Price of Ice Cream Cone-(Ret.)- $2.00 - $2.00 x 63 servings- $126.00
Divided by $23.52 (fd. cost) = 18.7%.   Gross profit is $102.48
(Total sales per batch = $126 less food cost of $23.52 = $102.48.)

Fixed costs component: Fixed costs are those costs that are fairly constant from month to month. These include:

Rent:	not to exceed 15% of sales
Wages:	not to exceed 25% of sales
Utilities:	not to exceed 3% of sales
Advertising:	not to exceed 3% of sales
Telephone:	not to exceed 1/2% of sales
Insurance:	not to exceed 3% of sales
Acct/legal:	not to exceed 1% of sales

PROFORMA FINANCIAL PROFIT & LOSS STATEMENT

WEEKLY SALES	7,692	6,731	5,769	5,288	4,800	4,322	3,846	3,365
DAILY SALES	1,099	962	824	755	687	618	549	481
TOTAL SALES	$400,000	350,000	300,000	275,000	250,000	225,000	200,000	175,000
RENT	48,000	48,000	48,000	48,000	48,000	48,000	48,000	48,000
RENT-COMMON	4,800	4,800	4,800	4,800	4,800	4,800	4,800	4,800
PAYROLL MGR.	35,000	35,000	30,000	25,000	25,000	25,000	25,000	25,000
PAYROLL 15%	60,000	52,500	45,000	41,250	37,500	33,750	30,000	26,250
PAYROLL TAXES 15%	14,250	13,125	11,250	9,938	9,375	8,813	8,250	7,687
INSURANCE 3%	12,000	10,050	9,000	8,250	7,500	6,750	6,000	5,250
FOOD COST 18%	72,000	63,000	54,000	49,500	45,000	40,500	36,000	31,250
PACKAGING 3%	12,000	10,050	9,000	8,250	7,500	6,750	6,000	5,250
UTILITIES 3%	12,000	10,050	9,000	8,250	7,500	6,750	6,000	5,250
ADVERTISING 2%	8,000	7,000	6,000	5,500	5,000	4,500	4,000	3,500
REPAIRS 1%	4,000	3,500	3,000	2,750	2,500	2,225	2,000	1,750
MISC. 3%	12,000	10,050	9,000	8,250	7,500	6,750	6,000	5,250
LEGAL & ACCT.	4,000	3,500	3,000	2,750	2,500	2,225	2,000	1,750
TOTAL EXPENSES	$ 298,050	271,425	241,050	222,488	209,675	196,813	184,050	170,987
NET PROFIT	$101,950	79,375	58,950	52,512	40,325	28,187	15,950	4,013

- **NET SALES:** Your yearly sales minus any sales tax collected.
- **RENT:** The yearly rent paid to your landlord.
- **RENT-COMMON:** Approximate yearly rent of 1-1.5% of sales paid for common charges in a mall operation where there is a food court. Your lease will probably specify this as a dollar cost per square foot of space. You have to arrive at the correct cost.
- **FOOD COST:** This yearly total is the cost of your ice cream product. If you produce your own ice cream, the percentage is approximately 16-18%. Add another 6% for sundaes, milk shakes, ice cream sodas and ice cream cakes.

- **PAYROLL:** Yearly rent paid to both part-time and full-time employees including any overtime or bonuses.
- **PAYROLL TAXES:** Yearly amount paid for any taxes regardless of whether they are employee or employer paid that might include federal FICA, state, or local taxes. Approximate percentage is 15% of total payroll.
- **ADVERTISING:** Yearly amount paid for any kind of promotion, print ads etc. not to exceed 3-5% of sales.
- **INSURANCE:** Your lease requires both property (fire) and public liability insurance. Also, included in this figure is workers' compensation insurance. For budgeting purposes, use a figure of approximately 3% of sales.
- **PACKAGING:** The yearly amount (3%) paid for any paper items like cups, napkins, ice cream cones etc.

CASH FLOW ESTIMATE

A cash flow statement is the amount of cash you actually have available at the end of each month and is calculated by starting out from the first day you are in business. The starting amount of cash flow is the amount you have left over after constructing and equipping your store. Depending on whether you have made or lost money each month, the cash flow figure will go up or down. It is recommended that you have a positive cash flow figure at day one equal to at least six months rent.

A marketing plan that demonstrates to you and others how your business will succeed. Here is where you set out all the reasons why your proposed ice cream business is sure to be profitable. Some of the specific questions you must answer in your business plan are the following:

- Who and what is your competition and how will your ice cream business be special or distinctive?
- What do your potential customers need or want that they are not getting from your competition? Or, to phrase the question another way, how is the competition failing to exploit the potential market you have identified?
- How many potential customers are in your geographical area? How many of them can you expect to do business at your ice cream store?

- How will you efficiently let your potential customers know about your ice cream business?
- Have you talked to your potential customers? Have they given you any feedback about whether your idea is a good one? What did they say?

Be creative, and even outlandish. Remember, ultimately innovators succeed, copiers fail in business.

A convincing capital spending plan: Describe in detail how you will spend your money. That means every piece of equipment and leasehold improvement needed to open your business.

START-UP COSTS: EQUIPMENT & CONSTRUCTION

Constructing a batch freezer production facility requires between 300 to 800 square feet of production space. You will need the following equipment:

Ice Cream Manufacturing Equipment

Batch freezer: 20-quart freezer to make the product	$14,500
Blast freezer: to blast freeze product after production	4,700
Freezer storage cabinet: to store product blast frozen 24-hours after production	3,200
Refrigerator: needed to store ice cream mix and ingredients	2,500
Three-compartment sink: for overall cleaning of equipment, tubs, etc.	750
Handsink: needed for washing hands.	300
Tables: stainless steel, six feet long (2@500/ea)	1,000
Shelving: for storing ingredient flavorings, tubs etc.	1,000
Blender and food processor: for pureeing fruit, nuts, etc.	2,000
Plastic or cardboard tubs: 2 1/2 or 3 gallon tubs and lids (150 pieces)	600
Hot water boiler: enough hot water for overall cleaning	500
Scale: to weigh ingredients	350
Timer: to time a batch of ice cream during production	25
Misc. equipment: spatulas, measuring bowls etc.	1,500
Ingredients: to start ice cream production	5,000
TOTAL	**$ 37,925**

Front of the Store Equipment

The equipment needed for the front of the store is based on a frontage of 20 by 50 feet. The equipment quoted below is for new equipment unless otherwise noted.

2- 16 hole dipping cabinets	$6,000
2- soft serve machines -	20,000
Chairs and tables for approximately 26 customers	5,000
Menu boards	4,000
Ice cream cake case	4,500
Outside signage	2,500
2 cash registers	4,000
Espresso/coffee package	5,000
Drop safe	500
Ice machine	1,500
2- Neon signs (front of store)	2,000
2- Fudge warmers	600
1- milkshake machine (3 heads)	400
Small wares (misc.)	3,000
TOTAL EQUIPMENT	**$59,000**

Leasehold Improvements

Electrical	$15,000
Plumbing	10,000
Mill work (counter and backwall)	20,000
Carpentry	20,000
Tile work	10,000
Architectural fees	10,000
Alarm system	2,000
Building permit	500
Painting	1,000
TOTAL LEASEHOLD IMPROVEMENTS	**$88,500**
Grand Opening Package	**$5,000**
Cash Flow	**$25,000**
GRAND TOTAL	**$177,500**

DON'T GO INTO BUSINESS WITHOUT ENOUGH MONEY

Lack of capitalization to support the start-up over the first 18 months is a major reason for most failures. The ice cream business is unique in that in most cases it is seasonal. If you don't make it in the summer, you aren't going to make it at all. Simple logic, but very true. If you listen closely and follow this scenario, you can greatly improve your opening day jitters and enhance your chance for an initial success.

- Don't overbuild your location with money you don't have. Pay as you go, there is always a day of reckoning.
- Pay C.O.D. for everything you buy the first year. It keeps you on your toes.
- Don't hire an architect until you have signed a lease.
- Open between February and April.
- Ask for a free rent period while you are constructing your business.
- Forget about paying yourself a salary the first six months. In most cases the money should be in the business, not in your pocket. What really happens is that we go through our first selling season and boom it's September. You ask yourself, where has all the business gone, or more importantly, where has all the money gone? So, be careful because when winter comes, there is nothing worse than looking at an empty store and having no money in the bank.

WRITING THE BUSINESS PLAN
INTRODUCTION: REQUEST FOR FUNDS

With all the information you now have on hand, it's time to write the introduction. You may wonder why I have waited until now to talk to you about this. It's simple. Until now, you were just researching your idea and putting a lot of research down on paper. By now, you have come a long way in your thought process and you should have a realistic idea of whether you have a good idea or not. So now it's time for the introduction, probably the most important element of your business plan. So pay attention! Most everyone you give this business plan to will probably never read the entire plan. They will make a preliminary decision as to whether they will lend you money or invest in your idea on the basis of the introduction. If they like your idea, they will read on. So be sure to put all the strong points in the first few paragraphs, saving the details for later. **You must absolutely adhere to the following rule**:
KEEP IT SHORT AND SPECIFIC

MALCOLM'S NATURAL

JANUARY 2001

MALCOLM STOGO ASSOCIATES

2727 PALISADE AVENUE
RIVERDALE, NEW YORK 10463
718-884-5086

This is a business plan.
It does not imply an offering of any securities.

(THE FOLLOWING BUSINESS PLAN IS PRESENTED HERE AS AN EDUCATIONAL TOOL TO HELP YOU DESIGN AND WRITE YOUR OWN. IT IS A FAIR, BUT FICTITIOUS VERSION OF WHAT A BUSINESS PLAN SHOULD LOOK LIKE.)

TABLE OF CONTENTS

INTRODUCTION

This business plan represents all of the requirements necessary to develop, design and operate a successful frozen desserts retail and wholesale manufacturing business. This plan will explain in detail:

- **Our Overall Strategy**
- **Expectations for Further Development and Adjustments**
- **Financial Requirements**

It will state our specific objectives and demonstrate how and why each objective will be achieved. Certain aspects of the business plan may change, for example- parts of the marketing plan or product categories. The one part of this plan that will not change is: **Producing and Selling a Great Product.**

All of the cost estimates and financial projections are consistent with a conservative business philosophy. We are confident this business plan will be the starting point for what will become New York's first choice for a frozen dessert of any kind.

THE VISION

Our vision is to develop a strong retail and wholesale manufacturing presence in the New York metropolitan area producing the finest ice cream, sorbet and Italian water ice and ice cream cakes possible.

The first Malcolm's Natural store is planned to open in Manhattan in the spring of 2001. It is the beginning of a chain of frozen desserts stores in the metropolitan New York area. Long term plans (two or three years down the line) are to expand into other warmer climates throughout the United States. Location choices include the states of Florida, California and Georgia. The plan includes smaller versions of Malcolm's Natural stores with limited space, production capacity and product offering for franchise or company owned stores.

The vision includes the development of new products and novelty items for retail as well as wholesale.

EXECUTIVE SUMMARY

Malcolm's Natural will be the first location of a storefront retail chain operation specializing in the production and distribution of Ice Creams, Italian Ices and Sorbets on a retail and wholesale level. The business will target young people ages 14- 24, their parents and other adults ages 25-45. The wholesale market will target fine restaurants throughout Manhattan and the outlying areas.

Malcolm's Natural will also offer a variety of fresh fruits with an assortment of unusual toppings and fresh fruit juices and frozen smoothies. Unique flavors, products and store design will be the hallmark of Malcolm's Natural stores. Manufacturing will be done on the premises of the first store, which will be located in Manhattan.

Malcolm's Natural Ice Creams will be made from the finest fruits, cocoas, nuts and chocolates to insure the **best taste** and **texture**.

Malcolm's Natural Sorbets and Italian Ices will be made from the freshest fresh and frozen fruits regardless of where they are produced in the world.

Most Italian Ices and sorbets contain only processed cooked fruits, fruit added flavorings and artificial color. We will be different!

Marketing will be done through retained public relation firms and local media extolling the many accomplishments of Malcolm Stogo during the last 15 years.

Malcolm Stogo will oversee the management of the first store in Manhattan.

Malcolm is the president of both Malcolm Stogo Associates and Ice Cream University and has a long history of creating the most discriminating fabulous desserts for the frozen desserts industry. Malcolm will use his knowledge and experience in the industry to develop Malcolm's Natural into a national chain.

Malcolm's Natural is seeking $1,000,000 in financing to build and open the three stores in Manhattan. Malcolm's Natural expects the first three stores to be profitable by the second year.

We expect that other store openings will come from franchisees or licensing agreements and should not impact on Malcolm's Natural capital structure.

MAJOR OBJECTIVES: SHORT TERM

For Malcolm's Natural to have a successful start and experience real long-term profitability, the following short-term objectives must be achieved:

1. The finest tasting ice creams, sorbets and ices must be produced.
2. The products must offer variety and novelty to create its own demand.
3. The place of operation, both the store and wholesale manufacturing facility, must be friendly, clean, comfortable and inviting.
4. The store must be located in an area where foot traffic is heavy.
5. The management team must have experience in business, especially the frozen desserts industry.
6. The business should be well capitalized and show a profit by the second year.
7. The retail design portion of this concept should be easily replicable to allow for the development of additional locations.

DESCRIPTION OF BUSINESS

Malcolm's Natural will be a storefront operation, which will include manufacturing facilities on the premises. Ice Creams, Sorbets, and real fruit Italian Ices will all be produced and distributed at the retail and wholesale level on a daily basis. The business will commence with one storefront located in Manhattan and will expand by direct sales to restaurants and specialty stores, that will carry our pints. The business will be subject to ebbs and flows in revenues and profitability attributable to seasonal changes. The first store here in New York will peak in the months of May through September and ebb in November through March.

We expect that wholesale revenues will supplement retail store revenues especially during the slower winter months. As the store network increases, emphasis will be placed on locating stores in regions where the peak season is longer. Future plans include a store design that will not only include a retail frozen desserts location but also a bakery-type restaurant or portion of the store designed specifically for food service.

The business will target youths ages 14-24, their parents and other adults ages 25-45. Malcolm's Natural offers this market a rich super premium ice cream and a natural fruit, dairy free Sorbet and Italian Ice.

The decor of the store will be beautifully pleasing to the eye and suggest an atmosphere of fun and entertainment. This, in conjunction with the quality of the product and service, will help to create a buzz among the target population in the area surrounding the site.

TARGET MARKET & LOCATION OF BUSINESS

Malcolm's Natural has a number of criteria that will be used to determine if a particular area is suitable for a store opening. These include:

- **PROPER DEMOGRAPHICS**

While Ice Cream and Italian Ices are for everyone, Malcolm's Natural expects the greatest response from young people and adults ages 24-45 with incomes between $25,000 and $100,000.

- **LOCATION WITH HIGH DEGREE OF FOOT TRAFFIC**

This will be the mechanism for attracting new business. Additionally, every effort will be made to be close to a college or other type of institution that will ensure that a larger percentage of that foot traffic is from the target population.

- **MINIMAL COMPETITION FROM OTHER DESSERT STORES**

In the long term, Malcolm's Natural sees itself as distinct from competitors such as Joe's Ice Cream. Accordingly, placing a store too close to a Joe's Ice Cream will not hurt short-term performance. With this in mind, Malcolm's Natural has identified the SoHo area of Manhattan as the location for the initial store. This area is heavily traveled by college students and tourists and has a reputation for its diverse restaurants and eclectic arts community.

The resident population is comprised of our two key target consumer groups:
- Young People
- Working Professionals

Malcolm's Natural unique theme store format will integrate well with the strong artistic culture and community that already exists in the East Village. Our proximity to New York University will help ensure foot traffic.

In addition, some general demographics include:

Total population	109,042
Median income	$31,175

The exact site has not been determined, but the requirements have been laid out and Malcolm's Natural has begun to identify certain real estate properties. Given rental prices in the area, Malcolm's Natural expects the rent to be between $3,500 and $7,000 per month. The space should be approximately 1,500 square feet.

PRODUCT DESCRIPTION

The Ice Creams will be made with the finest ice cream mixes and flavorings. Fresh nuts, fine chocolates and real fruits will be used to produce our ice creams as well as many other varied specialty ingredients. Malcolm's Natural will also offer the most incredible tasting choice of two soft-serve Ice Creams using fruit purees as well as the hard Ice Cream choices. There is a strong resemblance between Italian Ices (for retail stores) and Sorbets (for wholesale). Generally, Italian Ices uses a greater amount of flavoring additives and added color and because of this, Sorbets are often considered to be more of an upscale gourmet product than Italian Ice. However, Malcolm's Natural hopes to change this perception. Malcolm's Natural Italian Ices are made with real and often fresh fruits and juices so that Malcolm's Natural Italian Ices will be the top-of-the-line in quality compared to other Italian Ices. Our Sorbets, to be made specifically for our wholesale customers, will be produced in the same fashion.

Fresh fruits such as oranges and apples and an assortment of exotic fruits from other countries will be used. Peaches, nectarines, cantaloupes, bananas, etc. will all be sliced or chopped for sale as fruit sundaes with Ice Cream or Ices, blended into drinks, or served alone with a choice of toppings like superfine sugar, flavored whipped cream and honeys.

Malcolm's Natural will offer a limited number of beverages. The most unique will be our **Signature Slush:** Lemon Slush with Fresh Strawberry, chopped, mixed in and served with a tall spoon. Italian Ices and fresh fruits will be served in combinations as sundaes, cones or in cups of various sizes. Products targeted for our wholesale market will include Ice Creams, Sorbet and combination Sorbet and Creams sold in 1.25-gallon tubs.

WHY WILL WE SUCCEED?

The success of our business will be the result of the quality and uniqueness of our products, our superior service and attention to detail throughout our operation. Our ability to deliver quality products in a timely, personal and professional manner will be due to the talents of our key personnel, which is another reason for our success.

We can compete on price by making an aggressive sales effort and strategy to target a specific niche in the wholesale restaurant and gourmet food store market as well as in our retail stores.

We believe we have a special formula for success that includes the reputation of Malcolm Stogo together with:

- **Unique products**
- **Unique store design**
- **Our unique combination of personalities**
- **A very special history**

WHO'S INVOLVED?

Malcolm Stogo will oversee the management and frozen desserts production of the first store in Manhattan. He has a long history in the frozen desserts business. Malcolm is the president of Malcolm Stogo Associates and of Ice Cream University.

Malcolm has put together a team of partners with a significant amount of experience in the frozen desserts industry; in sales and marketing, frozen desserts retail store operations, food preparation, legal issues and technical product knowledge. Together this team will leverage this knowledge and expertise in growing Malcolm's Natural into a national chain.

RECENT ACCOMPLISHMENTS

The following is a brief description of the accomplishments of Malcolm Stogo.

- Successfully completed assignments for Joe's Ice Cream, Jane's, and Jimmy's Ice Cream.
- Founder and President of **ICE CREAM UNIVERSITY**, a hands-on seminar series dealing with production, retailing and merchandising of ice cream.
- Publisher of **BATCH FREEZER NEWS**, a quarterly newsletter involving every phase of batch freezer ice cream production and marketing.
- Publisher of **ICE CREAM STORE NEWS**, the most aggressive newsletter published on operating, marketing, and merchandising a retail ice cream store.
- Author of **ICE CREAM** *and Frozen Desserts*: **A Commercial Guide to Production and Marketing** published by John Wiley & Sons, Inc. This book is now the standard for how ice cream is produced and sold worldwide for both continuous and batch freezing operation processes.
- Co-author of **ICE CREAM CAKES**, an authoritative book on creating, producing, and decorating ice cream cakes.
- Author of **FROZEN DESSERTS, A Complete Retailer's Guide**, the most complete worldwide commercial book on batch freezing production and marketing of ice cream and other frozen dairy desserts.

- Conceived, constructed, and implemented ice cream retail concepts and ice cream production factories in Saudi Arabia and Tunisia.
- Achieved 1st place prize in **"NEW PRODUCT DEVELOPMENT" for Prepared Foods Magazine** with entry of a 9" frozen yogurt Raspberry Cheesecake.
- Creator and developer of many of the most popular ice cream, Italian gelato, frozen yogurt and sorbet flavors sold today including Cookies & Cream (1976), Snickers (1978), Milky Way (1978), Rice Pudding (1998) among others.
- Renowned author and speaker with published articles in THE ICE CREAM SUNDAE MAGAZINE, SDI, EDM Magazine and MICA on merchandising, retailing, and trends for the dairy industry.
- Implemented successful store refurbishing programs for many franchise operations (Joe's & Ben's Frozen Yogurt).
- Invented chocolate dipped waffle cone, a cone that is now being produced and marketed worldwide.
- Won 1st place runner-up for producing two successful television commercials for clients in Saudi Arabia sponsored by the International Bottled Water Association (IBWA).
- With the sponsorship of the Nicola Company of Bologna, Italy, originated an annual Gelato tour of Italy in January 2001.

BUSINESS EXPERIENCE
MALCOLM STOGO ASSOCIATES- International Ice Cream **Consultants-1981-Present**
Consultant to leading worldwide ice cream and dairy companies for new product development, purchasing, concept strategies, packaging and franchise retail marketing and merchandising plans.

Author of four books and two quarterly newsletters:

BOOKS
- **How to Succeed In the Incredible Ice Cream Business (2001)**
- **ICE CREAM and Frozen Desserts- A Commercial Guide to Production and Marketing (1998)**
- **ICE CREAM CAKES (1995)**
- **FROZEN DESSERTS- A Complete Retailer's Guide, (1991)**

QUARTERLY NEWSLETTERS
- *Batch Freezer News*
- *Ice Cream Store News*

ICE CREAM UNIVERSITY- (1995-Present)
- Founder and President of a series of nationwide seminars and newsletters on production, retailing and marketing of ice cream. Successfully graduated over 300 participants (companies) already in business or going into ice cream manufacturing and retail business.

JIMMY'S ICE CREAM (1999-2000)
- Served as their product development specialist in designing and reformulating all ice cream flavors and strategic advice as needed.

SAL'S (1999- Present)
- Consulted in creating and opening the most "talked-about" new ice cream and European café concept to hit Florida in years with its first store opening in November 1999.

MARC'S FAMOUS ITALIAN ICES (1998-Present)
- Designed a reformulation of their entire Italian Ice flavor line and helped them launch a super premium foodservice ice cream and sorbet line of products.

JIMMY'S ICE CREAM- Memphis, TN and Chicago, IL (1988-Present)
- For over ten years have been consulting on the site-selection, leasing, and product development for this multi-unit franchisee resulting in the opening of over ten stores nationwide.

BAGELS- (1999-Present)
- Created first American-style ice cream concept in Tunisia
- Constructed an ice cream manufacturing facility for client
- Purchased all equipment and ingredients for the production plant

CONES- (1992-Present)
- Created first American-style ice cream concept in Saudi Arabia
- Constructed two ice cream manufacturing facilities for client
- Purchased all equipment and ingredients for both production plants
- Designed corporate logo and sales brochure plus a new graphic image for the client's product packaging

POPPY'S MAIN STREET ICE CREAM- (1997-Present)
- Helped create a concept from beginning to opening its first store, including training personnel, flavor development, purchasing equipment/ingredients, and marketing.

RASPBERRY QUENCH- (1994-Present)
- Developed a sorbet flavor line (Lemon, Raspberry Lemon and Strawberry Lemon) for distribution to foodservice companies and supermarkets throughout North Carolina.

PERFECTO- (1995-Present)
- Helped launch a new retail frozen sorbet product line using ethnic Mexican fruit flavors for the California retail and commercial market.

BEN'S FROZEN YOGURT- (1990-1991)
For this 125 store frozen yogurt franchise chain located in California that offered a full variety of frozen yogurt products:
- Developed a new product line of upscale frozen yogurt cakes and pies resulting in sales increases of over 50% in the first year. The new line won a first place national prize for the best new foodservice dessert in 1991.
- Conceived new merchandising programs for "Take-Out Sales" that showed incremental sales gains of over 25% annually.

THE JIMMY COMPANY- (1988-90)
For the premier ice cream company in the world:
- Involved in concept strategies that helped turn around a declining franchise system to a new growth vehicle for both Jimmy's and its franchisees.
- Created and implemented successful marketing and refurbishing programs for over 175 shops.
- Helped conceptualize strategy for Jimmy's to become the exclusive ice cream vendor for the NEW OPEN TENNIS TOURNAMENT.

MARKET ANALYSIS
The ice cream industry (supermarket and retail shops) continues to grow at an annual rate of approximately 3% for the last three years as of December 31, 2000. Since most of the ice cream produced in the United States is eaten within the country, it is estimated that Americans now eat about 24 quarts of frozen desserts a year, per capita. Growth was mostly fueled by increases in both super premium and regular ice cream production of frozen desserts across the main regions of the United States, with the Midwest and West leading in production numbers. Frozen yogurt, in particular, continues its downward trend in the supermarket area. Sorbets, Italian ices, ice cream and premium ice cream bars showed the most significant growth. The most popular ice cream flavors continue to be vanilla, chocolate, fruit flavors, candy, and nut flavors. The most popular new flavor today is Dulce de Leche.

THE COMPETITION

Our main competitor at the retail level is Jimmy's. We feel their dominance of the market opens the door for us to offer a choice "that is unique and different" for the consumer. Malcolm's Natural will be that unique kind of store. Our customers will be offered products, entertainment and services that will not be found at a Jimmy's store. The biggest competition for us in the wholesale market is a company called Belluca. This company appears to control the wholesale Ice Cream and Sorbet market in New York. It is because of this fact that Malcolm's Natural feels that it is now the perfect time to break into the wholesale market. The advantage may be that we are their only competition and that so far no one else has taken the challenge. Smaller competition may be Snoopy's on Charles Street in Greenwich Village. They sell Gelato and Sorbets. The store itself has no warmth or personality. We believe that our main advantages lie within the uniqueness of our offerings:

- The product
- Our attitudes about positive customer service
- Our personal relations
- Our very special store design concept
- Malcolm Stogo's experience as one of the premier consultants in the ice cream industry

FINANCIAL NEEDS

Malcolm's Natural is seeking $1,000,000 in financing to build and open its first three stores in Manhattan.

Ideally, April 1st is our planned Grand Opening for wholesale operations. This would require that funding be completed by January 31st. The money will be used for construction, design, legal and licensing fees, to purchase equipment, product inventory, and to implement our marketing plan that will help us to build name recognition and generate revenues.

STRATEGY

Our strategy is to build a strong retail and wholesale brand identity. The brand will stand for quality, both in products and customer service. We want to send the message that we provide fun and entertainment as well as warm, personal and prompt service. Our marketing plan will support this name brand strategy. It is important that we send a positive message to our customers and create a pleasant atmosphere for them. We must also maintain a firm, strong business-like image. We will do this by:

1. Creating and setting certain company guidelines as well as personal standards
2. Maintaining these standards by consistently supporting them and by maintaining company as well as personal integrity at all times
3. Interviewing, hiring and training all employees with these objectives in mind.

Since Malcolm's Natural market will be local customers and tourists, part of our marketing strategy will be focused at local papers and magazines. Local media will be interested in Malcolm's Natural and the story behind Malcolm Stogo's newest enterprise.

Overall Strategy

Our strategy also includes maintaining low costs by incorporating simplicity wherever possible. We intend to streamline our focus to have a relatively narrow line of products and services in the beginning in order to maintain better control over the business.

Our sales marketing effort will be based on an aggressive sales effort where the wholesale market is concerned. In-store presentations will be the core of our selling effort. We will also send out announcement flyers or cards to local businesses and customers.

Our strategy also includes promoting the store through promotional and incentive offers. We may choose to use a company like Val Pack that specializes in business promotions.

Our service strategy will be to offer the best, most highly personalized service in the marketplace. We are an owner-operated company, and we intend to use that to our advantage to be absolutely certain that all of our customers receive excellent service.

We will go out of our way to make sure that our customers know that they truly matter to us.

START-UP COSTS: EQUIPMENT & CONSTRUCTION

Constructing a batch freezer production facility requires between 300 to 800 square feet of production space. We will need the following equipment:

Ice Cream Manufacturing Equipment

Batch freezer: 20-quart freezer to make the product	$14,500
Blast freezer: to blast freeze product after production	4,700
Freezer storage cabinet: to store product blast frozen 24-hours after production	3,200
Refrigerator: needed to store ice cream mix and ingredients	2,500
Three-compartment sink: for overall cleaning of equipment, tubs, etc.	750
Handsink: needed for washing hands.	300
Tables: stainless steel, six feet long (2@500/ea)	1,000
Shelving: for storing ingredient flavorings, tubs etc.	1,000
Blender and food processor: for pureeing fruit, nuts, etc.	2,000
Plastic or cardboard tubs: 2 1/2 or 3 gallon tubs and lids (150 pieces)	600
Hot water boiler: enough hot water for overall cleaning	500
Scale: to weigh ingredients	350
Timer: to time a batch of ice cream during production	25
Misc. equipment: spatulas, measuring bowls etc.	1,500
Ingredients: to start ice cream production	5,000
TOTAL	**$ 37,925**

Front of the Store Equipment

The equipment needed for the front of the store is based on a frontage of 20 by 50 feet. The equipment quoted below is for new equipment unless otherwise noted.

2- 16 hole dipping cabinets	$6,000
2- 754 soft serve machines -	20,000
Chairs and tables for approximately 26 customers	5,000
Menu boards	4,000
Ice cream cake case	4,500
Outside signage	2,500
2 cash registers	4,000

Espresso/coffee package	5,000
Drop safe	500
Ice machine	1,500
2- Neon signs (front of store)	2,000
2- Fudge warmers	600
1- milkshake machine (3 heads)	400
Small wares (misc.)	3,000
TOTAL EQUIPMENT	**$59,000**

Leasehold Improvements

Electrical	$15,000
Plumbing	10,000
Mill work (counter and backwall)	20,000
Carpentry	20,000
Tile work	10,000
Architectural fees	10,000
Alarm system	2,000
Building permit	500
Painting	1,000
TOTAL LEASEHOLD IMPROVEMENTS	**$88,500**
Grand Opening Package	**$5,000**
Cash Flow	**25,000**
GRAND TOTAL	**$177,500**

Appendix A:

PRO FORMA PROFIT AND LOSS STATEMENT
YEARLY RETAIL SALES TO BREAK EVEN
MALCOLM'S NATURAL

WEEKLY SALES	7,692	6,731	5,769	5,288	4,800	4,322	3,846	3,365
DAILY SALES	1,099	962	824	755	687	618	549	481
TOTAL SALES	$ 400,000	350,000	300,000	275,000	250,000	225,000	200,000	175,000
RENT	48,000	48,000	48,000	48,000	48,000	48,000	48,000	48,000
RENT-COMMON	4,800	4,800	4,800	4,800	4,800	4,800	4,800	4,800
PAYROLL MGR.	35,000	35,000	30,000	25,000	25,000	25,000	25,000	25,000
PAYROLL 15%	60,000	52,500	45,000	41,250	37,500	33,750	30,000	26,250
PAYROLL TAXES 15%	14,250	13,125	11,250	9,938	9,375	8,813	8,250	7,687
INSURANCE 3%	12,000	10,050	9,000	8,250	7,500	6,750	6,000	5,250
FOOD COST 18%	72,000	63,000	54,000	49,500	45,000	40,500	36,000	31,250
PACKAGING 3%	12,000	10,050	9,000	8,250	7,500	6,750	6,000	5,250
UTILITIES 3%	12,000	10,050	9,000	8,250	7,500	6,750	6,000	5,250
ADVERTISING 2%	8,000	7,000	6,000	5,500	5,000	4,500	4,000	3,500
REPAIRS 1%	4,000	3,500	3,000	2,750	2,500	2,225	2,000	1,750
MISC. 3%	12,000	10,050	9,000	8,250	7,500	6,750	6,000	5,250
LEGAL & ACCT.	4,000	3,500	3,000	2,750	2,500	2,225	2,000	1,750
TOTAL EXPENSES	$ 298,050	271,425	241,050	222,488	209,675	196,813	184,050	170,987
NET PROFIT	$101,950	79,375	58,950	52,512	40,325	28,187	15,950	4,013

Definitions

- **NET SALES:** Yearly sales minus any sales tax collected.
- **RENT:** The yearly rent paid to the landlord.
- **RENT-COMMON:** Approximate yearly rent of 1-1.5% of sales paid for common charges in a mall operation where there is a food court. The lease will probably specify this as a dollar cost per square foot of space.

- **FOOD COST:** This yearly total is the cost of the ice cream product. If you produce your own ice cream, the percentage is approximately 16-18%. Add another 6% for sundaes, milk shakes, ice cream sodas and ice cream cakes.
- **PAYROLL:** Yearly rent paid to both part-time and full-time employees including any overtime or bonuses.
- **PAYROLL TAXES:** Yearly amount paid for any taxes regardless of whether they are employee or employer paid that might include federal FICA, state, or local taxes. Approximate percentage is 15% of total payroll.
- **ADVERTISING:** Yearly amount paid for any kind of promotion, print ads etc. not to exceed 3-5% of sales.
- **INSURANCE:** The lease requires both property (fire) and public liability insurance. Also, included in this figure is workers' compensation insurance. For budgeting purposes, use a figure of approximately 3% of sales is used.
- **PACKAGING:** The yearly amount (3%) paid for any paper items like cups, napkins, ice cream cones etc.

PRO FORMA PROFIT AND LOSS STATEMENT
<u>WHOLESALE SALES</u>

TOTAL SALES	$300,000	250,000	200,000	150,000	100,000	50,000
FOOD COST @ 26%	78,000	65,000	52,000	39,000	26,000	13,000
PACKAGING @ 3%	9,000	7,500	6,000	4,500	3,000	1,500
PAYROLL @ 17%	51,000	42,500	34,000	25,550	17,000	8,500
PAYROLL TAXES	11,220	9,240	7,480	5,621	2,890	1,445
DELIVERY @ 5%	15,000	12,500	10,000	7,500	5,000	2,500
INSURANCE	9,000	7,500	6,000	4,500	3,000	1,500
REPAIR MISC.	3,000	2,500	2,000	1,500	1,000	500
@ 5%	15,000	12,500	10,000	7,500	5,000	2,500
TOTAL EXPENSE	$ 182,220	159,240	115,480	86,671	62,890	31,445
PROFIT	$ 108,780	90,760	84,520	63,329	37,110	18,555

PROJECTED PROFIT AND LOSS STATEMENT
THREE YEAR PROJECTION
COMBINED RETAIL & WHOLESALE BUSINESS-ONE STORE

TOTAL SALES	YEAR 3	YEAR 2	YEAR 1
RETAIL	$500,000	400,000	350,000
WHOLESALE	300,000	250,000	200,000
TOTAL SALES	800,000	650,000	550,000
TOTAL EXPENSES			
RENT	48,000	48,000	48,000
PAYROLL-MANAGER	35,000	35,000	35,000
PAYROLL 17%	136,000	110,500	93,500
PAYROLL TAXES	30,770	24,690	21,730
INSURANCE	24,000	19,500	16,050
FOOD COST 16.5%	160,500	131,000	109,750
PACKAGING 3%	24,000	19,500	16,050
DELIVERY 5%	15,000	12,500	10,000
UTILITIES 3%	24,000	19,500	16,050
ADVERTISING 2%	10,000	8,000	7,000
REPAIRS	8,000	6,500	5,500
MISC. 3%	30,000	24,500	20,050
LEGAL & ACCOUNTING	5,000	4,000	3,500
TOTAL EXPENSES	$550,270	464,190	402,180
PROFIT	$ 249,730	185,810	147,820

CHAPTER 3
SHOULD I MAKE MY OWN ICE CREAM
"Honestly, would you rather buy someone else's product?
Not me!"- Malcolm Stogo!

For those of you already in this business, the question of whether to make or not to make your own ice cream is really a mute point, but for those just starting out, the decision is "HUGE."

So, for this reason only, let's have a discussion on the merits.

Whether or not you are going to make your own ice cream is a decision that will influence the path your concept takes. The subject is complex and the ramifications of operating a business based on either option requires that you understand what it takes to operate each.

The decision is even more important today then 5-10 years ago. The business environment today is much more difficult with overhead factors such as water and electricity playing a more important role than ever before. Profit margins are constantly shrinking because of huge increases in rents, cost of products and ingredients, taxes and utilities.

The best thing to do is visit ice cream manufacturers and retail shops that are run both ways and take a good look at the differences and similarities of each.

So why should I make my own ice cream products? Without a doubt, 90% of everyone contacting me about going into business talk about the idea of being creative and making and selling the best ice cream imaginable. Well, we all know there is only one way to do that, and that's by making it yourself.

So if you decide to make your own product, you will have to prepare a product list of what you want to sell. Selecting products and flavors to make is one of the most enjoyable aspects of the business because of the research involved, such as traveling to other dairies, ice cream manufacturers and retail shops for taste-testing. The quality of producing your own products is usually superior to a ready-made product, and the costs are less in many cases. Most frozen dairy desserts have a large profit margin. The costs of ingredients and ice cream mix and the percentage of air pumped into the finished product (overrun) vary, depending on the quality level of your product. Buying a finished product from a dairy is more expensive for a shop owner because of the dairy's overhead, delivery costs, advertising expenses and profit margin.

At first look, it would seem that the main reason for making your own product is profit. But years of experience has shown me that the real reason is having control over the quality of the product you are featuring. You share what you sell with the public. If your goals are long term, you should seriously consider making your own product instead of selling someone else's. <u>You can make the best ice cream in town for the same cost as purchasing the cheapest ice cream from a dairy.</u>

You shouldn't be intimidated by the fear of failure or by a lack of knowledge. Certainly, there are difficulties at the start and costs are high because of having to buy equipment and ingredients. You will need help in learning how to use the equipment and in developing flavor recipes, but getting such help is not as difficult as it may seem. Equipment manufacturers, ingredient and mix companies, consultants, seminars and books can get you started on the right path.

So, why would anyone choose to sell someone else's finished product? For many, an ice cream shop is operated as a secondary source of income, with absentee ownership, or as a franchise of a major chain. Other attractions for buying a finished product include knowing beforehand the cost of a uniform product and a low labor factor for the daily operation of the business. Also, fear of the unknown and not fully understanding the real costs and opportunities involved keeps many people from making their own products.

Will the Concept Support Making Your Own Ice Cream?

If you expect your first store to do more than $200,000 a year in sales, purchasing a batch freezer and making your own product will save you an amount equivalent to 10-15 percent of ingredient costs (see the following section on the costs of making your own ice cream). Based on a sales volume of $200,000, the costs for purchasing a finished product from an established ice cream manufacturer will be 28-35 percent of sales, depending on the butterfat content and quality of the product purchased. Using a 30 percent cost factor for purchasing a finished product versus 18 percent for producing your own, a savings of $24,000 a year (without allowing for the labor costs) may be possible.

To make your own products you need to purchase the following:

START-UP COSTS: PRODUCTION ROOM EQUIPMENT

Constructing a batch freezer production facility requires between 300 and 800 square feet of space. The equipment needed is as follows:

Ice Cream Manufacturing Equipment

Batch freezer: *(20 Quart) to produce the product*	$14,000
Hardening cabinet *(blast freezer): to blast freeze product*	4,500

Additional Equipment Needed to Make Your Own Ice Cream

Freezer storage cabinet: *a freezer used to store product that has been blast frozen 24 hours after production*	2,600
Refrigerator: *to store ice cream mix and ingredients*	2,000
Three compartment sink: *for cleaning of equipment, tubs, etc.*	750
Hand sink: *for washing hands*	300
Tables: *stainless steel, six feet long (2)*	1,000
Shelving: *for storing ingredient flavorings, tubs etc.*	1,000
Blender and food processor: *for pureeing fruit, nuts, etc.*	2,000
Plastic or cardboard tubs: *2 1/2 or 3 gallon tubs and lids (150)*	400
Hot water boiler: *enough hot water for overall cleaning purposes*	500
Scale: *to weigh ingredients*	350
Timer: *to time a batch of ice cream during production*	25
Misc. equipment: *spatulas, measuring bowls etc.*	500
Ingredients: *to start ice cream production*	5,000
Leasehold improvements: *plumbing, floor drain and electricity*	5,000
TOTAL	$39,925

Ingredient Costs In Making Your Own Ice Cream

By totaling the ingredient and labor costs of producing your own ice cream and comparing those costs to the selling price of the product, you can establish a food cost percentage. Here's an example of the merits of making your own ice cream:

VANILLA ICE CREAM
INGREDIENTS:
2 1/2 gallons ice cream mix $6.92 per gallon $17.30
4 ounces two-fold vanilla extract- $47.40 gallon   1.48
10 ounces pasteurized egg yolks-$45.93-30 pounds   .96
TOTAL $19.74

Total batch size-334 OUNCES
5 % LOSS FACTOR- 317 OUNCES
6.2 CENTS PER OUNCE ($19.74 divided 317 ounces)
COST PER GALLON - 6.2 cents x 128 ounces- $7.93
5 OUNCE SERVING- 31 CENTS
CONE- NAPKIN- 6 CENTS PER SERVING
TOTAL COST SERVING- 37 CENTS- 63 SERVINGS
FOOD COST- $19.74
CONE-NAPKIN   3.78
TOTAL FOOD COST- $23.52
16.6% FOOD COST
TOTAL BATCH 317 OUNCES
TWO 2 1/2 GALLON TUBS
5 OUNCE SCOOP-63 FIVE-OUNCE SCOOPS
SALE PER SCOOP- $ 2.25
TOTAL RETAIL- $141.75
PER SCOOP COST-   .373
COST   23.52
FOOD COST   16.6%
EXCLUDING LABOR AND OVERHEAD

A single ice cream cone selling for $2.25 will have a cost of 37 cents for a five ounce serving portion based on a batch final cost (includes cost of napkin, cone or cup) of $23.52 ($11.76 per 2- 2-1/2 gallon tubs- food cost 16.6%) to produce the ice cream.

Comparable Costs- Making Your Own Versus Purchasing From a Distributor or Dairy

The following example illustrates the merits of making your own ice cream.

If the ice cream purchased from a distributor costs $19.00 per tub for an ice cream product that has a 100% overrun (37 servings per tub- food cost 26.1%) anyone making his/her own ice cream can produce a much higher quality ice cream at the same overrun for $9.87, a difference of $9.13. The $9.13 dollar spread works out to a difference of $35,607 per year saving assuming 3,900 tubs are used during the whole year. The 10 percent difference is due to the distributor's profit mark-up and delivery charges. That difference is considerable and is magnified with increased volume.

For example, on a business grossing $400,000, the food cost of producing your own is approximately $66,400 as compared to about $104,400 for purchasing a finished product. When you consider the depreciation of the production equipment, the profits on making your own become even greater. The fact is, a high-quality ice cream can be produced at the same cost or lower as purchasing a finished product of lower quality. In terms of butterfat, a 16 percent butterfat ice cream can be produced for the same cost as buying a 12 percent finished product.

The construction of a production room, and the total cost of purchasing the initial inventory of ingredients and equipment will add about $40,000 to the price of setting up your retail ice cream operation.

An average business doing in excess of $200,000 a year will recoup this initial investment in approximately 18-24 months or two summer seasons.

The timing of your opening can play a major role in your success or failure. The best time of year to open a retail business is February or early March, just before the spring selling season and just after the slowest sales months of the year. Most new operations take at least three full months of construction for building or renovating, and almost every new retail business is late opening for one reason or another. So, planning is extremely important to allow for contingencies. You should figure on beginning construction in September or October of the year preceding your planned opening.

WHAT KIND OF BATCH FREEZER SHOULD YOU BUY?

Outside of picking your location, this is probably the most important decision you will have to make.

There are three major batch freezer manufacturers in the United States. Each has its advantages and disadvantages, but the most important question you must answer for yourself is what kind of ice cream do you want to make? So, let me give you some free advice.

First of all, I am asked over and over again by people wanting to start an ice cream business if I know of any used batch freezers around. Well,

I will be honest with you, it's not a very smart idea and doing so can be costly. While there is a large market for used batch freezers, not knowing anything about how old they are, freon used, or the condition of the barrel and blades can make the purchase of a used batch freezer a costly one.

My advice to you is to purchase your first batch freezer new. When and if you want to add a second batch freezer to your operation, that decision will be easier for you to make because by that time you will have had an idea of how they work, have a good refrigeration person on hand to advise you and correct any deficiencies a used one might have, and frankly by this time your confidence level will enable you to make the right decision.

Carpigiani-Coldelite

FIGURE 3-1. Carpigiani batch freezer LB-250, LB-502, and LB1000.

If you are interested in making a gelato type product, your choice should be any one of the following Carpigiani-Coldelite models:

LB-502 and LB- 502G Batch Freezers

The LB-500 batch freezer makes a 75-90% overrun type ice cream product while the LB 502G batch freezer makes an outstanding 35-45% overrun super-premium type gelato or ice cream product.

Advantages:

- Features automatic touch pad operation using a computer type panel with an audible alarm signal that goes off when the product is ready to extract
- Built-in faucet hose that makes cleaning fast and easy

- Minimal waste of finished product left in the barrel
- Clam door latch does provide for quick interior access
- Batch time is less then nine minutes

Disadvantages:
- Wire safeguards on both the ingredient hopper and extrusion opening makes it difficult to use pieces of fruit, chocolate chunks or nuts as part of the actual ice cream making
- Ingredient hopper opening is narrow making it difficult to put thick type fruit or cocoa paste into the barrel before production starts
- Foreign made parts are sometimes difficult to obtain when the unit needs repair
- Barrel size is only 18 quarts
- Because of the speed of production, both water ice and sorbet type products can over-process if product is not extruded fast enough from the barrel chamber

LB-1002 and LB-1002G Batch Freezers

The LB-1002 batch freezer makes a 75-90% overrun type ice cream product and the LB-1002G batch freezer makes an outstanding 35-45% overrun super-premium type gelato or ice cream product.

Advantages:
- Features automatic touch pad operation using a computer type panel with an audible alarm signal that goes off when the product is ready to extract
- Built-in faucet hose that makes cleaning fast and easy
- Minimal waste of finished product left in the barrel
- Clam door latch does provide for quick interior access

Disadvantages:
- Wire safeguards on both the ingredient hopper and extrusion opening makes it almost impossible to use pieces of fruit, chocolate chunks or nuts as part of the actual ice cream making
- Ingredient hopper opening is narrow making it difficult to put thick type fruit or cocoa paste into the barrel before production starts
- Foreign made parts are sometimes difficult to obtain when the unit needs repair
- Barrel size is only 38 quarts
- Because of the speed of production, both water ice and sorbet type products can over-process if product is not extruded fast enough from the barrel chamber

Emery Thompson

FIGURE 3-2. Emery Thompson batch freezer model 40BLT.

Emery Thompson manufactures both single and two speed batch freezers for making either a high or low overrun ice cream, Italian water ice, gelato, or sorbet type products. (Emery Thompson batch freezers are also manufactured and sold under the Electro-Freeze brand name.)

20 Quart Batch Freezers
The 20 quart single speed batch freezer can make up to a 100% overrun type ice cream product. The 20 quart two speed batch freezer can go as low as a 45% overrun super-premium type gelato or ice cream product on low speed and up to a 100% overrun ice cream product on its high speed. The two speed batch freezer also has two-3 horsepower drive motors for either low or high overrun production.
Advantages:
- Features stainless steel construction
- Metal dasher blades
- Easy access ingredient hopper
- Extrusion opening allows finished product to flow out easily
- Excellent repair record and parts are easy to obtain
- Re-sale value very high
- United States manufacturer
Disadvantages:
- Production time at least 9-11 minutes
- Excess finished product tends to stick to dasher blades

40 Quart Batch Freezers

The 40 quart single speed batch freezer can make up to a 100% overrun type ice cream product. The 40 quart two speed batch freezer can go as low as a 45% overrun super-premium type gelato or ice cream product on low speed and up to a 100% overrun ice cream product on its high speed. The two speed batch freezer also has one 5 horsepower drive motor for low overrun production and one 7 1/2 horsepower drive motor for high overrun production.

Advantages:

- Features stainless steel construction
- Easy access ingredient hopper
- Extrusion opening allows finished product to flow out easily
- Excellent repair record and parts are easy to obtain
- Large barrel allows almost nine gallons of a water ice mixture to be filled up in the barrel
- Re-sale value very high
- Metal dasher blades
- United States manufacturer

Disadvantages:

- Production time at least 9-11 minutes
- Excess finished product tends to stick to dasher blades

Taylor Company

FIGURE 3-3. Taylor batch freezer Model 220.

While the Taylor Company is known for it's soft serve machines, it does make two batch freezers, one a counter-top unit producing low overrun ice cream and a floor model producing high overrun ice cream.

Model 104 Counter-Top
This unit is ideal for restaurants or very small ice cream stores
Advantages:
- Features stainless steel construction
- Easy access top of unit ingredient hopper
- Automatic timer control
- Produces both low and high overrun ice cream
- Extrusion opening allows finished product to flow out easily
- Excellent repair record and parts are easy to obtain
- United States manufacturer
- Excellent distributor network in USA for repair service when needed

Disadvantages:
- Production time at least 9-11 minutes
- Excess finished product tends to stick to dasher blades

Model 220
This unit is ideal for ice cream shops that want to produce a high overrun ice cream product.
Advantages:
- Features stainless steel construction
- Easy access top of unit ingredient hopper
- Automatic timer control
- Extrusion opening allows finished product to flow out easily
- Adjustable shelf
- Excellent repair record and parts are easy to obtain
- United States manufacturer
- Excellent distributor network in USA for repair service when needed

Disadvantages:
- Production time at least 9-11 minutes
- Excess finished product tends to stick to dasher blades

CHAPTER 4
LOCATION, LOCATION, LOCATION
"Make No Bones About It, Without It You Will Not Succeed!"- Malcolm Stogo

All the money in the world cannot buy you success without a good location for your business. It's as simple as that! A secondary location with a cheaper rent will greatly increase your chance of failure that critical first year, period! Nothing drives a new business more the first year of operation than a good location. The longer you are in business, the less important it is, but no matter how good your product or service is, you will struggle that first year without a good location. Ask around of those who know, your fellow retailers, and they will tell you that location-finding takes time, perseverance, hard work and luck (being in the right place at the right time).

The food industry, which we are part of, is rife with massive egotists who have all the answers; and some actually do. Most, however, do not! Unfortunately, ego often gets in the way of wise decisions, resulting in loss of money and considerable grief. So simply, what I must tell you is finding the right location should never be about "finding the best deal" or a "simple gut reaction."

EVALUATING A POSSIBLE LOCATION
Competition
Frozen desserts are impulse items. Customers will go to the closest place to buy an ice cream cone, frequently without regard to quality. If the area is already saturated with ice cream shops, you should seriously consider avoiding the area. In other words, in an average residential area, if there is an ice cream competitor within one mile with volume over $250,000, you should avoid the potential site.

Traffic Density
There is nothing more important than traffic density when assessing whether the location you are looking at is the right one for you. One way

or another, enough people must pass by to provide a potential customer base. A location with cheaper rent but less traffic won't help you succeed. The following must be seriously considered before a rational decision is made that this location is the right one for you:

- *Visibility along the main street:* Standing on the main street approximately 50 yards away from where you are considering a location, can you see the store? Will your store sign be visible from that distance? What are the zoning regulations regarding signs? You need answers to those questions. Visibility is so relative that a logical rating on visibility should be simple: either the store is visible or is not. If it is not, this is a major reason not to accept the location.

- *Visibility from a major highway:* It's very important to be seen, but don't get fooled by the number of cars passing by near your location. If the traffic travels at an excessive speed (more than 35 mph) past a location, this distracts from a site. Thruway and interstate highways are exceptions when off and on ramps are convenient to the site.

- *Accessibility from a major highway:* While visibility is important, accessibility is more important. A right turn onto a lot is the best accessibility. A left turn onto the lot is only okay if there is no lane blockers or a traffic light that might hinder a turn being made.

- *Number of people who walk in front of the store you are thinking about leasing on a particular day:* This is a key criterion because people walking in front of your store are your most desirable future customers. A strip center must have at least 5,000-7,500 either walking by or entering the center each day for a site to be considered.

Length of the Lease
If the lease is available for less than five years, the site should be avoided at all costs. A lease of five to ten years is what it takes to get established and it will also enable you to have some resale value if, at the end of two or three years, you might want to sell the business.

Zoning
If the potential site is not zoned for use as a foodservice establishment and it is not likely that it can be rezoned, there is no point in pursuing that site further.

Traffic Count and Neighborhood Profile

The best location for the average ice cream shop is a residential-shopping area, a community with abundant street traffic and accessible parking. For a population to support an ice cream shop, a resident population of 20,000-35,000 within a two-mile radius is required, and/or no more than 15-18 minutes away from the location.

Traffic count itself can be either an asset or a liability. In general, the higher the traffic count, the greater the opportunity to attract sales to the site. Even more important, the denser the residential community within two miles of your location where there is a large percentage of young families is a real plus. However, what is the quality of the traffic count? If the traffic is a high percentage of commuters (non-shoppers), and cars flying by at 55 mph or trucks, than the traffic count for that potential site is a liability.

Growth or Decline of the Area

Is the area getting better or worse economically? Is the population rising or declining? The answer to these two questions must be "better" and "rising." If the answer is no to either one, avoid the site.

Overhead Expenses

The rent and utilities must be within your opening cash flow budget, not your future sales projections.

Professional Opinion

Before you make the plunge, ask other retailers and professional real estate people about your concept and potential location.

LOCATION INFORMATION CHECKLIST

To avoid overlooking some location factors, you should develop a checklist of information for evaluating a site. While all the information called for in the following checklist may not be needed; the list can call attention to factors that must be addressed by you at some point in time.

1. *Dimensions and total square footage of site:* If you make your own ice cream, you will need at least a total of 900-1,000 square feet of space, in which 250-300 can be used for ice cream production purposes.

2. *Linear feet of site frontages:* Frontage must be at least 16 feet wide.

3. *Distance and direction from nearest major streets:* If you are on a side street, you must not be more than 25 feet from a major street.
4. *Average 24-hour traffic on each frontage street:* This is a guide to determine viability of the space. This is good knowledge to have, but it is not a deal breaker one way or another.
5. *Number of moving traffic lanes past location, widths, and medians:* A median separating traffic going in different directions is not a desirable situation for customers trying to enter into your parking lot.
6. *Traffic controls affecting the location:* Cars must be able to enter the parking lot in front of your store directly from a stop sign or traffic light.
7. *Posted speed limits of adjacent streets:* Speed limits should not be more then 25 mph. on any road facing your store location.
8. *On-street parking:* Is there on-street parking? Knowing this is very important if your main customer base is day traffic.
9. *Parking lots that are available:* What lots are available and for how many cars?
10. *Existing structures on either side of possible location:* Who are your neighbors and are they helpful to drawing traffic to your shop?
11. *Type of energy available:* Was your possible location used previously for a food establishment? If so, what utilities are available?
12. *Present zoning classification:* How is the space zoned? The space must be zoned for foodservice use.
13. *Building limitations:* What is the space being used for now? What uses or restrictions is the landlord making regarding the use of the space? Are you allowed to have tables outside your space on the sidewalk?
14. *Character of surrounding area within one mile:* Besides the one-two mile radius, what retailing surrounds the area of your space going in every direction at least 100 yards?
15. *Population and income characteristics:* Is the population and income base sufficient to support your business?
16. *Allowable signage requirements:* This is very important to find out because signage for a new establishment is a key to success.
17. *Building codes that must be adhered to:* What restrictions if any are placed on the space by the local government?

18. ***Competition within one mile radius:*** While you are particularly interested in what your major competition is, what other foodservice establishments, like restaurants, sell ice cream?

19. ***Lease price requirements:*** Don't consider any lease where the rent is going to exceed more than 15% of annual budgeted sales. The following example illustrates how a 15% rent structure might work:

    Example: sales- $300,000

    Based on 15% rent- $45,000 per year or $3,750 rent per month

    Square footage- 800 square feet at $55 per square foot = rent of $44,000 per year comes out to a rent percentage of $3,666.66 per month.

20. ***Length of lease available:*** What kind of lease did the previous tenant have in monthly rental cost and length of lease? Knowing the answer to this question will enable you to guide yourself in negotiations with the landlord.

Finally, and critically, can the concept and the potential market support the location being considered?

An ice cream store has two potential values:

- **Real Estate Value**

  The value of the real estate is very important when one is considering selling the business, but it is also a detriment if the value of the property increases and the landlord wants to increase the rent at renewal time.

- **Value as Profit Generator**

  As a profit generator, the real estate value or rent paid to the landlord plays to the ice cream store owner's benefit in that the upside potential has no limits if the business exceeds the sales projected.

The two values should always be considered separately in deciding whether to lease a chosen site or not, but the main consideration is whether the value of your investment will increase over time based on the profits earned from the business?

DOING YOUR HOMEWORK - A TRUE STORY

Let's be frank! Picking a location is very difficult. It's almost like a romance. First there is lust, and then there is reality. Do I love the site? Will I be happy there? Is the space big enough? Can I afford the rent? Will the lease negotiation be fair? Am I making the right decision?

You will have to come to terms with all of the above in a way that you are completely satisfied that you have made the right decision, and the only way to find out is by doing your homework.

Now I am going to tell you a true story of how one of my clients, with my help, did his homework in order to come to the decision to rent a space or walk away. It wasn't easy, but in the end all the work paid off.

The location was Union Station, Washington, D.C. The client was Haagen-Dazs. The store's owner was Jerry Siegel of New Orleans. After three years of pursuing the possibility of opening a store at Union Station, the rental agent offered my client the space. The rent was approximately $9,500 per month for 600 square feet of space. A large nut to crack. And our first reaction was, could we do enough business to afford the rent? The rental agent told us what the current tenant was reporting in yearly sales. Did we believe the numbers? Yes and no. Yes, it was possible they were doing those numbers. No, rental agents tend to embellish.

There was only one way to find out. And that was to do an on-site examination of the current business being done by the current tenant, an ice cream store. The way we did it was the hard way. There is no doubt about it. Over a two-week period of time, we sat at a table in the food court and did the following:

- Counted the heads of every person buying an ice cream product at that store
- Counted how long it took to get a person served
- Counted how long the line was at lunchtime
- Counted how many people left the line to go elsewhere

How did we actually do the count? With a pad of paper showing the day of the week and a line for every hour of the day the shop was open for business. The head counts were inserted into the hour boxes. By the end of two weeks, we had a fairly good estimate of the business being done.

Next, we took these head counts and put a monetary number to it, using the price of a single dip cone as the gauge and added a percentage for toppings. Once, we calculated the weekly tally of the store, we expanded it to a monthly total by season, and then a yearly total. We then took those numbers and put Haagen-Dazs pricing to the head count, took the wait time and the people who left the line into consideration and came up with a yearly sales of what we could do in that spot by doing the following:

- Having more employees behind the counter at peak times of the day
- Moving people faster through the line
- Raising the price of an ice cream cone to what the market could bear.

What we came up with was a sales figure that was 30% above what the current tenant was doing in that spot. Matching our sales figure next to the yearly rental cost, we came up with a percentage rent of about 16% of sales. At that point, we knew we could afford the spot, and make it work to our benefit from day one. Four years later, we have lowered the rental percentage to below 15%.

Yes, it was hard work sitting there counting heads and figuring out whether we should do this deal. But by the end of two weeks, we had spent so much time there, that we had a gut feeling we had a winner on our hands.

And that is what I am trying to convey to you here. You just can't look at a space, look around and just say this is a good location. You have to do your homework, and most important you have to really fall in love with the space. If you have any doubt about the space you are looking at, walk away.

Because walking away from a particular location might be the best decision you will ever make in contemplating going into business.

CHAPTER 5
THE RETAIL ICE CREAM STORE

What's it like to be an owner, what equipment you will need, and how to get the store built. All very important issues, but equally important are the words of my good friend, Tony Lana of A. Panza & Sons.
"Your distributor's sales rep could turn out to be your best friend."

Ice cream stores are everywhere. They come in all shapes and sizes. In some parts of the country like New England, they are literally blocks apart. But they have not nearly reached their saturation point. Americans love ice cream, so the public is still ready, willing, and able to seek out the new kid on the block.

So now it's your turn. You want to open your own retail ice cream store? You have gotten the bug. You now have a concept. But I have a question for you. Do you really have any idea what life is like working in an ice cream store? Probably not, so let me give you a day in the life....

A DAY IN THE LIFE- A TRUE STORY

This is a true story, because it is all about me. For five glorious years I lived it, 24 hours a day, seven days a week, 12 months a year. The store

was called Ice Cream Extravaganza (I.C.E.) and it was located at the South Street Seaport in New York City.

By it's year, it was the largest grossing single ice cream store in the United States. While our sales numbers were large, my daily experience running the store and making ice cream was not much different than any other ice cream store in the country doing one-fourth the business we were doing.

So this is how it went.

I usually arrived by about 7:30 AM each day. Got my cup of coffee and looked around the store to see how clean or dirty it was. I say dirty because no matter how clean a store is, an owner can always find something that was not cleaned.

LESSON TO LEARN
STARTING EARLY IS A GOOD IDEA
BECAUSE IT'S QUIET AND YOU CAN GET A LOT OF WORK DONE

Next, I read our diary book to see what happened the night before and then onto opening the safe to see what business we did the night before.

LESSON TO LEARN
HAVE YOUR MANAGERS WRITE THE HAPPENINGS OF THEIR SHIFT. IT WILL HELP SOLVE A LOT OF PROBLEMS THE VERY NEXT DAY

By 8:00 AM, the first crew is expected and as usual each comes in haphazardly, some on time, some ten minutes late, and some not at all. The phone rings and Ricki, my ice cream maker-manager, says he's sick and can't make it today. Thanks Ricki, that means I have to make the ice cream today. Sabina, one of my three store managers finally comes in looking tired. I can't blame her since she closed the night before. "How did it go," I asked her? Busy, very busy, especially the last hour (1:00 AM), but the guys as usual just took their time cleaning up.

LESSON TO LEARN
GIRLS ARE A LOT BETTER WORKERS THAN GUYS

While the morning crew sets up the dipping case, my ice cream production crew who did show up, gets the three batch freezers sanitized and ready to go, I change my clothes to begin my eight to ten hour shift making ice cream. Sabina pops in to tell me we only have one tub of vanilla ice cream in the display case. Oops, I say to myself, we are in trouble because we need at least four every morning, one for each case. Okay I say to her, we will make some vanilla real fast. I get out my clipboard and look at the inventory.

LESSON TO LEARN
MAKE VANILLA EVERYDAY, YOU CAN NEVER HAVE ENOUGH

Thanks Ricki, I say to myself. Where's all the vanilla? My ice cream makers have everything all set, so we make six batches (22 tubs) of vanilla ice cream right off the bat. Of course during this process of making the vanilla ice cream, which did take almost one hour, the telephone started to ring with wholesale orders coming in for delivery to restaurants all over Manhattan by five in the evening. Next, came the calls from my ingredient and ice cream mix suppliers. What do you want tomorrow, each asked? Frankly I didn't have a clue, so I just ordered everything we got the day before, but doubled the order since Ricki was not here and sometimes he is lax about ordering.

LESSON TO LEARN
WITHOUT ADEQUATE INVENTORY CONTROLS
YOU WILL HAVE A LOT OF WASTE AND GO BROKE TO BOOT

Sabina pops in and says, "we got a problem," the dipping case in front of the store is not cold enough. Something is wrong. I go out and check and sure enough she is right. Immediately, I get on the telephone and call Nino, my refrigeration guru. Where are you I say? He tells me he's in Staten Island and can't get to me for at least two hours. I look at my clock. Since it is only 9:00 AM, that means 11 AM and he's here. With a little bit of luck, he will get it fixed by lunchtime. After all, Nino is my number one man. I love him and he knows it. I pay him so well why shouldn't he love me.

LESSON TO LEARN
FIND A GOOD REFRIGERATION REPAIR PERSON THE DAY YOU
OPEN FOR BUSINESS. YOU WILL BE LOST WITHOUT HIM

But really, I have treated Nino as my friend. I make a birthday cake for each of his four kids every year, and believe me that $15.00 ice cream cake to his family is worth the equivalent of a diamond ring to someone else. If you get the picture, treat your refrigeration repair person with respect, and pay him/her well, and you will never have a problem getting your refrigeration fixed.

Nino, of course, shows up, fixes the problem in ten minutes, eats a scoop of ice cream, and out he goes. By now I am into my fifth cup of coffee. My ice cream makers are now into making their third flavor without my help, but now I have to go and flavor the next three flavors because I don't trust their eyes measuring out the ingredients needed for these tough ones coming up. With that done, I look at the schedule for the weekend. Everything looks okay; thank goodness something is right. We are now into lunch, the store is hopping with everyone wanting to get their dessert at the same time. After all, it's 1:45 PM and everyone has to get back to work by 2:00 PM!

During this whole time the telephone rang constantly. The problem is that half the calls are for my employees, not for me. With lunch over, it's time to go to the bank and make my deposits and get change for the weekend. And do I mean change, $400 worth, all in quarters and one-dollar bills. You see, we have everything priced so we only have to worry about having enough quarters and singles on hand to handle any emergency. By Sunday afternoon, every food store in our food court will be coming around asking the same question, do you have any quarters and singles to spare. Seriously, this is a very big problem. Holding up a line giving out change can take a lot longer than scooping an ice cream cone, believe me.

LESSON TO LEARN
HAVE PLENTY OF CHANGE FOR THE WEEKEND BUSINESS

Back from the bank, I am hungry. All I have eaten all day was the ice cream just made, seven licks in all, which I spit out once I decided that I liked what I tasted. Too many times an owner starts making his/her own ice cream with good results, but then over time turns the ice cream making over to an employee. And before you know it, the quality of the ice cream has changed, and the owner isn't even aware of it.

LESSON TO LEARN
TASTE YOUR ICE CREAM EACH DAY: IT'S IMPORTANT THAT IT MEETS YOUR STANDARDS

Walk over to Pizza Del Ponti, my partner's pizza joint (the largest pizza joint in the USA), get my slice with anchovies, grab a coke, and back to my desk to pay some bills.

LESSON TO LEARN
IF YOU PAY YOUR BILLS ON TIME: IT'S AMAZING WHAT YOUR SUPPLIERS WILL DO FOR YOU

It's now 4:00 PM, and my ice cream makers are humming along, working incredibly well without Ricki. Does that mean they are well trained, or are they happy Ricki is not here today to boss them around?

LESSON TO LEARN
IF YOUR EMPLOYEES MAKE YOUR ICE CREAM AND THEY ARE NOT TRAINED OR SUPERVISED YOU WILL END UP WITH INCONSISTENCIES AND LOUSY ICE CREAM

By this time we have made most of the ice cream we need for tomorrow, ordered all our ingredients, dealt with a refrigeration problem, went to the bank, paid some bills, and even had a slice of pizza to balance out all the coffee I drank so far today. Get the picture, you will be very busy indeed.

It's now 5:00 PM and we are up to our last batches of ice cream to be made today. Since they are our most difficult ones, I take charge and with my crew, I mix the batches up, get the ingredients measured, pour the variegating sauce into the water cans we used to variegate our product and off we go making three separate flavors in three separate batch freezers, two batches for each flavor. I go from one machine to the next, check for taste and help my crew extrude out the flavors when they are ready to be extruded. All of this takes about one hour.

LESSON TO LEARN
DON'T FORGET WHY YOU GOT INTO THIS BUSINESS
IT'S BECAUSE YOU LOVED THE IDEA OF MAKING ICE CREAM

It's now 6:00 PM, the night crew is fully assembled, staggering in from 4:00 PM on replacing the day crew one by one. The night crew fills up the dipping case with new tubs, gets the place cleaned up and mopped, and one by one each goes on a dinner break. Dinner, what's that? If I eat before 9:00 PM, I am lucky.

By now we are finished making ice cream for the day, the production room is cleaned up. I make up a list of everything we made today and enter it onto the computer. All of this took 15 minutes. I am pooped, so I decide to get something to eat. I call up my partner and we agree to meet for dinner.

At dinner, we talk about expansion and cash flow. I want to expand and he wants the cash. An interesting twist of fate. But that's business. Everyone has his/her own priorities.

It's now 8:30 PM, back from dinner and the place is hopping with over 40 people waiting to be served by my 13 scoopers. I can tell this is going to be a good night. I go back into the office and open up the mail I got at 10:00 AM. It's actually relaxing to read the mail after a long day.

Well, by now, I think it's time to go home and rest my feet. It's been a long day, but all in all, it's a lot better than working for someone else.

BUYING THE EQUIPMENT, GETTING THE STORE BUILT

So the next question is, what will it cost and how will it get built?

For someone new getting into this business, all of the equipment needed and how to get your place built can be a traumatic experience in ignorance. But relax, it's not that difficult and within six months you will think you are an expert.

Equipment- Old, Inherited or New

There is no question about it; many people entering our business ask me the same question: where can I buy used equipment, especially a batch freezer? While I understand why they ask, I am frankly surprised about the ultimate situations and decisions many end up with purchasing used equipment. It's like learning how to walk before you start to crawl. Unless, you know exactly what you want and the manufacturer who makes the equipment you are looking for, buying used equipment can end up costing you a lot more than you ever expected.

A perfect example is the purchase of a used batch freezer. Many think every batch freezer on the market will do the same job. For me, probably the answer is yes, but I have been in this business over 25 years, and I know the in-and-outs of each batch freezer on the market today. If you are new to this business, saving a $1,000 between one make of batch freezer or another is worth nothing if it's not the batch freezer you really need for your kind of business.

If you are so inclined to purchase used equipment, here are a few tips:

58

- The best time to purchase used equipment is from September to February.
- A 20 quart batch freezer over three years old is worth no more than $5,000. One over 10 years old is worth no more then $2,500.
- Always get a serial number of the unit and check it out with the manufacturer. They will tell you how old the unit is.
- If you are going to pick it up yourself, have a refrigeration repair person look at it first before buying the unit.
- Never buy a dipping case older than four years old. The possibility of a compressor failing is very great.
- Buying a used shell of a walk-in freezer is always a good idea because in most cases you will only have to purchase a new compressor. The panels of the shell are in most cases always in good shape.
- Small items like milkshake machines and fudge warmers are excellent buys in used condition.

It is very important to take into consideration the replacement of freon in any piece of refrigeration equipment. Any piece of refrigeration equipment more than six years old does not have the right kind of freon and if you purchase a piece of equipment more than six years old, you will pay dearly to get it repaired. The cost to replace freon can be over $500 a shot with the older freon. Imagine having purchased a used piece of equipment and you have a freon leak at least twice a year.

If you take over an existing ice cream store, as is likely, you may inherit a certain amount of basic equipment. It isn't free, you paid for it. You may reject it, of course, in favor of new equipment of your own preference. But you still may have to pay for it. There are considerable savings to be made from using inherited equipment, even though it may sometimes look depressingly old and decrepit and quite out of sympathy with your brave new hopes.

A practical eye is required. A walk-in is a walk-in, as long as it works, whether it's brand-new or 20 years old. Any old refrigeration equipment that proves unreliable and beyond cheap local repair should be replaced promptly. A breakdown on a busy day is the worst thing imaginable, especially when you are waiting for the refrigeration repair service to come to your shop. So, a word of caution, a bargain is only good if it works well, everyday, not just some of the time.

Equipment- New

Buying brand new equipment is like buying a car. It's shiny, looks great and you are afraid to get it dirty. Brand-new equipment is the most expensive kind. The bank will be more inclined to lend you money for new equipment, but you'll pay top price. Sometimes equipment can be leased, especially ice machines and batch freezers.

One thing can be said about buying new ice cream manufacturing and dispensing equipment. Almost without exception, every manufacturer I know makes reliable equipment. What is important is the distributor you buy it from. The reason for this is because the distributor is responsible for the warranty on the equipment and getting the piece of equipment repaired in case of a breakdown as soon as possible.

Dipping Cases

There is very little difference in manufacturing quality in purchasing a dipping case from either Kelvinator or Masterbilt. Below is a list of things you should consider regardless of which manufacturer you ultimately buy your dipping case from:

- Buy new equipment and make sure the compressor has a good 5-year warranty.
- Look at the width of the counter on top of the case. A one-half to one-inch difference in width makes a lot of difference when you want to display something on top of the case.
- If you can buy a used dipping case in good condition, grab it.
- Since most manufacturers use compressors that never burn out, a used dipping case can save you a lot of money, in many cases, half the cost of a new one.
- Dipping cases that come with frost shields are a lot easier to maintain when defrosting a case on a weekly basis
- European cases offer a lot more visibility of product than most domestic conventional cases.
- Make sure all water piping coming from your dipper well is at least 1" to 1 1/2" in diameter. Piping less than that will drive you nuts with clogged up drains of ice cream particulars such as nuts, fruits etc.
- Customers like to see the product, so don't even think you can get away with using a reach-in storage freezer as a dipping case. It just doesn't work.

- Never empty the contents of an empty tub on top of a new ice cream tub. It's simply disgusting!

MENU BOARD SIGNAGE

A great majority of ice cream storeowners feel that if their product is terrific, everything else is unimportant; that means, customer service, cleanliness, and signage. Well, let me tell you, I know of many ice cream stores that are no longer with us because they were too shortsighted in understanding what it takes to run a "complete" successful establishment.

How many times have you gone into an ice cream store and spent more time trying to figure out what flavors the store offered, the different sizes, and at what price?

Even worse, if there is one thing that is lacking in most ice cream stores, it's both the menu board and flavor signage inside the dipping cases.

Whereas a repeat customer has previous experience to rely on, a new customer, in particular, must be able to make eye contact with your products and have access to clear, concise signage in order to make a decision.

Pitfalls to Avoid

By paying close attention to detail when designing your signage and graphics, you can avoid the following common mistakes:
- Sign boards that are too small to accommodate all your menu items
- Menus lacking distinctive and descriptive selling copy to communicate to the customer
- Item descriptions that are too long; be concise
- Type that is too small to be read easily
- Handwritten notes attached to the menu or signboards; these look shabby and rarely help sales
- Poor interior lighting over or near signboards that are not illuminated

Designing a Menu Board

The basic criterion you want to consider when designing a menu board is that it is clear and striking so that the customer can make a purchasing decision. In particular, you must make sure the following is considered:

- Targeting the menu board to attract the customer, enhance the beauty of your store, and increase your sales
  <u>Bottom line: People buy what they see!</u>
- The use of simple and concise language of the items and flavors available
- How the menu board should reflect the image of your operation
- How the menu board should appeal to children; simply how to have a fun and lighthearted design.

The signboard is one of the first things a customer sees when entering the premises, so it's important that it projects a positive image consistent with your environment.

ICE CREAM SCOOPS

Believe it or not, most owners of ice cream stores know very little about what size ice cream scoops to use and worse yet, how to care for them so they don't have to be replaced every summer season.

So here's a primer course on both.

Size and Portion Control

Each ice cream scoop when filled properly will yield the amount set forth below for each cone or cup. Many ice cream stores like the idea of a regular scoop and a cap to get the desired weight per cone or cup. In other words, if you want a 4-ounce portion with a scoop and cap, you should use a number 12 scoop for the regular scoop and a simple fill in the same scoop for the cap.

Size	Description
10	4 ounces of ice cream
12	3 ounces of ice cream
16	2 1/2 ounces of ice cream
20	2 ounces of ice cream
24	1 1/2 ounces of ice cream
30	1 ounce of ice cream

Taking Care of Your Ice Cream Scoops

The following cleaning tips will help you get longer life out of your ice cream scoops:

- Abrasive or caustic cleaners mar the finish, reduce scoop's life and dipping efficiency
- Use fine grade cleaning pads daily to preserve finish
- Use mild detergents
- Do not put in dishwasher or water over 140 degrees F.
- If surface darkens, rub hard with cleaning pad and detergent
- Always rinse, rinse, and rinse, then wipe down and air dry
- If water in your area is hard or highly chlorinated, look for an ice cream scoop with a Teflon finish

WHAT DOES IT TAKE TO OPEN AN ICE CREAM STORE?

Depending on your specific location you have chosen, the cost of constructing your store and purchasing equipment to fill it will be approximately as follows:

Front of the Store

Equipment

The equipment needed for the front of the store based on a frontage of 20 ft. x 50 ft. The equipment quoted for new equipment unless otherwise noted.

2- 16 hole dipping cabinets: *to sell 32 flavors*	$6,000
2- soft serve machines: *to sell 4-6 flavors*	20,000
Chairs and tables: *for approximately 26 people*	5,000
Menu boards: *2 back-lit boards*	4,000
Ice cream cake display case: *to display ice cream cakes and novelties*	4,500
Outside signage: *sign to be placed in front of store*	2,500
2 cash registers: *store of more then 300 sq. ft. needs two cash registers*	4,000
Espresso/coffee package: *a full blown espresso/coffee set-up*	5,000
Drop safe: a drop safe is needed if you are not *going be there everyday*	500
Ice machine: *if you are going to sell smoothies or soda from a machine*	1,500
2 Neon signs (front of store): *to highlight or add visibility to your location*	1,000
2 Fudge warmers: *for hot fudge and caramel*	500
1 Milkshake machine: *three head machine a must to sell*	

milkshakes	400
1 Smoothie blender: *high powered mixer a must to sell smoothies*	400
Small wares misc.	3,000
Total Equipment	$58,300

Leasehold Improvements

Electrical	$15,000
Plumbing	10,000
Mill work (counter and backwall)	10,000
Carpentry	10,000
Tile work	5,000
Architecture fees	10,000
Alarm system	2,000
Building permit	500
Painting	1,000
Total Leasehold Improvements	$63,500
Grand Opening Package	5,000
Cash Flow	25,000
TOTAL	$151,800

Ice Cream Production Room

If you are going to make your own ice cream, the cost=	$39,925
GRAND TOTAL	$191,725

LEASEHOLD IMPROVEMENTS

Once you have signed your lease, the clock begins to start ticking. In most cases a new tenant is given anywhere from two-six months of free rent to get the store built and ready to open. If you have anticipated what you need to get done in advance of signing your lease, you will have been well ahead of the game.

Design

What is really interesting is that while many new people coming into our business have no idea about the equipment to purchase or use, many have a very good idea of what kind of ambience they want for their concept. A lot of these ideas depend on the age of the owner. Many want to relive their childhood while younger people go for a more modern upscale look.

Let's face it, décor is in the eyes of the beholder, and the beholder here is the owner of the store. If he/she likes it and the décor is well executed, lit properly with clear looking signage, and the product is well displayed, you will have a winner on your hands as far as décor is concerned.

Ultimately, the object of all ice cream stores must be to provide the maximum delight to the customers while efficiently serving as many customers as possible. And all ice cream storeowners juggle these two factors constantly. Some emphasize efficient service, others are big on ambiance, and others just crowd people in wherever they'll fit or have them wait in a long line outside the store.

Hard though it may be to believe, many people like being crowded. Perhaps it gives them an illusion of being part of something special waiting for the incredible treat or just enjoying the group experience.

Once you have signed a letter of intent to rent your space you should begin the design process as soon as possible. The importance of this is to be ready to start construction the moment you have signed your lease. As soon as the design process is finished and you have approved them, you should begin lining up your electrical, plumbing, and carpentry people you will need to turn your drawings into reality. Don't of course begin construction until you have the signed lease in hand.

Demolition
If you rent a space, and it is not a clean shell, then once you sign your lease, the first thing you should do is evaluate what is there, retain what you might need and use, and clear out the rest as soon as possible.

Electrical
Have your electrical contractor do a survey of what power is in your space. Next, submit a "spec" sheet of every piece of equipment you will be purchasing and a layout drawing given to you by your architect of what you visualize your space to look like. Once they have this information, they can advise you of your future electrical needs, let you know what you can keep and use, and begin adding more power as needed. You should do this work well in advance of any painting and carpentry work you will be doing to the space. Remember, more power is better than less, so you should anticipate future possible needs now. Doing this will save you lots of money later on.

Plumbing

If the space you are renting was a food establishment before you took over, evaluate closely what plumbing is there and how you can use it for your operation. When laying out the space, make sure you have a floor drain both in the front of the store behind the counter preferably near your dipping cases and soft serve machines and another floor drain in your ice cream production room near your batch freezer. Floor drains are an absolute necessity for fast, proper cleaning.

GETTING READY TO OPEN

You have done all you can do, and you are now ready to open. So step back and take a good hard look at your store through the eyes of the customer. This is how you can do it:

Right before you are set to open, one morning come to your store and pretend you are the customer. Take you time and look around. What you will discover will astound you. First, look at the outside area:

- Is the sidewalk and front window clean?
- Is the lighting good and the menu signage easy to read?
- Is the front counter clean and are all the signs hung straight?
- Is all the equipment in place?
- Are the toilets in the bathrooms operating correctly, and clean?

At this point, do you feel comfortable at what you just saw? If you are, you are ready to open your store. If you are not comfortable, write down all your thoughts, set a timetable to get them fixed. Once fixed, take a deep breath, and kick open the doors.

You are now in business!

CHAPTER 6
EVERYDAY MARKETING

"How do I know I have made and marketed a good product? When the customer buys it again a second, third, and fourth time."
Robert Ellenger, Baked To Perfection, Port Washington, NY.

To many starting out in the retail ice cream business, marketing is a mystery word. So much effort has gone into the idea, raising the money, building the store, that once the front door is open, most owners simply think customers will flock to the store, rave about the ice cream and come back again and again. Wrong!

If you don't begin to think about how you are going to market your ice cream store from the moment you began thinking of this wonderful idea, then your ultimate chance for success is diminished greatly.

When it comes to marketing an ice cream store, the most important thing you can come up with is creating for your customer the WOW experience.

WOW EXPERIENCE

The genesis for the following comes from a great husband and wife team, Norm & Pat LaPalme, the owners of THE PIAZZA*, Keene, New Hampshire. Through a lot of trial and error, they made their little shop of 400 square feet of inside space into a rock and roll establishment serving hundreds of soft serve flavors creating what they call for their customers the WOW experience.

So what is the WOW experience?

Creating a niche for their business
Developing a vision
Taking action to make it happen

- **Creating a Niche:** They looked around and focused on doing business totally the opposite of their competition; literally offering hundreds of soft-serve flavors everyday of the week.

- **Clear Vision:** They encouraged their customers to try these new flavors. Be outlandish. They wanted their customers to walk away from the store saying I had that crazy flavor today, it was even better then the weird one I had last week. They wanted the word OUTLANDISH to stick with their customers.
- **Taking Action:** It took Norm and Pat two years of being in business to figure out what their vision was and it was only after ALMOST GOING BROKE that they got it. I make this statement for one reason only. **Going broke forced them to really think.** That is something most owners never do. They get caught up in their problems, get bogged down in their thoughts and lose total control of why they got into business in the first place. To Pat and Norm, their vision was simple: Give value to their customers, implement these values over time, not just for the moment they were in crisis. It has worked for them.

Simply put, the WOW experience is all about the customer from the moment he/she enters your shop till the moment he/she leaves. And this experience is all about the following:

- **Customer Service:** Employees that have a smile on their face, and with that smile every time a customer enters your store, the following two lines-should always sing out- "hello, may I help you" and when they leave, "good-by, hope to see you again."
- **Quality Product:** Products that are always fresh; it's as simple as that.

Do you have the idea now? So let's talk further about the WOW experience. Put yourself into your customers' shoes. When they come into your store, wouldn't it be nice if they think the following of you and your employees?

- They know what I always order
- They make me feel comfortable
- They give me great personal service

So, in summary, how can you create a WOW experience for your store? Take a second now and think and answer the following:

- Relive those moments when you have had a WOW experience at either your store or someplace else.
- Try to put these experiences into values.

- Identify no more than three specific values that you are willing to totally live; focus resources, time and energy in making these values a total reality; make decisions based on them. Now, hold them foremost in your mind.
- Put these values into a vision phrase and use the phrase over and over and over so people know your message and your servers project the message. Phrases like:
  Vision Phrase- An ice cream a day brings a smile your way
  Values- Personalized attention, country charm
  Target Population- Who are you serving?
- Act out the values at every opportunity; play your vision video often until the fog clears from your crystal ball.
- Create specific actions, behavior, policies, specials, expectations that get you closer to your vision video.
- Direct resources and energy toward your vision video; involve others in helping to provide ways to get there.
- Use your energy well, it's all for nothing if you don't know where you are going.

EVERYDAY MARKETING TRICKS

It takes years to learn all the marketing tricks of a frozen desserts shop, but since learning is part of life, whatever you can grab onto should be cherished. Considering myself an old hand at all of this, I am amazed at everything new I learn about marketing and merchandising from others as I travel around the world.

Bar none, day in and day out, the best marketing trick of the trade is making sure you have a "smiling" customer. How you get there is by having a clean looking store, happy employee faces, great customer service, and great tasting products.

Marketing Arousal

A powerful word! If you can arouse your customers with your shop and the quality of your products, you will become a long-term winner. Rethink this word at the beginning of each new summer season. "Arousal " takes many forms:
- Opening day banner
- Season opener, "BUY ONE GET ONE FREE" single scoop
- Specific product sales special to begin the season

- Bright new paint job for your shop
- New ice cream flavors and products broadly announced on your front window and counters
- To take arousal a step further, even the simplest and less expensive things get the best results. As I said before, a simple hello and smile arouses interest. An example is instructing your employees simply to say to each customer entering your shop, "Hello, may I help you? May I serve you a sample?" The result of all of this is arousal and satisfaction: Getting something for nothing always works.

Be an Originator, Not a Follower
Use your creative juices to be different.
- Create flavors and products no one else has. The only criterion is that they taste good. Don't copy your competitors because long-term there is no value in it.
- Evaluate your competition. Find your niche against them and exploit it. I have never seen a successful follower, especially one who copies what the competition is doing down the street.
- Always out-price your competition with specials one after another all season long.

Catering to Children
Catering to children is one of the most neglected areas of our business. We simply forget what they like. Yes, they like Vanilla, Chocolate and Strawberry, but as they get older their choices change dramatically. Kids love the following:
- Candy flavors, Bubble Gum and Cookies & Creme
- Flavors that have a lot of color to them
- Small sizes
- Colorful character ice cream cakes for birthdays
- Rainbow sprinkles with different color combinations

Promotions
A retail business that doesn't promote is a business asking to go out of business.
- Bar none, the best ice cream promotion is: "BUY ONE GET ONE FREE."
- All you need is a poster in your front window and a sign sitting on

top of your counter or dipping case.
- Couponing works wonders for short-term sales promotions.
- After each sale, give the customer a new coupon with his/her change. It promotes repeat business.

Birthday Clubs
Ice cream shops and birthday clubs go hand in hand. This is simply a fantastic way to promote customer loyalty and repeat business. To get started, you need the following:
- Create a program with a sign up book, poster and card for each participant.
- Go to a printer and print a birthday club card the size of a normal business card with your company logo on it and in bold, print "BIRTHDAY CLUB" on it with a space for the customer's name, address, telephone number and date of birth.

Serving Sizes
What does serving sizes have to do with marketing? It's all about perception and eye contact. When it comes to ice cream, customers like to know that they are getting a large serving no matter what size they are ordering. Mainly, this rationale is based on the theory that customers feel they are being cheated versus the price paid for the serving. With this in mind:
- Serve large servings and price them accordingly
- A happy customer is repeat business
- Use cups that allow space for toppings
- Serve three sizes, small, regular, and large. This is a wonderful marketing idea because in most cases, consumers will opt for the regular size giving you a larger unit sale.

Selling Your Logo T-Shirts
Go to a T-shirt manufacturer and purchase "irregular" T-shirts. Put your logo on them and give them away as part of a special occasion. For the most part, these shirts cost no more then $2.00-3.00 apiece because they are slightly damaged. If you decide to purchase regular T-shirts for your logo, price them competitively.

Your Store Club

Make your customers part of your own WOW experience. Create a store club and issue a "Club Card." Make this card worth something and offer benefits to go along with being a member like simply having each member show the card at a specific moment and get something for it.

For example,
- 1/2 price on anything every Monday
- Free ice cream cone on a birthday
- One free ice cream cake once a year

School Colors

Offer, on a specific day of the week, sprinkles in the colors of a school near your store. Every school has two colors as its logo, so as a special for anyone buying a large size cone, offer the school color sprinkles FREE. Simply dip half the cone with one color and the other side of the cone with the other color.

School Visits

Nifty Fifties* in Philadelphia has a program called "Milk Shake Days." Every year they visit over 20 elementary school classes that have achieved something worthy of a special event.

Students work very hard in school. They read books. They hold food drives. They often have perfect attendance. Nifty Fifties rewards their hard work with a visit from "Shakeman." Milk shakes are a treat that children love, so no wonder that "Milk Shake Days" are a super treat for deserving students.

"Shakeman" goes into the classroom and dresses the children in aprons, hats, and gloves and teaches the children the art of milk shake-making. Each student has the opportunity to select a favorite flavor and mix his/her own milk shake. Prizes are handed out to the students with the best-prepared shakes. All of this activity takes about one hour.

Store Contest: Getting Your Customers Involved

What I am about to tell you is a wonderful story and a fabulous contest idea. It comes from Maraline Olson of Screamin Mimi's* of Sebastopol, California. Maraline and her husband Kurt were about to have their first child and the due date was to be sometime in February. Everyone in town knew Maraline was pregnant and since the store was closed except for weekends during January and February, they decided to have some fun with their customers. They devised a contest around the big event.

Customers were asked to choose the date of birth, weight, and sex of the baby. Anyone choosing the correct date won a $5.00 gift certificate; choosing the correct weight won a $10 gift certificate; and choosing the correct sex won a free ice cream cone. Anyone who guessed all three won a $50.00 gift certificate.

Needless to say, the contest was great fun and a huge success.

They gave away 72- free cones, 16-$5.00 gift certificates, 2-$10.00 gift certificates, but no grand prize. The closest anyone got to the correct weight was two ounces. Carter Olson was born on February 24, 1999 at 9 pounds, 13 ounces. Maraline and I have been having a friendly feud about selling ice cream by weight so her response to me is "even if sold by weight, he's still priceless!"

Labor Day Sales
In my opinion, the best time to do business is when you are busy. Not necessarily in the winter when no one comes into your store. Is there any busier time then Labor Day weekend? Here are a few suggestions:
- 1/2 off the price of anything sold in the store
- Free ice cream to everyone on the evening of the last day of the weekend
- "Buy One, Get One Free" on the last day of the weekend
- Have a "special "PINT" sale

Using Coupons to Promote Your Ice Cream Cake Business
If you sell take-out pre-packed quarts, you have a wonderful opportunity to promote your ice cream cake business because a take-out quart customer is "a perfect ice cream cake customer." Simply place a coupon sticker somewhere on the face of the quart containers saying "$2.00 Off Any Size Cake." This "nifty idea" comes from Stan Zafran of Denise's Ice Cream* of Somerville, Mass.

Turning Sampling into a Sale
There is no better way to promote a sale and get new and repeat customers to try new things than through sampling. Customers love to be asked and the more you do it, the better your sales will be. Here are

a few ideas to try:

- Let your employees promote "their" favorite flavors
- Use taster spoons; they are relatively inexpensive
- Put up a sign:

IF WE DON'T ASK
THE SCOOP'S ON US

- Make sampling techniques a part of all new employee training
- Encourage customers to ask for more than one sample

The goal here is to increase check size and attract new customers. Sampling has been an effective method of stimulating trial of your store's products. It can also be effective in stimulating trial of your TAKE-OUT items.

The following are two methods you can use to sample the desserts in your store.

Hard Ice Cream- Scoop ice cream with a melon baller into taster cups. Place the taster cups on a silver tray, ready for sampling. Sample and pass these cups out at high traffic times (especially for customers waiting in line).

Ice Cream Cakes- Cut a cake into 1/2-inch chunks and store them in your back freezer. Serve chunks in small cups using toothpicks. Again serve them at high traffic times.

NOTE: It is essential that the employee handing out samples is completely knowledgeable about the products (ingredients, servings and price).

COUPONING: A WAY TO MAKE YOUR BUSINESS GROW

A customer saved is a customer earned! Sounds simple, but in today's tough economic times, it's a struggle operating a frozen dessert business. Now more than ever, marketing your establishment toward promotions that will get customers into your store is a necessity for survival. Look around you: loyalty is out the door.

Advantages of Couponing

- Keep old customers coming back
- Build product and store awareness
- Produce immediate results
- Compared to other forms of advertising, the costs of couponing are relatively inexpensive
- Create your own coupons, thanks to computers and color printers

Disadvantages of Couponing
- If you use an outside source to print them, it can be expensive
- Each coupon redeemed has a food cost
- If you are a franchise operation, there are royalties to pay on additional gross sales
- Today, everybody does it, so if the coupon isn't dynamic on its own, the beneficial effect is diluted

Do's and Don'ts of Couponing
Do's
- Use coupons to trade up in size proportions
- Use coupons as bag stuffers for take-out sales
- Use the word "FREE" as much as possible
- If at all possible promote on coupons "$1.00 OFF" instead of cents. That means $1.00 off sundaes, shakes, cakes, etc.

Don'ts
- Never have cents off if it's less than "50 CENTS OFF"
- Never use "% off" as an inducement
- Never have an expiration date less then three weeks to one month
- Never use set hours of the day or time. Words like mornings, afternoons or evenings work much better

TAKE-OUT BUSINESS: A GREAT WAY TO MARKET YOUR ICE CREAM STORE

Take-out is now considered the hottest means of increasing sales in the food service industry. It can be the critical margin of profit you need to fight high occupancy costs, limited seating or space capacity and cold winter months.

There are certain key elements that you must consider in order to make your TAKE-OUT business a success.

Your Investment in This Program

Yes, you will need to invest $$$$ to create and sustain a successful TAKE-OUT business. The program cannot exist without a plan that includes adequate front and backroom freezer storage space. Adequate freezer space means the front TAKE-OUT display freezer is always fully stocked. If you don't already have a front display freezer unit, then I highly recommend you purchase either a Masterbilt (BLG 27 or 52) or

Kelvinator (VGL26 or 48), one-or two-door, glass front, vertical merchandising unit.

FIGURE 6-1. Kelvinator Model VGL-48 two door glass front merchandising freezer.

Marketing Plan

You have to be committed to building sales with a great line of TAKE-OUT products. A full, beautifully merchandised freezer in your shop is essential to building sales and creating legs to a long-term TAKE-OUT business. You cannot rely on custom orders. The key to building sales is to maximize impulse purchases.

Once you have your marketing plan in place, there are many avenues you can follow to build your TAKE-OUT business. By focusing on the various days of the week, holiday occasions, organizations and segment groups, you will begin to get increased volumes in TAKE-OUT sales. It is imperative that you take the following steps before you begin any TAKE-OUT store-marketing plan.

You Must Have Good Operating Standards on How a TAKE-OUT Business Should Operate

1. Always have a clean, stocked, well-merchandised TAKE-OUT display freezer.
2. All employees must be trained in what TAKE-OUT products are available and the cost of each.
3. Think long term- six-month programs, not short events.
4. Identify your store's marketing strengths and weaknesses and take the time to do it right: Analyze, plan, execute.
5. All programs should be stated so that your customers understand what you are doing. Think of yourself as a customer.

6. When attempting to meet competitive programs, the rule is to meet and not exceed competitive offers. Your advantage is your quality, and you must emphasize that.
7. Deliver what you promise for every TAKE-OUT product. The best way to find out is to take a product home, just like a customer would, eat it and dissect it for its strengths and weaknesses regarding quality of product, packaging, and any message attached to the product.
8. Lead from your strength. You have your own brand awareness that you should be constantly emphasizing everyday to your customers throughout your branded cups, napkins and bags.
9. Apply rational and common sense to whatever you attempt.

The following strategies are a framework for developing and building TAKE-OUT sales. They are designed to increase profits through <u>volume</u> sales.

Attract New TAKE-OUT Store Business

1. Stimulate trial: done by sampling and daily specials.
2. Generate awareness of any new products: done by promoting the product as a special.
3. Target particular groups, e.g. kids, men, seniors: done by offering a special kind of product or product size to the targeted group.
4. Support special events for recognition and awareness: done by giving away freely. The rewards of doing this will come back to you in spades year after year.
5. Improve community relations: done by giving freely to any group in which its members are good customers of yours.
6. Enhance your store image: done by doing all of the above.

Products to Sell

The most popular products you can sell in your TAKE-OUT freezer area are pre-packed pints, quarts, ice cream cakes and ice cream pies.

Signage

Clear, striking signage is the marketing tool that creates interest and provides information to your customers. Interior store signage is one of the many vehicles needed in order for your store to have a pro-active TAKE-OUT business.

All of the graphics, TAKE-OUT menu board (on top of freezer unit or on a wall next to the display freezer unit) and the main menu board should satisfy four main objectives of a store primed to do a substantial TAKE-OUT business. Go into your store and ask the following questions:

1. Does your menu and existing signage target the market you are trying to reach?
2. Are your customers getting the message that you are in the TAKE-OUT business?
3. Are you using printed displays and mobiles in your store, and do they work? If they don't, ask yourself why not?
4. Is the existing signage expressing to your customer that your store is different than the competition?

Thinking about and defining how your store attracts a customer to purchase product once inside your store will go a long way towards targeting your marketing and merchandising efforts in successfully growing a TAKE-OUT business.

Situated above the TAKE-OUT freezer, this unit should list all your TAKE-OUT products with pricing, and if possible graphically display product photographs of some if not all of your cakes and pies. It is also helpful to have a separate TAKE-OUT Menu Board. This board should be completely realigned so that "TAKE-OUT" is emphasized with a category header as follows:

TAKE-OUT

Pint	$3.85
Quart	4.85
Ice Cream Cake 7"	14.95
Ice Cream Cake 9"	19.95
Ice Cream Pies	14.95

TAKE-OUT Freezer

It is very important that you have proper, clear, concise product signage **inside (not just outside)** your merchandising display freezer right in front of each product displayed. This signage should state the product name, price and size. If the product is an ice cream cake or pie, it should also state the amount of servings the product will serve.

If you have either a Kelvinator (FPD-5) or Masterbilt (FIP50), then you can insert a translite lettered plate of your store name and logo that goes into the large white space across the front of the unit.

78

FIGURE 6-2. Masterbilt Model FIP50 ice cream cake display freezer.

TAKE-OUT at the Office

"TAKE-OUT" at the office is an effective way to increase sales, increase check size and bring business to your store by way of repeat business.

> *It's 3:00 PM in the afternoon and everyone in the office needs a pick-me-up. Someone grabs your TAKE-OUT" menu and travels from desk to desk asking:" We're ordering, what do you want?*

In developing TAKE-OUT at the office, there are a number of avenues to pursue. Below are various ideas to consider:

- Free delivery of order over $15.00. Location will dictate if this is possible
- Special pricing of ice cream cakes, quarts, and pints for offices
- A free, medium-size, cup/cone, with a topping, to the person who calls in and picks up an order of $10.00 or more

Choose the office program that best meets your needs and demographics of your area. The following are steps you <u>must take</u> to get this program off the ground.

Inform Offices of Your Program

- Create a form letter that can be mailed or hand delivered
- Include your TAKE-OUT menu and bounce-back coupons

BRINGING BACK CUSTOMERS WHO NO LONGER PATRONIZE YOUR STORE

Now that is the $64,000 question! Once you have lost a customer, getting him or her back will take an enormous effort on your part. In fact, the effort is even harder than a brand new store just starting out. But you will be at least 50% there if you realize this has happened to you.

Because once you have come to grips with the situation, it's a lot easier to correct it.

What I propose is to have a promotion and call it:

Come Home Again, We Miss You

&

Have Some Free Ice Cream On Us

INCREASING CHECK SIZE OF YOUR CORE CUSTOMER

Here's a few hints:

1. Encourage sale of new TAKE-OUT products
2. Stimulate group or family sales
3. Build sales volume of existing TAKE-OUT sales

SAMPLING OUTSIDE THE STORE

The same method used to sample inside the store can be used outside. When sampling outside the store, offer a **bounce back coupon** to anyone who tries the product.

HAPPY HOUR

The main purpose for developing a "Happy Hour" program is to develop the following:

- Increase customer frequency
- Increase traffic from 5:00 - 7:OO PM
- Increase average unit sales from 5:00 - 7:00 PM

The "Happy Hour" can easily increase your customer count and sales between 5:00 -7:00 PM, Monday through Friday, or any day (s) of your choice. Sales incentives should be related to TAKE-OUT items only. This will target customers who are on their way home from work and want to bring home a "treat."

Suggested "Happy Hour" Prices:

- Free pint with Custom Quart
- $2:00 off a Custom Quart
- $1:00 off a Custom Pint
- $2:00 off any Cake or Pie
- Half price on pre-packaged Quarts & Pints

Promote your "Happy Hour" through newspaper advertising, coupons, and a large message on a stand-alone board inside your store.

PARTY PACKAGES

The goal of creating a party package is to attract new customers and garner repeat business on a long-term basis.

A birthday party in an office is a super way to generate trial of your store's desserts. The key to this program is to inform offices in your area that you will provide all the necessary ingredients to give someone a great birthday party, with little or no effort on the part of the office employees. All they need to do is pick up the phone and call you. *A party will soon arrive.*

What is a Party Package?
- One of your store's desserts (pie, cake, ice cream cups, etc.)
- A certificate for a free cup/cone of ice cream
- Bounce-back coupons for the party participants
- Balloons
- Serving utensils

Inform Offices of Your "Party Package" Program
- Create a form letter detailing the package that can be mailed or hand-delivered to office buildings.
- Person-to-Person contact is the most effective way to generate business. Hand delivering the letter with a complimentary dessert, a TAKE-OUT menu and some bounce back coupons will allow you the opportunity to get future customers and let them taste your great desserts.

Follow Up
- When your customers use the bounce-back coupons, ask them about the party and let them know about other items and services that are available from your store.

DON'T COMPETE AGAINST YOUR COMPETITION

That's right, don't compete! This is a marketing tool that really works, trust me. I know it sounds crazy, but competing, to a large extent, is copying, and in the end most copiers eventually fail. Whether in the retail frozen dessert or restaurant business, competing against company-owned, national or large franchise chains is simply a waste of time. So don't!

That's right, the biggest mistake many independents make is trying to figure out how to compete against their franchised neighbor down the block. What we all fail to realize is that they are our best competitive advantage. We own our business, lock, stock and barrel! They basically have a lease to sell someone else's products; they can't name their own flavors; they can't make a change in the décor; and finally, they can't add to their menu without calling out to a higher authority for approval. Even when they get approval, the time period involved in this process takes months for anything to happen.

We, on the other hand, can make a change in a second and adjust to our customer's whims and desires without asking for approval.

Most important of all, it's our money on the line, not some district manager or corporate executive who probably has never scooped a cone in his/her life.

Don't moan and complain about those neighbors of yours and let them start worrying about you.

Yes, opening, building and operating one's own business will give you a great sense of satisfaction of doing something for yourself, but make no mistake about it, it's tough.

So, before you take that big plunge, take in a good movie, have a good dinner and try to get a good night's sleep. You'll need it!

CHAPTER 7
GREAT CUSTOMER SERVICE

When a customer comes into your shop
forget about your vision and your product.
Just remember one thing- "how can I help you?"- Malcolm Stogo

Let's be frank. Great customer service is all about perception. You either have it or you don't. Regardless of how much you learned from a book or a seminar, if you don't practice what you have learned or if your customers don't perceive you to have great customer service, then you don't.

The flip side of perception is that most owners think they do have it. They are so blinded by their own ego or absentee-management style.

But once you get it, great customer service becomes great marketing. In the early years of every ice cream store's existence, every owner thinks the operation gets better with each passing year. It's a natural thought. But research tells us otherwise. Just giving good customer service is not enough. It's setting the bar too low. What we really want is for our customers to happily pay for their ice cream and say, "boy, that was great!"

Whether you have one store or three, the basics of giving great service is the same. And because you know your store better than the competition, you have a competitive advantage. So, let's be frank. People expect good service. And part of the reason they don't get it is because giving good service is really hard.

SMILE

If you view your ice cream store as entertainment, and not simply as a food establishment, then the way you and your employees interact with your customers in a positive way is very important. In reality, it's one way and the only way to market your business and offer great customer service.

The key word here is "SMILE." And that means you, your employees and your customers. We can only assume that when a customer comes into your establishment, the only reason is to get a treat, so in 95% of the cases customers are in a very positive mood with <u>smiles</u> on their faces.

How many times have you gone into an ice cream store and the employees have this glum look on their faces? It's really pathetic. Perceptually, there is probably nothing more important in the customers' eyes then seeing an employee with a smile on his/her face ready to serve. After all, this is a fun business, isn't it? A smile on an employee's face usually means that the employee is happy to be working for you, likes ice cream, and wants to make your customers' experience in your shop a pleasant one.

As I have said, if you view what we do as entertainment, and view your shop as a theater, we have created an atmosphere that will be fun for everyone. So let's start our theater production with a couple of scenes of acting out!

Scene 1
Customer comes into the store laughing and asks the clerk, "what new flavors do you have this week?"
Narration
Clerk: You must try this new Dulce de Leche flavor. It's incredible. It's now my favorite flavor. Customer: If you like it so much, can I have a sample?
Clerk: No problem, here.
Customer: You are so right! I must have an ice cream cone now and a pint to take home.

Scene 2
Customer comes into the store and asks for two flavors on a single cone.
Narration
Clerk: No problem!

PAYING ATTENTION TO SERVICE
All too often the attention paid to service takes aim at the servers (your employees) who are easy and convenient targets. The reality is that most dissatisfied customers are seldom critical of the server, but perceive the owner as not supporting the server or simply not caring how he/she runs the business. And that means everything from the strategic

marketing plan or the owner's vision to the cleanliness of the bathrooms. Servers stand on the front line and need the support of the owner behind them. It's the owner's responsibility to take care of the little things like teaching the servers how to look the customer in the eye when asking them what they would like to purchase and saying "thank you" after giving them their ice cream. When the server has the ability to read what each customer wants and can put aside assumption, that is great service, and great everyday marketing.

DOES GIVING GOOD CUSTOMER SERVICE COME AND GO?
Depending on the Time of the Year

You bet it does! In the busy summer season, when an ice cream shop is packed with long lines, good customer service is at its worst. Employees are usually tired from looking at hordes of customers, seeing no end to the line. They are in a rush to serve a customer and customers are tired at waiting in line. When business is slow and the weather is bad and there are barely enough employees to both serve customers or keep the shop clean, the situation is usually the same.

Is there a solution? Yes, there is. It's called <u>better training</u>: the training you give your employees the very first day they start to work for you. It's that initial block of time you spend training your employees about your philosophy of what your shop is that will stay with your employees to the day they leave you. Before you begin every new summer season, plan to spend at least one day training new and old employees on the following points regarding customer service:

- The importance of everyday customer service
- What flexibility they have to dispense recommendations and samples
- The following words-"hello," "good-by" and "thank you"- simple gestures on the part of your employees that will really work to enhance the friendly demeanor the customer had when he/she first entered your shop. You need to teach the importance of:
    Hello
    How can I help you?
    Would you like to try a sample of some flavor?
    What flavor would you like?
    How to pick up the scoop
    How to hand the cone to the customer
    How to take the money
    Saying thank you

KNOW YOUR CUSTOMERS

Try and learn who your customers are instead of trying to make them fit your image of who they are. This is a major mistake that many ice cream owners make:

- Don't create an image of your shop that is totally out of the realm of what your customer-base is.
- While comment cards are helpful, don't always depend on them to try to find out your customers' thoughts.
- Be the greeter, the master of ceremonies by spending time talking with your customers.
- Talk to your customers, and ask them why they come into your shop.
- And frankly, ask them, "Is there anything you are doing wrong?"

DELIVER WHAT CUSTOMERS WANT

A successful ice cream storeowner, for the most part, will give his customers anything they want. While this is not a 100 percent rule, it does work. The most common complaint I hear from owners is customers trying to get two flavors in a single-size cone or cup. So, what's the big deal? Are you going to lose a billion dollars over it? I say give it to them if they want it. Doing this builds customer loyalty. Even more important, you should authorize your employees to do whatever it takes to make the customer happy- just give it to them, accurately, politely, and enthusiastically. This leads me to the following fabulous words that will do wonders for your shop's image, "NO PROBLEM."

NO PROBLEM

If there are two words that you should consider as your trademark marketing tool, they are "NO PROBLEM." No Problem simply means that anything your customer wants "within reason" you should provide for them.

- It's an everyday marketing tool that your customers will remember.
- It's what will bring them back to you over and over again as a destination spot for their frozen dessert treats.

Why do these two words work so well? It's because in everyday life, as we know it today, everyone is in a hurry, materialism is rampant in our society, and people have no patience. The reality is that when they come into your establishment and ask for something out of the ordinary and your response is NO PROBLEM, they are taken aback.

Believe me, this everyday marketing tool works!

SAMPLING

Sampling is mentioned in many parts of this book because it is the essence of what we ice cream owners are all about. We want our customers to taste, purchase, and enjoy our products. We want them to love our establishment. We want them to talk about us, crave what we sell, come back time and time again to purchase our stuff, and we want them to tell their friends about us.

And there is no question about it, sampling is a key ingredient in making all of this happen.

And if you do it right, you will be offering great customer service because in the customer's mind there is nothing better than something that is free, even if it is a very small sample.

CHAPTER 8
<u>GETTING COMPETENT HELP</u>
<u>KEEPING THEM</u>

"Listen to your employees and ask their opinion about what your customers like or dislike. They are the heart and soul of your business."
Stan Zafran, Denise's Ice Cream,* Somerville, MA.

It's very simple. You can't operate your business without employees. And you especially need employees who have your interests at heart, know how to smile, and love ice cream. In other words, you want to hire special people. Once you hire them, you need to tell them they are special and you need to treat them that way. In that way they will know it is special to work for you.

<u>GETTING COMPETENT HELP</u>

Somebody said to me recently, does anyone want to work anymore? While this statement might sound a little crass, it's true that young people are very reluctant to do physical work, let alone work in a retail atmosphere that pays only $6.00-7.00 per hour. After all, it was only a few years ago that you could get help at $4.50 per hour. So what can we do about it? First of all, getting help is not a short-term thing.

It's a Long-Term Building Process

It's incumbent of you to build a "I want to work there" or a "fun place to work" attitude about your establishment. Since this will only occur after you have been in business a number of years, you will need to build up a reputation regarding working conditions, pay scale, flexibility with hours, bonuses, reward programs, and most important:

How You Trust and Respect Your Employees as Human Beings

Create demand for jobs. Students learn very fast who pays what, and seek out the better paying jobs early on during the spring hiring season. In the scheme of things, employers who try to save 50 cents an hour will find out that it can be very difficult to get employees when there is demand from other retail establishments. In the end, being greedy will hurt you in building sales. If I learned anything when I was in retail, it was if you didn't have employees behind the counter when you needed them, sales were lost. People simply don't wait for service. Ours is an impulse business. They will go elsewhere. That's right, straight to your competition.

Everyone in this business knows that the hardest time to find help is at the beginning of the season and at the end.

The Secret is Flexibility

Take advantage of their availability, but do it in a way that not only helps you, but them too. From March through June, while high school or college students might want to work, they have homework and activities to deal with. <u>So that means you should hire more than what you might need in people but not in hours worked</u>. A large pool of students to choose from is a lot better than scrounging around for someone to cover a shift. Remember that every student applying for a job will tell you how much he/she wants to work, but immediately discount 50%. Since in the spring, most of your business will be weekend oriented anyway, if you have a large pool to draw from, you will find that staffing will not be as difficult as it might seem.

Even getting summer employees is not that difficult, especially in June. You will find that everyone will be looking for a job, high school or college. What they won't tell you for the most part is when they are going to quit at the end of the summer, and that will be your dilemma. What usually happens is that in early August, your employees start telling you that they are going on a vacation with their parents, they have to go back to school the last week in August, and so on.

By this time you are stuck. You start saying to yourself, how am I going to operate the business the last two weeks in August and the first week in September? The answer is simple. Develop a:

Bonus System and Make it Part of the Hiring Process

Offer all summer employees a certain amount of extra money (bonus) for each week worked during the summer, but only paid to employees who work the whole summer selling season. The bonus ($25 for each week worked) is paid to them with their last paycheck at the end of the summer. What this accomplishes is your upfront notice to potential employees that you only want employees

Who Will Work the Whole Summer, Not Just Part of It

WHAT TO LOOK FOR WHEN HIRING EMPLOYEES

Setting standards helps you create a staff that will work together as a team. By following the guidelines below you will be in a position to hire the kind of employees you want versus just getting bodies to work for you.

- **Appearance:** They should be well groomed, have a wholesome appearance, be dressed properly, and **have a smile on their faces.**
- **Style:** They should have an All American look regardless of their nationality and **have a smile on their faces.**
- **Personality:** They should have a positive attitude, be outgoing, and **have a smile on their faces**.
- **Character:** They must be responsible for coming to work on time, honoring their commitment to you, and **have a smile on their faces**.
- **Abilities:** Prior work experience is not necessary as long as they are willing to learn. But they should have a love for ice cream.

So why is it so important that they have a smile on their faces? Because the environment of your store is supposed to be all about fun. What is the percentage of your customers who come into your establishment with a smile on their faces? Probably in the range of 75% to 90%. So if your customers come to you with a smile, why shouldn't your employees be that way also. After all, isn't ice cream enjoyable! Get the picture, let's move on.

Your employees will be your ambassadors to your customers and a major means to having good customer relations and a positive image for the store operation. While this language might sound simplistic, it's importance cannot be overstated.

Recruiting

The first step to filling a position is a clear understanding of the duties and characteristics for the maximum success of the position.

Ask yourself: What are the actual duties of the job?
                What qualities, characteristics are necessary?

Recruiting Sources
Probably the single best way to recruit is by meeting the standards of your operation so that your store and employees are providing a great experience for every customer. A clean, upbeat, "smiling" store is your best recruiting tool! And in most cases most of your employees at one time or another are and were customers of yours because for the most part they think of your store as a fun place to spend their summer, and earning money doing it.

Interviewing
Analyze the completed application. From this application, you can discover many things about a potential employee. Is the application neatly written and filled out properly? What is the applicant's availability to work for you? If it is a summer job, is the applicant willing to honor his/her commitment to the date the applicant says he/she will work for you?

The Actual Interview
Be extremely aware of the following:
- Is the applicant on time?
- Is the applicant dressed neatly and cleanly?
- Watch body language. It is normal for any applicant to be nervous, but if the applicant is fidgety or can't look you straight in the eye, you might have a problem.
- Be honest and follow through. If you say you will call back, make sure you do.
- Inform the applicant of the physical nature of the job.
- Know what you need as far as your schedule. You will be writing the schedule, not your employees.

PERSONNEL, THE EMPLOYER'S ROLE
As an owner there is perhaps no resource more costly, complicated, or valuable than your personnel, the people who have agreed to work with

you towards the realization of your business goals. As an employer, it is your role to lead, to take a diverse combination of personalities and create an environment in which you and they can all work together toward the attainment of your goals.

Because you cannot achieve your goals without the help of others, you must offer your employees a motive for joining you and working toward those goals.

Good leadership does not spring from some mysterious quality, and it is not the same as authority. Authority over people is a position of power, not acts of authority and not necessarily acts of good leadership. True leaders are concerned most with a personal sense of responsibility to those who follow them, to help them succeed.

Now, what's important here is knowing very clearly that although you cannot satisfy all of your employees all of the time, you will receive the highest performance by fulfilling a good portion of those needs a good part of the time.

What are those needs?

- *The need for money.* But money alone won't do it. Although wage and cash incentives will bring people in, they won't keep employees happy or keep them there.
- *Saying "thank you."* That's right, a simple gesture to your employees when they leave your establishment at the end of their daily shift or for doing a specific act during the day.
- *Promoting them.* There is nothing more positive than promoting a young employee to a higher position.
- *Listening to them.* They all have personal needs and concerns, and it's especially important to listen and answer questions regarding work. Don't ever ignore their work concerns!
- *The need to learn.* While this might sound like an intangible way to satisfy an employee's need, it does accomplish something every young person wants: To be cared for and shown something they knew nothing about before they met you. If you can teach them one thing, that is taking responsibility for doing their job to the best of their abilities. If you make this effort to make learning a part of the work experience, I will bet all the money (and even all the ice cream) in the world that 10-15 years from the time they worked for you they will remember that job they had at your place and what you taught them.

Above all, be true to yourself and straight and open with your employees. Remember, good employee relations is not just something to do. It is the only thing that will promote the success of your business.

THE TRAVAILS OF RETAIL TRAINING

In general, most ice cream store owners deem training important. Yet few are satisfied with their training. Most say they don't have the time to train their employees adequately, and if they did, they have no idea where to start.

Just because you learned quickly what to do in your store, don't necessarily think you can translate what you have learned to others without setting down the foundations of what the training program is expected to accomplish.

Most important of all, a good trainer must have confidence in his/her ability in order to convey that same message to the people he/she is training. And the largest failure of training is poor communication. Most owners are not explicit enough about what they expect from their managers and employees.

Since training costs are significant in any business, one of an owner's biggest nightmares is investing substantial time and money in training a new hire only to have the trainee leave. Answering, understanding, and implementing the following steps will make your training program a success:

1. ***What is expected of the trainee, and by when?*** You may think that if you hire someone to work in your ice cream store, it's obvious what you want them to do: sell and serve products to customers, become knowledgeable about your products, and give good customer service, etc. But to most new hires, it isn't obvious at all. Your trainees can't know what to focus on unless you tell them. Presenting expectations in writing is essential. Verbal expressions of expectations leave room for misinterpretation or misunderstanding. Written ones focus your staff on what you think is most important and invite questions of clarification. Expectations only make sense within a specified timeframe. So whatever training program you put into action, there must be a set time for it to end. A favorite expression heard often is- "Work without deadlines is work toyed with."

2. *How will the information be made available?* Once trainees know what's expected of them, they need to find out how they can accomplish these goals. Among the training tools you can use are on-shift buddy system, manuals, and videos. Out of all of the above, the most common training method is the on-shift buddy system- the trainee works alongside a trainer throughout a shift.

3. *How will we know when the expectations are being met?* You owe it to yourself, your trainees and your customers to measure whether employees are meeting your expectations. Your best trainees will be eager to demonstrate that they have met- or surpassed - your expectations. Passing a test of some sort is a concrete way of demonstrating achievement.

4. *What are the rewards/consequences for meeting/not meeting the expectations?* If there are no rewards for meeting your expectations and no consequences for not meeting them, don't be surprised if they're not met. Your trainees are not bad people, and they don't want to do a bad job. But it's human nature to tend to do things you get rewarded for and avoid doing things that have negative consequences. Bonuses, raises and promotions are rewards that most people think of first, but they aren't the only ones. Most employees appreciate recognition- especially in front of their peers and customers - and in most surveys, it ranks <u>higher</u> than money as a motivator.

The answer to the above four questions forms the framework for a successful training program. While there is no magic pill that can teach each new hire all they need to know overnight, it just makes sense that an employee who knows the answers to these questions will perform at a higher level than one who does not.

So the most important key here is **COMMUNICATING**. If you communicate well to your managers and they to your employees, you have done your job well. Here's a little experiment for you to try in your business. Ask a couple of your new hires and a couple of longer term employees to answer the four training questions for their jobs. At the same time you should answer them yourself. If they are the same or close, you're doing a good job of communicating and your training program will bring you long term positive results.

EMPLOYEE WORK SCHEDULES

Ice cream is a fun, impulse business. And because it is fun, the business revolves around the time of the year when people feel happy and carefree. So, it doesn't take a genius to figure out that your business will increase starting in the spring and gain full steam during the summer months. Starting from the spring and moving forward you will need employees for the most part from Thursday night through Sunday night with most of your emphasis on employees working the following shifts:

Spring

Thursday night- 7:00-10:00 PM
Friday night- 7:00-11:00 PM
Saturday- 1:00 to 4:00 PM
Saturday night- 7:00-11:00 PM
Sunday- 1:00-4:00 PM
Sunday night- 7:00-10:00 PM

Summer
Monday night- 7:00-10:00 PM
Tuesday night- 7:00-10:00 PM
Wednesday night-7:00-10:00 PM
Thursday night- 7:00-10:00 PM
Friday night- 7:00-11:00 PM
Saturday- 1:00-4:00 PM
Saturday night- 7:00-12:00 PM
Sunday- 1:00-5:00 PM
Sunday night- 7:00-10:00 PM

The shifts should be no longer than four to five hours in length. The amount of employees you need for each shift depends of course on the amount of business you will be doing. On average you should expect an employee to do approximately $175.00-250.00 per shift.

CHAPTER 9
THE FUN PART
PREPARING YOUR WARES

I truly believe that the fun part of this business is coming up with exciting creative specialty desserts like sundaes, shakes, sodas, smoothies and the syrups, toppings, and chocolate dipped cones that are needed to make these unique desserts the signature items that draw customers to your store. It's the part that drew most of us to the business in the first place. That's creating products that we first imagined in our sleep.

CHOCOLATE DIPPED CONES

One of the greatest successes I have had in the ice cream industry is my invention of the chocolate dipped waffle cone back in 1983 at Ice Cream Extravaganza, South Street Seaport, New York City, NY.

Over the years, all over the world, many people have copied this idea and have been successful in earning additional revenue for their shop. What has always mystified me is the failure of many shop owners to really promote the dipped waffle cone as a merchandising tool similar to the selling of an ice cream cone. Maybe the reason is that many think dipping the cones is labor intensive, and maybe it is. But getting an extra buck for a sale of an ice cream cone is enough incentive to me that it's worth the effort, and the extra money that can go into the bank.

Even better, consider the possibilities of creating chocolate dipped sugar and wafer cones. So in my opinion, get into the dipped cone business NOW!

Supplies Needed
- Warmer for melting chocolate
- Waffle, sugar, and wafer cones
- Acrylic waffle cone displays
- Tempered chocolate or chocolate discs similar to what is used for chocolate candy making
- Toppings

Peanuts	Roasted sliced almonds
Rainbow sprinkles	Coconut

- 4 round 8" cake pans to hold dry toppings
- Aluminum foil for full size sheet pan

Chocolate Warmer
- The temperature of the warmer should be set at 100 degrees F. during operating hours.
- In the morning, the temperature can be slightly higher (125 F.) to melt new chocolate added to the warmer faster. Within one hour of melting chocolate, reduce temperature to 95-100 degrees F.
- Every morning, and throughout the day, use a large spatula to constantly stir the chocolate to allow any chocolate at the bottom of the pan to mix and circulate with the new chocolate added at the beginning of the day.
- Never allow water to drop into the pan. This action will destroy the melted chocolate, causing a thickening of the chocolate to occur.

Operating Procedure: Melting the Chocolate

Melt chocolate in the morning at 125 degrees F. for one hour. Place fresh chocolate in pan so the pan is full. As chocolate begins to melt, stir constantly and reduce the temperature to 95-100 degrees F.

Dipping the Cones

1. Fill up cake pan with topping
2. Place waffle cones on counter next to melted chocolate. Take waffle cone and dip the cone approximately 1-1/2" from the top rim of the cone into the melted chocolate.
3. Lift dipped cone out of the warmer and shake off excess chocolate from the cone

Pouring the Dry Topping Over the Dipped Cone

1. Using a single serving plastic cup, fill the cup up with the dry topping that is in the cake pan. Holding the dipped cone in one hand, pour the filled paper cup with the dry topping into the cone itself, and then immediately empty the topping out of the inside of cone and back into the cake pan. This will result in the inside of waffle cone being coated with topping adhering to chocolate.
2. Next, fill the plastic cup again with the dry topping, holding the dipped cone in one hand, and the cup of dry topping in the other. Pour the topping over the outside of the cone, using a swivel motion of turning the cone over until the whole chocolate portion of the outside of the cone is covered with the dry topping.
3. Once the cone is coated inside and out with the dry topping, place it on a lined aluminum foil full size sheet pan. When the pan is filled up with the dipped coated cones, place the tray in the dipping cabinet for 10 minutes to allow the chocolate coating to dry and set.
4. After cones are dry, remove them from dipping cabinet and stack them by inserting them inside each other on a full size sheet pan and/or into the cone holders that are to be placed on top of the front counters for sale to the customers.

Selling the Dipped Cone

The secret is simple. Dip the cones attractively, and keep the cone holders filled up with cones. Failure to keep the cone holders filled to the top of the cone holder with dipped cones will dramatically decrease the possibility of sales; conversely, keeping the cone holder filled with dipped cones will dramatically increase the possibility of sales. If you want to expand your dipped cone business even further, consider dipping sugar or wafer cones in chocolate.

ICE CREAM TOPPINGS

If you make and/or purchase great ice cream for your store, it can be great by itself; there's no question about it. But if you want to make it really special for your customers, make sure you have terrific tasting toppings that can add something to your business and to its profitability.

PREPARING FRUIT FOR SUNDAE TOPPING

Use 2 heaping cups (1 pound) of CC-917* per 30 pounds frozen fruit mixture (which contains sugar- about 3 gallons) to thicken fruit to make sundae topping. Slowly sift stabilizer (CC-917) onto the fruit, stirring constantly. Allow at least 30 minutes (2-3 hours is better) for the stabilizer to hydrate.

Note: CC-917 can be purchased from Continental Colloids at 630-231-8650

MAKING YOUR OWN VANILLA EXTRACT

Place six long vanilla beans, split open and cut into pieces into one quart of good quality vodka. Cap tightly and place in a cool dark place. Leave for four to six weeks, shaking the bottle occasionally.

Before using, sieve through a strainer lined with cheesecloth (or use a coffee filter), rinse the bottle to remove residue, and pour back into the bottle. Add one whole bean and cap tightly until used.

STRAWBERRY TOPPING

Incredibly popular topping that will end up being number one in your shop.

Ingredients:

2 pounds	Fresh strawberries, leaves cut and washed
1 cup	Sugar
1/2 cup	Spring water
	Juice of 1 lemon

Preparation:

Combine the strawberries, water, and sugar in a blender or food processor and process until smooth. Add lemon juice.

Yield is approximately 1 1/4 quarts.

APRICOT TOPPING

Simply the most sensual topping you can ever make.

Ingredients:

2 pounds	Fresh apricots, peeled and pitted
1 cup	Sugar
1/2 cup	Spring water
	Juice of 1 lemon

Preparation:

Combine the apricots, water, and sugar in a blender or food processor and process until smooth. Add lemon juice. Yield is approximately 1 1/4 quarts.

RASPBERRY TOPPING

One of the most popular toppings you will sell.

Ingredients:

2 pounds	Fresh raspberries, washed
1 1/3 cup	Sugar
1/2 cup	Spring water
	Juice of 1 lemon

Preparation:

Combine the raspberries and water in a blender or food processor and process until smooth. For a silky topping, pass the puree through a fine-meshed sieve. Add sugar and lemon juice.

Yield is approximately 1 1/4 quarts.

KIWI TOPPING

Succulent flavor that is great over vanilla ice cream.

Ingredients:

12	Fresh kiwis
1 1/2 cups	Sugar
1/2 cup	Spring water
	Juice of 1 lemon

Preparation:

Peel the kiwis. Combine the kiwis, water, and sugar in a blender or food processor and process until smooth. Add lemon juice.

Yield is approximately 1 1/4 quarts.

BASIC NUT SYRUP

This syrup is great on ice cream, Belgian waffles, etc.

Ingredients:

4 cups	Sugar
1 1/2 cups	Water
1/2 cup	Dark corn syrup
1 teaspoon	Vanilla extract
2 cups	Chopped walnuts, pecans or almonds

Preparation:

In a small, heavy-bottomed saucepan, combine sugar, water, and corn syrup. Stir over medium heat until sugar dissolves. Raise heat and boil gently until mixture thickens to desired syrup consistency (3-5 minutes).

Remove from heat. Add vanilla and nuts. Refrigerate until needed.

Yield is approximately one quart.

MEXICAN CHOCOLATE TOPPING

The use of orange flavor and cinnamon combined with chocolate is a perfect balance of flavor to be enjoyed. Give your customers a free taste, they will buy a topping immediately. Trust me!

Ingredients:

2 pounds	Semisweet or dark chocolate
1/2 pound	Sugar
5 cups	Heavy cream
3 tablespoons	Triple Sec
1 ounce	Cinnamon

Preparation:

In a double boiler, combine chocolate, sugar and heavy cream, and bring almost to a point of a "very slow" boil. Remove mixture from the heat and add the Triple Sec and cinnamon.

Stir the finished topping and refrigerate overnight.

Yield is approximately 2 quarts.

FRESH BERRY SYRUP

Take advantage of whatever berries are at their peak of sweetness.

Ingredients:

2 quarts	Fresh berries, such as strawberries, raspberries, blueberries, or blackberries, or a combination of any of the above
2 cups	Sugar
2 cups	Water

Preparation:

Hull and clean berries if necessary. In a 4 quart saucepan, combine berries, sugar, and water. Stir over medium heat until sugar dissolves. Raise heat and boil gently until mixture thickens. Simmer for 10 minutes. Cool to lukewarm and strain through a fine sieve into a large container, pressing hard to extract all the liquid. Chill thoroughly before using.

Yield is approximately one quart.

CHOCOLATE RASPBERRY TOPPING

This is one instance in which frozen berries are better than fresh.

Ingredients:

1 1/4-1 1/2 quarts	Frozen raspberries (frozen in syrup)
2 cups	Water
1/2 cup	Sugar
1 1/4 pounds	Semisweet chocolate (chopped) into 1/2-inch pieces
4 tablespoons	Unsalted butter, softened
2 teaspoons	Pure vanilla extract

Preparation:

In a mixing bowl, thaw raspberries in their syrup. Mash berries to a mush-like consistency.

In a heavy-bottomed 2-quart saucepan, bring sugar and berries to a boil. Add chocolate and butter and cook, stirring constantly, until melted. Cool to room temperature and refrigerate. Add the vanilla extract.

Yield is approximately 1 to 1-1/2 quarts

PISTACHIO TOPPING

A perfect match and a great topping especially when served over coffee ice cream.

Ingredients:

8 ounces	Sugar
8 ounces	Egg yolk
2.2 pounds	Milk
1 ounce	Fabbri pistachio paste
2 ounces	Pistachios, granulated
1 teaspoon	Pure vanilla extract

Preparation:

In a small, heavy-bottomed saucepan, combine sugar, milk, egg yolk and pistachio paste and cook to 187F. degrees.

Remove from heat. Add vanilla. Refrigerate until needed.

Yield is approximately 1 1/2 quarts.

CARAMEL TOPPING

Over the last few years, caramel has become very popular. So this is your chance to make your own.

Ingredients:

3 cups	Boiling water
6 cups	Sugar
1 cup	Heavy cream
1 1/2 tablespoons	Pure vanilla extract

Preparation:

In a double boiler, heat sugar over moderate heat. As sugar just barely begins to melt, lower heat to a bare simmer and stir constantly until the sugar turns a golden brown. Continue stirring over low heat until it becomes medium dark brown.

Slowly stir in the boiling water until sugar and water are well blended and mixture thickens. Remove from heat and add the heavy cream. Let caramel cool down slightly and stir in the vanilla.

Yield: Approximately 1/2 gallon.

BUTTERSCOTCH TOPPING

If you prefer to make a Butterscotch Topping instead of Caramel, here's your chance. It just tastes great!

Ingredients:

6 cups	Brown sugar
3 cup	Heavy cream
6 ounces	Light corn syrup
6 ounces	Butter
2 ounces	Pure vanilla extract

Preparation:

In a double boiler, heat sugar, corn syrup, butter and cream over moderate heat. Bring mixture to a boil. Cook, stirring constantly, until mixture thickens, about 235 F degrees on a candy thermometer.

Remove from heat and cool down slightly and stir in the vanilla. Store mixture in refrigerator for 6 hours. It is now ready to be served.

Yield is approximately slightly more than a 1/2 gallon.

COFFEE TOPPING

This is a great topping to serve over any vanilla or chocolate ice cream as part of a sundae preparation or even as a simple topping.

Ingredients:

6 cups	Granulated sugar
6 cups	Water
6 ounces	Instant coffee powder
6 ounces	Butter
24 ounces	Heavy cream

Preparation:

Place the sugar and water in a double boiler over moderate heat and bring to a boil. Cook, stirring constantly, for about 5 minutes, or until the sugar has melted and you have a clear, smooth syrup. Add the coffee, stir to dissolve, then remove from the heat. Gradually stir in first the butter, then the cream, blending well. The topping is now ready to be served.

Yield is approximately 3 quarts.

BLACK CHERRY TOPPING

A wonderful topping that works incredibly well in the wintertime with either sundaes or as a topping for Belgian waffles.

Ingredients:

2 cups	Black cherries
2 cups	Black cherry jam
2 tablespoons	Butter
2 ounces	Kirsch or brandy
1/2 ounce	Lemon juice
5 cups	Water
2 teaspoons	Pure vanilla extract

Yield: Approximately 1/2-3/4 gallon

Preparation:

In a double boiler, combine the black cherries, jam, butter, and water and place over moderate heat. Remove from heat and introduce the lemon juice, kirsch or brandy. Continue to heat for 2 minutes.

PRALINE NUT TOPPING

If you want a terrific topping for your topping bar, make your own pralines. Making your own will provide you with a more refreshing tasting nut than anything you can buy elsewhere.

Ingredients:

2 cups	Sugar
3 cups	Shelled pecans or almonds

Preparation:

In a double boiler, dissolve the sugar in 1 cup water. Add the pecans or almonds and boil for about 15 minutes until golden brown. Pour onto a cold, oiled surface and leave until set. Place nuts in a plastic bag and hit with a rolling pin until the praline nuts are broken into small pieces.

MARSHMALLOW TOPPING

Here are some marshmallow toppings and some variations that are both delicious and easy to make.

Ingredients:

64	Regular marshmallows
2 cups	Water
4 cups	Sugar
8	Large egg whites
2 teaspoons	Pure vanilla extract

Preparation:

In a mixing bowl, beat the egg whites until soft peaks form. Set aside. In a double boiler, combine the sugar and water and place over moderate heat. Stir until the sugar dissolves, then let the mixture boil for 3 minutes. Reduce the heat to low.

Add the marshmallows, and stir until they are completely melted and the mixture is smooth. Remove from heat and slowly beat the hot marshmallow mixture into the egg whites. Continue to beat for 2 minutes. Beat in the vanilla extract. Yield: Approximately 1/2-3/4 gallon

VARIATIONS

MARSHMALLOW CARAMEL TOPPING

Add 32 small caramel candies with the marshmallows. Stir until the candies are completely melted.

MARSHMALLOW COCONUT TOPPING

Add 1 cup shredded coconut with the vanilla. Optional: add 1 ounce of coconut flavored rum.

MARSHMALLOW MINT TOPPING

Substitute 2 teaspoons peppermint extract for the vanilla extract.

MARSHMALLOW NUT TOPPING

Add 2 cups chopped toasted almonds, hazelnuts or pecans when the topping is completely finished.

MARSHMALLOW PEANUT BUTTER TOPPING

Add 32 ounces peanut butter after the marshmallows are melted.

OLD FASHIONED ICE CREAM SPECIALTY DESSERTS

Over the years, the retail ice cream store segment of our business has gone through many changes. The days of the old-fashioned ice cream parlor for the most part are gone, but a newer reincarnation has occurred. And it's because ice cream is back in all its glorious forms.

It's time to re-create the image, the reasons why our customers really like to come to our shops, and to enjoy themselves and leave the outside world at the front door.

It's all about marketing and merchandising, and there is no better time than the summer to be outrageous in offering unusual sundaes that attract attention.

If you market them in a way that your customers know about them, you will be surprised how many you might sell.

ICE CREAM SUNDAES

The ice cream sundae has never really left the scene, but for many years was definitely downplayed to one or two favorites like the traditional Hot Fudge or Caramel Sundae. Use your imagination and try out one of these sundaes on your customers.

PEANUT CUP SURPRISE SUNDAE

There is no question that for those people who love peanut butter, any way they can get it- it's a treat! This sundae goes a long way in making that happen.

Ingredients:

2 scoops	Vanilla ice cream
2-3 ounces	Hot fudge
2 ounces	Peanut Butter Cups, crushed
1 ounce	Granulated peanuts
	Whipped cream
1	Maraschino cherry with stem

Preparation:

Place some fudge on bottom of the sundae dish. Place 2 large scoops of vanilla ice cream over the fudge. Spoon the crushed peanut butter cups and peanuts over the ice cream.

Spoon remaining hot fudge over the topping. In a circular pattern swirl the whipped cream over the fudge and ice cream.

Place a maraschino cherry on top of the sundae.

BLACK FOREST SUNDAE

Any sundae with a brownie in it has to be delicious!

Ingredients:

1	3 inch square brownie
2 scoops	Vanilla ice cream
1 ounce	Hot fudge
2 ounces	Cherry topping
	Whipped cream
1	Maraschino cherry with stem

Preparation:

Place brownie in bottom of sundae dish. Place some fudge on top of the brownie. Place both scoops of vanilla ice cream over the fudge. Spoon cherry topping over the ice cream.

In a circular pattern swirl the whipped cream over the fudge and ice cream.

Place a maraschino cherry on top of the sundae.

STRAWBERRY MARSHMALLOW SUNDAE

If your store sells a lot of sundaes, then featuring this one is a can't miss opportunity. Enjoy!

Ingredients:

1 scoop	Vanilla ice cream
1 scoop	Strawberry ice cream
2 ounces	Strawberry topping
1 ounce	Marshmallow topping
	Fresh strawberries

Preparation:

In a sundae dish place a scoop of both ice creams side by side. Cover ice creams, first with the strawberry topping and then the marshmallow topping.
Garnish the sundae with a fresh strawberry.

CARAMEL PEANUT SUNDAE

If you use Peanut Butter ice cream in this sundae, your customers will love it to death!

Ingredients:

2 scoops	Peanut Butter ice cream or a commercial brand
2 tablespoons	Caramel topping
3	Chocolate covered wafers
2 tablespoons	Chopped salted peanuts
	Whipped cream

Garnish with Peanuts

Preparation:

In a tall parfait glass or container, place a teaspoon of caramel in the bottom of the parfait glass.
Lay a wafer on top of the caramel, and top with a scoop of Peanut Butter ice cream. Add more caramel, another wafer, another scoop of ice cream, and more caramel.
Add whipped cream and sprinkle some peanuts on top of the whipped cream.

PEANUT BRITTLE SUNDAE

If you use Peanut Butter ice cream in this sundae, your customers will love it to death!

Ingredients:

2 scoops	Peanut Butter ice cream
2 tablespoons	Peanut Butter topping
2 ounces	Chopped up Peanut Brittle candy
	Whipped cream

Garnish with Peanut Brittle candy

Preparation:

In a tall parfait glass or container, place a teaspoon of peanut butter topping in the bottom of the parfait glass followed by a scoop of Peanut Butter ice cream. Next, place a spoon full of Peanut Brittle candy on top of the ice cream. Add more Peanut Butter topping and another scoop of ice cream.

Add whipped cream and sprinkle some Peanut Brittle candy on top of the whipped cream.

A SPLIT WITHOUT THE BANANA

Since there is a little bit of everything in this sundae, you could almost say it's a banana split, but it isn't because there isn't any no banana in this sundae!

Ingredients:

2 scoops	Chocolate and Vanilla ice cream
1 ounce	Almonds
1 ounce	Chocolate fudge
1 ounce	Marshmallow topping
1 tablespoon	Jimmies

(Jimmies is the name used for sprinkles in certain parts of the country)
Whipped cream
Maraschino cherry

Preparation:

Place 2 large scoops of Chocolate and Vanilla ice cream into the bowl. Spoon the chocolate fudge over the ice cream. Next, spoon the marshmallow topping over the fudge. Top the sundae with almonds and whipped cream. Spoon the jimmies over the whipped cream and place a stem cherry on top of the sundae.

Garnish the sundae with more almonds.

GOLDRUSH SUNDAE

The name "Goldrush" conjures up the feeling of lots of something. In this case, it's lots of butterscotch and chocolate fudge. In other words, a very gooey sundae.

Ingredients:

2 scoops	Chocolate and coffee ice cream
1 ounce	Diced almonds (to look like pieces of gold)
1 tablespoon	Jimmies
1 ounce	Butterscotch topping
1 ounce	Chocolate fudge
	Whipped cream
	Maraschino cherry

Preparation:

Place 1 large scoop each of Chocolate and Coffee ice cream into the bowl. Spoon the Butterscotch topping over the ice cream. Next, spoon the chocolate fudge over the butterscotch. Top the sundae with diced almonds and whipped cream. Spoon the jimmies over the whipped cream and place a stem cherry on top of the sundae.

Garnish the sundae with diced almonds.

HEAVENLY HAWAIIAN SUNDAE

Very refreshing, need I say more!

Ingredients:

2 scoops	Vanilla ice cream
2 ounces	Pineapple cubes
1 ounce	Pineapple sauce
1 ounce	Coconut, flaked
	Whipped cream

Garnish with pineapple cubes

Preparation:

Place pineapple cubes in bottom of a sundae dish. Place both scoops of vanilla ice cream over the pineapple cubes.

Place pineapple sauce over the ice cream. Spoon coconut over the sauce. Top with whipped cream and a stem cherry.

Garnish top of the sundae with pineapple cubes and flaked coconut

SORBET SURPRISE SUNDAE

This sundae believe it or not comes from Saudi Arabia.

Ingredients:

2 scoops	Mango sorbet
1 scoop	Lemon sorbet
3 ounces	Mixture of mango cubes, strawberries, and kiwis
	Whipped cream
1	Maraschino cherry with stem

Preparation:

In a sundae dish place the Lemon sorbet in the middle between the two scoops of Mango sorbet into the bottom of the bowl.

Cover the sorbet with the fruit mixture. In a circular pattern swirl the whipped cream over the ice cream.

Garnish sundae with slices of mangos, strawberries, and kiwis and a maraschino cherry.

ALMOND JOY JUBILEE SUNDAE

If your customers like coconut and almonds, they will love this outrageous sundae.

Ingredients:

2 scoops	Vanilla ice cream
1/2 ounce	Almond liqueur
1/2 ounce	Crème de cocoa
1 ounce	Hot fudge
	Whipped cream

Preparation:

Place 2 large scoops of vanilla ice cream into the bowl. Spoon the almond liqueur and crème de cocoa over the ice cream.

Top the sundae with whipped cream.

Garnish the sundae with coconut chopped almonds.

TROPICAL TREAT SUNDAE

Let your customers dream about being on a tropical island as they enjoy this sundae.

Ingredients:

1	Banana, sliced
2 scoops	Vanilla ice cream
3	Pineapple spears
2 ounces	Strawberry topping
1 ounce	Coconut, flaked
1/4 teaspoon	Cinnamon
	Whipped cream
	Maraschino stem cherry

Preparation:

Place sliced bananas in bottom of sundae dish. Place both scoops of vanilla ice cream over the bananas. Place pineapple spears pointing downward into the side of the sundae dish into the ice cream. Spoon strawberry topping over the ice cream.

Top with whipped cream and a stem cherry.

Garnish top of the sundae with coconut.

MMMM....MOCHA SUNDAE

If your customers like coffee and chocolate, then this sundae is a winner.

Ingredients:

2 scoops	Chocolate ice cream
2 ounces	Oreo cookies, broken
2 ounces	Coffee liqueur
1 ounce	Marshmallow topping
	Whipped cream
	Peanut butter topping
	Shaved chocolate
1	Maraschino cherry with stem

Preparation:

In a sundae dish place the ice cream into the bottom of the bowl.

Cover ice cream, first with the Oreo cookies and then pour the liqueur over the cookies.

Top with whipped cream and a stem cherry.

Garnish sundae with peanut butter sauce and shaved chocolate.

TROPICAL DESSERT SUNDAE

This is like sleeping on the beach dreaming your heart away!

Ingredients:

2 scoops	Vanilla ice cream
3 ounces	Mango cubes
2 ounces	Pineapple, crushed
1 ounce	Chocolate sauce or hot fudge
	Whipped cream
	Banana slices
1	Maraschino cherry with stem

Preparation:

In a sundae dish place the ice cream into the bottom of the bowl.

Cover ice cream, first the hot chocolate sauce or hot fudge, and then with the mango cubes and crushed pineapple.

In a circular pattern swirl the whipped cream over the ice cream.

Garnish sundae with slices of bananas and a maraschino cherry.

LOTS OF STUFF SUNDAE

Lots of stuff make this a sight to behold.

Ingredients:

1 scoop	Toasted Almond ice cream
1 scoop	Vanilla ice cream
1 ounce	Butterscotch topping
1 ounce	Hot fudge sauce
2 ounces	Roasted diced almonds
1	Maraschino cherry
	Whipped cream

Preparation:

In a tall parfait glass or container, place one scoop of Toasted Almond ice cream topped with butterscotch topping and diced almonds. Then add one scoop of Vanilla ice cream smothered with hot fudge topping, topped with whipped cream, diced almonds, and a maraschino cherry.

THE CHOCOLATE EXPLOSION SUNDAE

When you combine chocolate ice cream with hot fudge sauce and chocolate chunks, you have an explosion of chocolate. Adding raspberry sauce just tempers it down a little, but makes this sundae even more sinful.

Ingredients:

2 scoops	Chocolate ice cream
1 ounce	Raspberry sauce
1 ounce	Hot fudge sauce
2 ounces	Chocolate chunks
1 ounce	Chocolate shavings
1	Maraschino cherry
	Whipped cream

Preparation:

In a tall parfait glass or container, place one scoop of Chocolate ice cream, topped with raspberry sauce.

Then add one scoop of Chocolate ice cream smothered with hot fudge topping and chocolate chunks, topped with whipped cream, shaved chocolate, and a maraschino cherry.

RAILROAD CAR

Looks like a banana split, but it's a railroad car just chugging along! It's outrageous.

Ingredients:

1 scoop each	Chocolate, Rocky Road, and Chocolate Chip ice cream
1 ounce	Marshmallow topping
2 ounces	Hot fudge sauce
1 ounce	Chocolate chunks
	Maraschino cherry
	Whipped cream
	Diced almonds

Preparation:

In a banana split dish, place one scoop each of Chocolate, Rocky Road, and Chocolate Chip ice cream. Between the first and second scoop, pour some hot fudge. Over the Rocky Road ice cream, pour some marshmallow topping. Next pour some chocolate chunks over all three ice creams, and top off this dish with whipped cream, diced almonds, and a maraschino cherry.

THE TORNADO

You can really shake things up with a dessert of epic proportions! Imagine 8 scoops of ice cream, 8 different toppings, topped off with a banana, whipped cream and a maraschino cherry. The price, upwards of $16.00 for this creation.

Ingredients:

8 scoops	Ice Cream (customer's choice)
8 each 1/2 ounce	Toppings (customer's choice)
1	Banana
1 ounce	Caramel topping
1 ounce	Hot fudge
1	Maraschino cherry
	Whipped cream

Preparation:

In a very large bowl, place a spoonful of hot fudge followed by the eight scoops of ice cream. Next, place a spoonful of each topping over each ice cream ball and spoon the caramel topping over the whole bowl. Cut the banana lengthwise, and place each half on the side of the bowl and top off this creation with whipped cream and a cherry.

BRANDIED PEACH SUNDAE

When peaches are in season, this sundae stands out!

Ingredients:

2 scoops	Vanilla ice cream
2-small	Freestone peaches, ripe
1 ounce	Brandy
1 tablespoon	Grenadine
	Whipped cream

Preparation:

Halve the peaches, remove the pits and cut into 1/2 inch sections. Place 2 scoops of vanilla ice cream into the bowl followed by the peaches around the ice cream. Spoon the brandy and grenadine over the ice cream. Top the sundae with whipped cream. Garnish the sundae with chopped walnuts.

BAKLAVA SUNDAE

Ingredients:

1 two inch square	Baklava
2 scoops	Pistachio ice cream
1 ounce	Honey
1 ounce	Chopped pistachios
1/4 teaspoon	Cinnamon
	Whipped cream

Preparation:
Place baklava in bottom of dish. Place vanilla ice cream and honey over the baklava. Garnish the sundae with pistachios and cinnamon.

BUTTERSCOTCH MARSHMALLOW SUNDAE

Ingredients:

2 scoops	Vanilla ice cream
2 ounces	Butterscotch topping
1 ounce	Marshmallow topping
1	Maraschino cherry with stem

Preparation:
Place the ice cream into the bottom of a sundae bowl. Cover ice cream with the butterscotch and marshmallow topping. Garnish with a maraschino cherry.

CAPPUCCINO SUNDAE

Ingredients:

2 scoops	Coffee or Espresso ice cream
1 ounce	Fabbri coffee or hazelnut syrup
	Whipped cream
1	Maraschino cherry with stem
2	Almond macaroons

Preparation:
Place the ice cream into the bottom of a sundae bowl. Cover ice cream with the coffee syrup. In a circular pattern swirl the whipped cream over the ice cream. Garnish sundae with almond macaroons and a maraschino cherry.

ICE CREAM SHAKES

For the smart ice cream operator, creating a repeat ice cream shake business is "smart business." What it accomplishes is filling a lunchtime hole where most ice cream stores are shaking there heads trying to figure out how to get more business.

Making good malts and shakes isn't rocket science. But the difference between a good and great one depends on the quality of the ingredients, and the sequence in which they're packed, and technique.

Before we start, below are some "Soda Jerk Secrets" that can help you make a great milkshake.

Soda Jerk Secrets

- Ice cream that is too hard will eventually blow the motor of the blender.
- Brian Johnson of The Malt Shop* in Minneapolis, MN claims the best temperature for using ice cream in milkshakes should be at 32F.
- A good milkshake should take no longer than 25 seconds to blend in the mixer.
- Tomfoolies* Restaurant in Kansas City, Kansas uses French Vanilla ice cream and adds whipping cream as one of the ingredients for their shakes.
- Whitey's* in Moline, IL uses no milk in their shakes, just softened ice cream and flavorings.
- Nifty Fifties* in Philadelphia, PA judges whether their shakes are ready when the spoon stands up straight in the cup.
- When using malt powder, make sure it is added after you pour in any liquid ingredients like milk. Never put malt powder at the bottom of the blender canister.

BLACK FOREST MALT

From Nifty Fifties* of Philadelphia, PA comes this terrific shake.

Ingredients:
13 ounces	Chocolate ice cream
1 ounce	Chocolate syrup
1 ounce	Cherry syrup
1 ounce	Canned cherries, drained and chopped
2 ounces	Malt powder*
4 ounces	Whole milk
4 ounces	Whipped cream

*Note: Malt Powder is a combination of milk and malted barley that is cooked, dried and ground into a mellow, slightly sweet flavored powder.

Preparation:
Mix ice cream, syrups, cherries, powder and milk in blender. Blend for 30-45 seconds, depending on hardness of ice cream. Check for smooth texture. Cherries should appear as specks. Drink is proper thickness when spoon stands straight up in the cup. Garnish with whipped cream.
    Serve immediately.

Note: Many years ago, many operators used partially frozen milk to create a very cold thick shake. It still works.

BROWN VELVET SHAKE

This shake is a real treat. I wish I could have one right now!

Ingredients:
2 ounces	Root beer syrup
8 ounces	Vanilla ice cream
6 ounces	Milk
	Whipped cream
	Dust of cocoa powder.

Preparation:
Into a cold mixing cup place the ingredients. Blend thoroughly. Garnish with whipped cream and dust with cocoa powder. Serve in a 16-ounce container or glass.

TOP BANANA SHAKE

Nothing more refreshing than a banana combined with ice cream and rum.

Ingredients:

12 ounces	Vanilla soft or hard ice cream
3 ounces	Milk
1 tablespoon	Rum or "drop" of rum extract
1	Banana
	Whipped cream
	Grated nutmeg for decoration

Preparation:
Combine the ice cream, milk, banana, vanilla extract, and rum into a cold mixing cup. Blend thoroughly. Garnish with whipped cream and nutmeg.

MEXICAN MALTED SHAKE

Strictly for coffee lovers!

Ingredients:

9 ounces	Chocolate soft serve or hard ice cream
6 ounces	Milk
3 tablespoons	Chocolate syrup
1 tablespoon	Malt powder
1/2 teaspoon	Cinnamon

Preparation:
Mix milk and chocolate syrup. Add ice cream, cinnamon, and malt powder and all the ingredients through blender until smooth. Garnish with cinnamon.

CHOCOLATE "CHIMP" SHAKE

A great shake! Bananas mixed with chocolate always throws off a terrific taste.

Ingredients:

9 ounces	Chocolate soft serve or hard ice cream
6 ounces	Milk
1	Banana
1 ounce	Chocolate syrup

Preparation:
Into a cold mixing cup place the ingredients. Blend thoroughly. Garnish with a banana slice.

ISLAND MILKSHAKE
This rum-laced treat is the next best thing to an island getaway.

Ingredients:

9 ounces	Vanilla ice cream
6 ounces	Milk
2 tablespoons	Pineapple syrup
1	Banana
2 ounces	Dark rum

Preparation:
Into a cold mixing cup place the ingredients. Blend thoroughly. Garnish with a slice of banana

APPLE CINNAMON HERBAL SHAKE
The flavor from the apple cinnamon teabag blends in real well with vanilla ice cream. It's a sure winner!

Ingredients:

12 ounces	Vanilla soft or hard ice cream
3 ounces	Milk
2 tea bags	Apple Cinnamon
1/4 teaspoon	Cinnamon

Preparation:
Cut open tea bags and mix contents with the ice cream. In a cold mixing cup, blend the ingredients thoroughly. Garnish with whipped cream and cinnamon.

WILD BLACK CURRANT ESCAPE SHAKE
The strong flavor of a black currant tea bag adds a real zest to this shake.

Ingredients:

12 ounces	Vanilla soft or hard ice cream
3 ounces	Milk
2 tea bags	Black Currant tea bags
1/4 teaspoon	Blackcurrant syrup
1	Fresh mint leaf

Preparation:
Cut open tea bags and mix contents with the ice cream. Into a cold mixing cup place the ingredients. Blend thoroughly. Garnish with fresh mint leaf.

RASPBERRY DREAM SHAKE
A sweet refreshing drink!

Ingredients:

12 ounces	Vanilla soft or hard ice cream
3 ounces	Milk
2 tea bags	Raspberry tea bag
1/4 teaspoon	Raspberry syrup

Preparation:
Cut open tea bags and mix contents with the ice cream. Into a cold mixing cup place the ingredients. Blend thoroughly. Garnish with a fresh raspberry.

MANGO PASSION FRUIT FIESTA SHAKE
A terrific summer drink that has great body and texture.

Ingredients:

12 ounces	Vanilla soft or hard ice cream
3 ounces	Milk
2 tea bags	Mango passion fruit tea bags
1/4 teaspoon	Passion fruit syrup
	Whipped cream

Preparation:
Cut open tea bags and mix contents with the ice cream. Into a cold mixing cup place the ingredients. Blend thoroughly. Garnish with whipped cream.

PEPPERMINT FIELDS SHAKE
For the customer who likes any kind of peppermint dessert product, this shake is a winner and very refreshing!

Ingredients:

12 ounces	Vanilla soft or hard ice cream
3 ounces	Milk
2 tea bags	Peppermint
1/4 teaspoon	Vanilla syrup

Preparation:
Cut open tea bags and mix contents with the ice cream. Into a cold mixing cup place the ingredients. Blend thoroughly. Garnish with a touch of cinnamon and whipped cream.

COFFEE FROST

This shake is strictly for coffee lovers. The vanilla extract really boosts the coffee flavor to its fullest.

Ingredients:

5 ounces	Coffee
2 teaspoons	Sugar
7 ounces	Vanilla soft serve or hard ice cream
5 ounces	Milk
1 tablespoon	Vanilla extract

Preparation:
Mix coffee and sugar and stir until sugar is dissolved. Add milk and vanilla extract. Add ice cream, run through blender until smooth.
   Garnish with a chocolate covered coffee bean.

MUD SLIDE MILK SHAKE

Offering this milk shake is an easy sell. Prepared with coffee syrup, Oreo cookies and fudge, it's really delicious. The name itself conjures up excitement!

Ingredients:

5 ounces	Very cold milk
8 ounces	Vanilla or Coffee ice cream
1 1/2 ounces	Coffee syrup
3 ounces	Oreo cookies
1 ounce	Fudge

Preparation:
Into a cold mixing cup put in all the ingredients and blend them thoroughly.

CHOCOLATE MINT MILK SHAKE
Very, very good, that's all I can say!

Ingredients:

6 ounces	Very cold milk
9 ounces	Chocolate ice cream
2 drops	Peppermint extract or 1/4 teaspoon- Crème de Menthe
3 ounces	Peppermint Pattie candy (broken pieces)

Preparation:
Into a cold mixing cup pour 5 ounces of very cold milk. Add peppermint extract or Crème de Menthe. Add ice cream and Peppermint Pattie candy.
Place on the mixer long enough to blend thoroughly.

GRAPEFRUIT FRAPPE
While this might sound like an unusual drink, I can assure you it tastes wonderful.

Ingredients:

3 ounces	Fresh grapefruit juice (Tropicana Grovestand Ruby Red)
2 (number 10) scoops	Vanilla ice cream
8 ounces	Milk

Preparation:
Into a cold mixing cup pour 8 ounces of very cold milk. Add grapefruit juice and ice cream. Place on the mixer long enough to blend thoroughly.

LEMON COOLER SHAKE
This is one great "refreshing" shake!

Ingredients:

3 tablespoons	Frozen lemonade concentrate
9 ounces	Vanilla ice cream
6 ounces	Milk

Garnish with lemon zest or slice

Preparation:
Into a cold mixing cup place the ingredients. Blend thoroughly.
Garnish with a slice of lemon or lemon zest.

ICE CREAM SODAS & FLOATS

Not to confuse anyone, there is a difference in terminology, depending on where one resides between a float and a soda. In New England a soda is milk, syrup, seltzer and ice cream. In New York and the rest of the country we leave out the milk. A good soda or float requires:
- Quality syrups
- Very cold highly carbonated water (seltzer)
- Not messy looking
- Served immediately or they lose their carbonation
- There should be a good froth on top

Here are a few sodas that I think are terrific:

BLACK & WHITE

From the good old days! A very traditional ice cream soda that you got at the corner drug store.

Ingredients:

2 (No.10) scoops	Vanilla ice cream
3 tablespoons	Chocolate syrup
1 ounce	Milk
12 ounces	Chilled carbonated water (seltzer)
	Whipped cream

Preparation:
Place syrup in bottom of container (glass). Add milk and stir. Gently pour in the soda, mixing the syrup mixture with the water. Add the ice cream, top with whipped cream and serve.

BROADWAY SODA

Another great soda from the good old days! But this one is strictly with coffee ice cream.

Ingredients:

2 (No.10) scoops	Coffee ice cream
3 tablespoons	Chocolate syrup
1 ounce	Milk
12 ounces	Chilled carbonated water (seltzer)
	Whipped cream

Preparation:
Place syrup in bottom of container. Add milk and gently pour in the soda, mixing the syrup with the soda. Add the ice cream, top with whipped cream.

CLASSIC ROOT BEER SODA

A simple drink, but one that tastes terrific.

Ingredients:

1 1/2 ounces	Root beer syrup
8 ounces	Chilled carbonated water (seltzer)
3 ounces	Ice

Preparation:
Place syrup in bottom of container. Gently pour in the seltzer, mixing the syrup mixture with the water. Add the ice and serve in a 12-ounce container or glass.

CLASSIC ROOT BEER SODA (With a Twist)

That's right, a twist of lemon to give the drink some "zest."

Ingredients:

1 1/2 ounces	Classic root beer syrup
3/4 ounce	Lemon syrup
12 ounces	Chilled carbonated water (seltzer)
2 ounces	Ice
	Garnish with a lemon slice

Preparation:

Place both the root beer and lemon syrups in bottom of container. Pour in the soda, mixing the syrups with the water. Add the ice. Garnish with a slice of lemon and serve in a 16-ounce container or glass.

HOT CHOCOLATE FLOAT

This float comes from the <u>Ben & Jerry's Ice Cream Cookbook.</u> Try it!

Ingredients:

2 scoops	Chocolate ice cream
2 ounces	Hot fudge sauce (warmed up)
12 ounces	Milk
2 ounces	Semi-sweet chocolate- shaved
	Whipped cream

Preparation:

Pour fudge into a container. Heat milk in saucepan over low heat. Next pour milk into container and stir until mixture is blended. Scoop ice cream onto the top of the container. Top with whipped cream and shaved chocolate.

CALIFORNIA FLOAT

You have to be a way-out thinker to grasp making this float. It does work.

Ingredients:

8 ounces	Orange sorbet
6 ounces	Orange juice (fresh)
1/2	Avocado, mashed
2 tablespoons	Sugar

Preparation:

Blend orange juice, avocado and sugar together. Pour into a container. Add the Orange sorbet. Top with whipped cream and orange slice.

RED SPLASH

I found this drink in an issue of Nielsen-Massey's* newsletter. Their version had no ice cream in it. Of course, this one does! Enjoy!

Ingredients:

2 scoops	Vanilla ice cream
3 ounces	White grape juice
6 ounces	Cranberry juice
1/4 teaspoon	Pure vanilla extract- (Madagascar -single fold)

Preparation:
Into a 20-ounce container or glass, pour in the white grape juice and cranberry juice. Add the ice cream, top with whipped cream and serve.

GOLDEN CUP

Blending apricot nectar, mango juice and ice cream, how can you go wrong.

Ingredients:

2 scoops	Vanilla ice cream
5 ounces	Apricot nectar
5 ounces	Mango juice
1/4 teaspoon	Madagascar bourbon pure vanilla extract

Preparation:
Into a 20-ounce container or glass, pour in the apricot nectar and mango juice. Add the ice cream, top with whipped cream and serve.

ALL AMERICAN

Is there a healthier drink than this? It could be a customer's lunch!

Ingredients:

8 ounces	Non-fat vanilla soft serve ice cream or frozen yogurt
1 tablespoon	Wheat germ
10 ounces	Skim milk
1 tablespoon	Honey

Preparation:
Pour milk into the container. Add the wheat germ and honey. Stir. Next, add the ice cream or frozen yogurt, and serve in a 20-ounce container or glass.

CHOCOLATE & VANILLA CREAM SODA

You would be pretty hard pressed to offer an ice cream soda that is richer than this one.

Ingredients:

1 scoop	Vanilla ice cream
1 scoop	Chocolate ice cream
2 ounces	Chocolate syrup
3 ounces	Half and Half
3 ounces	Seltzer
1 teaspoon	Pure vanilla extract (single-fold)
	Whipped cream

Preparation:

Place chocolate syrup, half-and-half, vanilla extract, and 1 scoop of chocolate ice cream in a blender and blend 1 minute.

Into a 20-ounce container or glass, pour in the seltzer and blended mix. Next, drop in the vanilla ice cream. Top with whipped cream and serve.

STRAWBERRY BLONDIE FLOAT

A very different soda made with strawberry ice cream and either ginger ale or ginger syrup.

Ingredients:

2 scoops	Strawberry ice cream
2 tablespoons	Ginger syrup or 2 ounces ginger ale
12 ounces	Chilled carbonated water (seltzer)
	Whipped cream

Preparation:

Place ginger syrup in bottom of container (glass). Gently pour in the seltzer, mixing the syrup mixture with the water. Add the ice cream, top with whipped cream and serve in a 20-ounce container or glass.

COCONUT-GINGER ICE CREAM SODA

This tropical soda is sure to delight ginger lovers. The ginger has to steep in water for 8 hours, so start a day in advance.

Preparing Ginger Syrup

20 ounces	Fresh ginger, peeled and cut into quarter sized pieces
2 quarts	Water
4 cups	Sugar

In a food processor or in a blender in small batches, process ginger until it becomes pulpy. In a saucepan boil ginger in water for five minutes. Set aside and let steep at room temperature for at least 8 hours. Strain through a fine sieve into a clean saucepan, pressing hard to extract all the liquid. Add sugar and boil over medium heat until the mixture is slightly reduced (about five minutes). Refrigerate the mixture.

Ingredients:

2 scoops	Coconut ice cream
2 tablespoons	Ginger syrup
12 ounces	Chilled carbonated water (seltzer)
	Whipped cream

Preparation:

Place ginger syrup in bottom of container (glass). Gently pour in the seltzer, mixing the syrup mixture with the water. Add the ice cream, top with whipped cream and serve in a 20-ounce container or glass.

RASPBERRY ICE CREAM SODA

If you are a lover of raspberries, then this delicious refreshing ice cream soda is a must for your establishment.

Ingredients:

2 scoops	Raspberry ice cream
3 tablespoons	Raspberry sauce
8 ounces	Seltzer
	Whipped cream
	Fresh mint leaves, for decoration

Preparation:

Into a 20-ounce container or glass pour in the raspberry sauce and half of the seltzer and stir until well blended. Add the ice cream and the remaining seltzer to fill the container. Stir gently, and top with whipped cream and mint leaves.

DULCE de LECHE ICE CREAM SODA

When I was in Argentina, I had this ice cream soda. It's absolutely one of the best tasting sodas I have ever tasted, bar none!

Ingredients:

2 scoops	Dulce de Leche ice cream
3 tablespoons	Caramel sauce
8 ounces	Seltzer
	Whipped cream
	Pecan pralines, for decoration

Preparation:
Into a 20-ounce container or glass pour in the caramel sauce and half of the seltzer and stir until well blended. Add the ice cream and the remaining seltzer to fill the container. Stir gently, and top with whipped cream and pecan pralines.

PEACH CINNAMON DELIGHT SODA

This is a soda version of peaches and cream ice cream.

Ingredients:

2 scoops	Vanilla or Peach ice cream
1/4 cup	Fresh or frozen peaches, diced-(defrosted)
pinch	Cinnamon
5 ounces	Seltzer
1 tablespoon	Light rum
1 tablespoon	Triple Sec
	Whipped cream

Preparation:
Using a blender, blend the peaches with seltzer. Next pour this mixture into a 20-ounce container or glass. Add the ice cream, light rum and triple sec. Top with whipped cream and cinnamon. The soda is now ready to be served.

SUGAR FREE MONKEY MOCHA

After drinking this drink, you won't care whether it is a sugar free drink or not. It's that great!

Ingredients:

2 ounces	Sugar free caramel syrup
3 tablespoons	Cocoa
4 ounces	Espresso (liquid)
1/2	Banana
9 ounces	Ice

Preparation:
Blend thoroughly the caramel syrup, cocoa, espresso, bananas and ice. Pour mixture into a container and serve in a 16-ounce container or glass.

SUGAR FREE CHOCOLATE LATTE

For a sugar free drink, this is a good choice for someone to enjoy.

Ingredients:

1 ounce	Sugar free chocolate syrup
11 ounces	Chilled milk
4 ounces	Espresso (liquid)

Preparation:
Place sugar free chocolate syrup into bottom of container. Gently pour in the milk, mixing the syrup mixture with the milk. Add the espresso, mix, and serve in a 16-ounce container or glass.

SUGAR FREE TRUFFLE SODA

You would never believe it was a sugar free drink!

Ingredients:

1 ounce	Sugar free chocolate syrup
1/2 ounce	Sugar free raspberry syrup
13-14 ounces	Sparkling water
1 ounce	Ice

Preparation:
Place both the sugar free chocolate and Raspberry syrups into bottom of container. Gently pour in the sparkling water, mixing the syrup mixture with the sparkling water. Add the ice, and serve in a 16-ounce container or glass.

CHAPTER 10
SMOOTHIES

What do Strawberry Paradise, Peach Smash, and Mocha Frappe have in common? Answer: They're names of popular smoothies, they're all highly profitable, and they're all positioned to drive beverage sales all year round, especially in the summer when the summer heat brings an unsatisfied thirst to customer appetites nationwide.

In every dining setting- ice cream parlors, fast food establishments, coffee houses, family restaurants, and even upscale cafes and bistros- the nonalcoholic frozen drink phenomenon has become a hook for capturing patrons who otherwise might be lured to a meal or a snack on the other side of town.

The Smoothie phenomenon started in California in the early 1990's with companies like the Juice Club (now called Jumba Juice) and Smoothie King being the driving force that has led the way for national fast food chains like Haagen-Dazs, Baskin-Robbins, TCBY, Starbucks and thousands of restaurants and coffee bars of every size and shape throughout the United States to follow suit.

That's right, smoothies are "in." They aren't simply just a frosty treat suited only to scorching summer days. Besides being refreshing and delicious, they're very healthy. They are geared to the needs of every kind of body that is in the process of growing, flexing and doing aerobic activity.

Whether it's a summer afternoon, when the appetite is stifled, or simply a normal pleasant day, a chilled Smoothie can provide:

- Healthy calories from which the body might otherwise be shortchanged in the heat of the moment.
- They offer an alternative to carbonated beverages that have dominated the foodservice industry for decades.
- They can make money for you. That's right, they offer foodservice establishments the opportunity to increase incremental sales with each customer's purchase.

Thanks to continued popularity of Italian espresso and cappuccino type drinks that have swept the country in the 1990's, consumers are now used to and even welcome other types of non-carbonated drinks. Smoothies fit that bill. They are unique, healthy, refreshing, and delicious.

Representing a small yet rapidly expanding "high-end" niche in the nonalcoholic frozen-beverage market, smoothies are fruit drinks that appeal to customers with a preference for natural foods or a nutritional diet.

WHAT IS A SMOOTHIE

A smoothie is a refreshing lowfat blended drink or dessert made up of the following:
- Fresh or frozen fruit
- Ice
- Fruit juice
- Combined with either yogurt, skim milk, ice cream or sorbet

Without fruit, the refreshing appeal of a Smoothie might never have been conceived. There are so many qualities of fruit that make them fun to eat and drink. They are, in a sense, a marketing term that is used to promote freshly prepared juices. Bananas are used in most smoothies to create a creamier texture to the prepared drink. Smoothies have been around since the invention of the blender. But I have always wondered who came up with the name Smoothie in the first place. In a way it does resemble the milkshakes and malteds of generations ago.

HEALTHY ADDITIVES

One way to promote and increase Smoothie sales is to offer healthy additives for a power breakfast, energy builder, or part of a workout snack. The additions go by a variety of names: fortifiers, extras, energizers, boosters and nutritional additives. Drinks made with these additions fit in very well with growing trends toward lighter eating, convenience, freshness, and exciting tastes. Customers who order the add-ins are into working out and are usually between 18-35 years old. Most add-ins go for an extra 50 cents per tablespoon. On average, they will increase your smoothie sales by 10%. Adding extras, which are virtually tasteless, does not change the formula or taste of a smoothie. People don't mind paying 50 cents each for several additives. They regard it as value-added. Some healthy additions are as follows:

- **Bee Pollen:** Said to increase sexual stamina and prolong life. It is considered an excellent source of vitamin B, 18 amino acids, 14 minerals and enzymes, which aid in digestion.
- **Ginseng Root:** Contains a caffeine-like chemical, which enters the bloodstream rapidly, giving a sense of increased vitality and mental alertness.
- **Lecithin:** Derived from soybeans, lecithin is found in every cell of the body. Its primary function is to emulsify fats and cholesterol in the body.
- **Vitamin C:** Best known for its ability to increase the body's immune system to help fight infection, pollution, and cancer.
- **Wheat Germ:** Provides an excellent source of vegetarian protein, vitamin E, trace minerals, copper, iron, and maganese.

COST OF MAKING A SMOOTHIE

It takes 1-2 minutes to prepare a smoothie from scratch with an average food cost of 30% for a standard 20-ounce drink. Little skill is required to whip up smoothies, equipment needs are minimal and food costs are flexible depending on the ingredients used. If a drink is made without ice and just whole berries, juice, sorbet and/or frozen yogurt, costs run 34% to 37%.

EQUIPMENT NEEDED

The major piece of equipment needed to make a smoothie is a high-powered blender and ice machine. Better yet, all you need to adapt an existing facility to get into the smoothie business is

- Fruit blender
- Fruit juicer
- Freezer to hold frozen fruit and ice
- Twelve square feet of counter space

Blenders can be purchased from Vita-Mix (800-4DRINK4), Blendex (800-253-6383), (Hamilton Beach (800-572-3331) or Waring (800-492-7464). The best source in the USA for smoothie ingredients, packaging etc. is Southwest Traders (California-800-275-7984) or A. Panza & Sons (800-ICE CREAM).

FOODSERVICE OPPORTUNITIES

Marketers in the foodservice industry love the idea of marketing and selling Smoothies. They are a product of the 1990's with huge upside potential for incremental sales. The more marketers focus on health and the more we try to stay young and healthy and alive and happy, the more opportunity there is going to be for Smoothies and fruit juices. Since your customers are already accustomed to coming to you to indulge themselves- in a morning cup of choice Mocha Java coffee, a buttery sweet scone or a crunchy biscotti dipped in chocolate or in the afternoon for a ice cream cone: the opportunity is simply there for foodservice operations to grab on to something else. But in these crazy fast moving times, people are grappling with the conflicting need to reward themselves with gourmet foods and the wish to not undo those countless hours on the treadmill. They are getting tired of feeling guilty.

The good news is that there is opportunity. People want to indulge with a product they feel good about consuming. And what could be healthier than a freshly made smoothie or fruit juice.

HOW SMOOTHIES ARE MADE

20 Ounce Serving With Ice

Using ice creates a colder, more granita texture to the smoothie drink:

    4-6 ounces of frozen fruit
    1/2 of a banana
    4-6 ounces of juice
    4-6 ounces ice cream, frozen yogurt, sherbet or sorbet
    2-4 ounces ice

Preparation and Presentation

Pour frozen fruit (including banana), juice, ice, and either ice cream, frozen yogurt, sherbet or sorbet into a regular size (28-ounce) metal tumbler or blender canister. Attach the tumbler to a mixer and mix for 30 seconds. Pour the finished smoothie into a 20-ounce container and serve with a napkin and straw.

If the order is "to go," put a lid on the container and gently place it in a bag along with a napkin and straw.

20 Ounce Serving Without Ice

For the most part, all the recipes in this chapter are made with ice. If you want to make smoothies without ice, simply follow the below recommended recipe:

    5 ounces of frozen fruit
    1/2 of a banana
    5 ounces of juice
    6 ounces ice cream, frozen yogurt, sherbet or sorbet

Preparation and Presentation

Pour frozen fruit (including banana), juice and either ice cream, frozen yogurt, sherbet or sorbet into a regular size (28-ounce) metal tumbler or blender canister. Attach the tumbler to a mixer and mix for 30 seconds. Pour the finished smoothie into a 20 ounce container and serve with a napkin and straw. If the order is "to go," put a lid on the container and gently place it in a bag along with a napkin and straw.

Tips of the Trade

If you are selling a lot of smoothies, then pre-portioning the fruit is a very good idea. Place 1/2 banana cut into 1 inch pieces with 4 ounces of fruit in a plastic bag and freeze the bag so you end up with pre-portioned frozen fruit packages.

SOME VERY COOL "OUTLANDISH" SMOOTHIES
All Smoothie Recipes Below-20-Ounce Portion

FRUIT BASED SMOOTHIES

- **SINGING THE BLUES ON BLUEBERRY HILL:** Pour 4 ounces frozen blueberries (including 1/2 banana), 8 ounces orange juice, 6 ounces ice and I tablespoon of Lecithin powder into a regular size (28-ounce) metal tumbler or blender canister. Attach the tumbler to a mixer and mix for 30 seconds.

SORBET BASED SMOOTHIES

- **PEACH SMASH:** Pour 4 ounces frozen peaches (including 1/2 banana), 5 ounces peach nectar, 2 ounces ice, and 5 ounces peach sorbet into a regular size (28-ounce) metal tumbler or blender canister. Attach the tumbler to a mixer and mix for 30 seconds.

- **STRAWBERRY BANANA PARADISE:** Pour 4 ounces frozen IQF (Individual Quick Frozen) strawberries (including 1/2 banana), 5 ounces orange juice, 2 ounces ice, and 5 ounces strawberry sorbet into a regular size (28-ounce) metal tumbler or blender canister. Attach the tumbler to a mixer and mix for 30 seconds.

- **MANGO ORANGE PASSION:** Pour 4 ounces mango cubes (including 1/2 banana), 5 ounces orange juice, 2 ounces ice, and 5 ounces mango sorbet into a regular size (28-ounce) metal tumbler or blender canister. Attach the tumbler to a mixer and mix for 30 seconds.

- **SMOOTH CHOCOLATE FREEZE:** Pour 5 ounces seltzer (including 1/2 banana), 1 ounce fudge, 2 ounces ice, and 6 ounces chocolate sorbet into a regular size (28-ounce) metal tumbler or blender canister. Attach the tumbler to a mixer and mix for 30 seconds.

- **PASSION FRUIT:** Pour 5 ounces frozen IQF strawberries (including 1/2 banana), 5 ounces orange juice, 2 ounces ice, and 6 ounces passion fruit sorbet into a regular size (28-ounce) metal tumbler or blender canister. Attach the tumbler to a mixer and mix for 30 seconds.

138

- **PINEAPPLE CRUSH:** Pour 4 ounces frozen IQF pineapple cubes (including 1/2 banana), 5 ounces pineapple juice, 2 ounces ice, and 5 ounces strawberry sorbet into a regular size (28-ounce) metal tumbler or blender canister. Attach the tumbler to a mixer and mix for 30 seconds.

- **PANAMA SLUSH:** Pour 1 cup seltzer into the blender with 6 ounces pineapple sorbet, 2 ounces mango juice, and 2 ounces ice into a regular size (28-ounce) metal tumbler or blender canister. Attach the tumbler to a mixer and mix for 30 seconds.

- **BLUEBERRY PASSION:** Pour 4 ounces frozen blueberries (including 1/2 banana), 5 ounces blueberry sorbet, 5 ounces orange juice, 3 ounces ice into a regular size (28-ounce) metal tumbler or blender canister. Attach the tumbler to a mixer and mix for 30 seconds.

ICE CREAM BASED SMOOTHIES

- **STRAWBERRY PARADISE:** Pour 4 ounces frozen strawberries (including 1/2 banana), 3 ounces orange juice, 2 ounces ice, and 5 ounces ice cream into a regular size (28-ounce) metal tumbler or blender canister. Attach the tumbler to a mixer and mix for 30 seconds.

- **APPLE HUMMER:** Pour 6 ounces vanilla ice cream, 7 ounces apple juice, 1 ounce white rum, 1-1/2 ounces of Apple Schnapps, 1 teaspoon vanilla extract, and 2 ounces ice into a regular size (28-ounce) metal tumbler or blender canister. Attach the tumbler to a mixer and mix for 30 seconds.

- **RAZ-MA-TAZZ:** Pour 6 ounces vanilla ice cream, 7 ounces orange juice, 1 ounce raspberry liqueur, 1/2 ounce of brandy, 1 teaspoon vanilla extract, and 2 ounces ice into a regular size (28-ounce) metal tumbler or blender canister. Attach the tumbler to a mixer and mix for 30 seconds. Garnish top of the smoothie with fresh raspberries.

- **DERBY DAY:** Pour 1 cup vanilla soda into the blender with 8 ounces peppermint stick ice cream, and 2 ounces ice into a regular size (28-ounce) metal tumbler or blender canister. Attach the tumbler to a mixer and mix for 30 seconds.

- **MOCHA FRAPPE:** Combine 3/4 (6 ounces) cup strong coffee, 2 tablespoons cocoa powder, 3 ounces ice, and 6 ounces vanilla or chocolate ice cream in a blender until smooth.

- **CHOCOLATE CAPPUCCINO SUPREMO:** Pour 5 ounces non-fat milk into the blender with 8 ounces chocolate ice cream, 2 1/2-3 ounces coffee syrup and 3 ounces ice into a regular size (28-ounce) metal tumbler or blender canister. Attach the tumbler to a mixer and mix for 30 seconds.

- **RED NECKTIE**
  Pour 1 cup cranberry juice into the blender with 5 ounces vanilla soft serve ice cream or frozen yogurt, 3 ounces apricot brandy, and 2 ounces ice into a regular size (28-ounce) metal tumbler or blender canister. Attach the tumbler to a mixer and mix for 30 seconds.

- **JAMAICA SUNRISE:** Pour 1 cup orange juice into the blender with 6 ounces vanilla soft serve frozen yogurt, 2 ounces Tia Maria, 1/2 banana and 2 ounces ice into a regular size (28-ounce) metal tumbler or blender canister. Attach the tumbler to a mixer and mix for 30 seconds.

- **HAWAII FIZZ:** 2 scoops of vanilla ice cream, 2 ounces pineapple juice, 2 ounces cream of coconut, 4 ounces lemon-lime seltzer, and 4 ounces ice into a regular size (28-ounce) metal tumbler or blender canister. Attach the tumbler to a mixer and mix for 30 seconds.

- **MIXED OREO BERRY:** 2 scoops of vanilla ice cream, 6 ounces milk, 2 ounces each of IQF strawberries, raspberries, and blueberries into a regular size (28-ounce) metal tumbler or blender canister. Attach the tumbler to a mixer and mix for 30 seconds. Pour into container and sprinkle on top 2 Oreo (broken up pieces) cookies.

FROZEN YOGURT SMOOTHIES

- **PEACH:** Pour 4 ounces frozen IQF peach slices (including 1/2 banana), 5 ounces orange juice, 2 ounces ice, and 5 ounces vanilla or peach nonfat frozen yogurt into a regular size (28-ounce) metal tumbler or blender canister. Attach the tumbler to a mixer and mix for 30 seconds.

- **BLUEBERRY PASSION:** Pour 4 ounces frozen blueberries (including 1/2 banana), 5 ounces orange juice, 2 ounces ice, and 5 ounces vanilla nonfat frozen yogurt into a regular size (28-ounce) metal tumbler or blender canister. Attach the tumbler to a mixer and mix for 30 seconds.

- **CHOCOLATE MOUSSE:** Pour 6 ounces seltzer (including 1/2 banana), 1 ounce fudge, 2 ounces ice, 3 ounces chocolate non-fat frozen yogurt and 3 ounces chocolate sorbet into a regular size (28-ounce) metal tumbler or blender canister. Attach the tumbler to a mixer and mix for 30 seconds.

- **CAPPUCCINO QUENCHER:** Pour 6 ounces non-fat milk, 2 ounces coffee syrup, 2 ounces ice, and 7 ounces vanilla non-fat frozen yogurt into a regular size (28-ounce) metal tumbler or blender canister. Attach the tumbler to a mixer and mix for 30 seconds.

- **MANGO MANIA CREAM:** Pour 4 ounces frozen mango cubes (including 1/2 banana), 5 ounces orange juice, 2 ounces ice, and 4 ounces vanilla frozen yogurt into a regular size (28-ounce) metal tumbler or blender canister. Attach the tumbler to a mixer and mix for 30 seconds.

- **PINEAPPLE DELIGHT:** Pour 4 ounces frozen IQF pineapple cubes (including 1/2 banana), 5 ounces pineapple juice, 2 ounces ice, and 4 ounces vanilla frozen yogurt into a regular size (28-ounce) metal tumbler or blender canister. Attach the tumbler to a mixer and mix for 30 seconds.

- **STRAWBERRY RUSH:** Pour 4 ounces frozen strawberries (including 1/2 banana), 5 ounces orange juice, 2 ounces ice, and 4 ounces vanilla or strawberry frozen yogurt into a regular size (28-ounce) metal tumbler or blender canister. Attach the tumbler to a mixer and mix for 30 seconds.

- **CAPRICORN DELIGHT:** Pour 1 cup orange juice into the blender with 3 ounces frozen pineapple cubes, 6 ounces vanilla soft serve frozen yogurt, 1/2 banana and 2 ounces ice into a regular size (28-ounce) metal tumbler or blender canister. Attach the tumbler to a mixer and mix for 30 seconds. Garnish top of the smoothie with shredded coconut and crushed cashews.

BREAKFAST SMOOTHIES

- **BREAKFAST BLAST:** Pour 1 cup Tropical Blend V-8 Splash with 1 banana, 3 strawberries (frozen), and 4 ounces milk into a regular size (28-ounce) metal tumbler or blender canister. Attach the tumbler to a mixer and mix for 30 seconds. Garnish with fresh strawberries or banana slices.

- **PEAR YOGURT GINGER:** Pour 1 cup Tropical Blend V-8 Splash with 2 pear halves, 12 ounces nonfat frozen vanilla yogurt and 1/2 teaspoon ground ginger into a regular size (28-ounce) metal tumbler or blender canister. Attach the tumbler to a mixer and mix for 30 seconds.

EXOTIC HEALTH SMOOTHIES

Especially at lunchtime, you can offer your customers some very interesting health drinks.

- **ALL AMERICAN:** Pour 10 ounces skim milk, 1 tablespoon wheat germ, 1 tablespoon honey, and 8 ounces vanilla frozen yogurt into a regular size (28-ounce) metal tumbler or blender canister. Attach the tumbler to a mixer and mix for 30 seconds.

- **ROSE GARDEN:** Pour 10 ounces skim milk, 2 ounces strawberries, and 8 ounces vanilla frozen yogurt into a regular size (28-ounce) metal tumbler or blender canister. Attach the tumbler to a mixer and mix for 30 seconds.

CHAPTER 11
ICE CREAM FLAVOR RECIPES

"Don't be afraid to venture where no one's gone before. Simply let your mind wonder. It's a lot of fun."- Bill Lambert, International Dairy Consultant, Des Moines, Iowa

The recipes in this section are all new creations that have either appeared in our newsletter, *Batch Freezer News* or for one reason or another, never made it into my book, ICE CREAM & FROZEN DESSERTS, A Commercial Guide to Production and Marketing. What is amazing is that even when you think there are no more flavors to create, more keep popping up.

It's also amazing how times have changed. When I first got into the ice cream business I used a small 5-quart White Mountain batch freezer. That was back in 1978. I learned the hard way, made my own ice cream mix, and made what I still think is the best ice cream I have ever produced. Now I use big batch freezers but I still think I make some pretty good ice cream.

HELPFUL HINTS
The following "helpful hints" will help you produce quality uniform products day-in and day-out. Take care in understanding them because these rules are the backbone of operating your batch freezer properly.
- The batch freezer must be cleaned at the end of each day and sanitized at

the beginning of each new day.

- Have a 60 minute timer sitting on top of your batch freezer, and time each batch. It will eliminate guessing whether a product is frozen or not.
- Use preset measuring containers to measure your ingredients (extracts, chips, fruits etc.). If you are interested in uniformity, this is a necessity.
- Keep the area around your batch freezer clean during production. Cleanliness makes the production process a more organized affair. Always use clean rags, paper towels or handi-wipes.
- Place a rubber floor mat in front of your batch freezer. This will eliminate slipping due to spills from dairy products and ingredients, etc.
- Plan in advance what you are going to produce each day. Being organized will enable you to produce better products.
- Immediately place all produced products into a blast freezer after extrusion. Less contrast in temperature between a product extruded and the temperature of the blast freezer will reduce iciness in the product.
- Sharpening your metal dasher blades at least once a year will produce better finished products and will allow you to operate your batch freezer on an 8-10 minute production cycle.

VANILLA-BASED ICE CREAM FLAVORS

The old adage is that you will always be judged by the quality of your Vanilla ice cream. Well, that is still true. So, it 's very important that you put your best foot forward in the standard Vanilla ice cream you will produce whether it is a French Vanilla or a regular Vanilla without egg yolk in it. What is really important is that you use a high quality pure vanilla extract in your Vanilla flavors.

FRENCH VANILLA ICE CREAM

The ultimate Vanilla ice cream recipe, straight from my book, ICE CREAM and Frozen Desserts, A Commercial Guide to Production and Marketing.

Ingredients:

2 1/2 gallons	14 or 16% ice cream mix
4 ounces	Two-fold vanilla extract (Madagascar bourbon)
13 ounces	Pasteurized egg yolks

Preparation:
Pour all ingredients into batch freezer. Turn on both dasher and refrigeration and begin batch.
   At end of batch, extrude out the finished product.
                    Batch time: 8-10 minutes

VANILLA ICE CREAM

A fabulous Vanilla ice cream recipe from The Grateful Bean Café*, of Oklahoma City, Oklahoma. The Grateful Bean is a non-profit café that employ young adults who are disadvantaged and are trying to better themselves. The Café won the best of Oklahoma City for its great ice cream and this flavor defines what the Café is all about: "excellence." The Irish cream extract is used to create color (dissipate the stark white look), and at the same time create a "slight" subtle taste to the overall flavor.

Ingredients:

2 1/2 gallons	14 or 16% ice cream mix
3 ounces	Single-fold Tahitian vanilla extract
4 ounces	Indonesian vanilla extract
4 ounces	Madagascar bourbon pure vanilla
1/2 teaspoon	Irish cream extract
1/4 pound	Malted milk powder

Preparation:
Pour all ingredients into batch freezer. Turn on both dasher and refrigeration and begin batch. At end of batch, extrude out the finished product.

Batch time: 8-10 minutes

OREO COOKIE ICE CREAM

From Denise's Ice Cream* of Somerville, MA is Stan Zafran's own creation! It's like eating cookies and cream, not just Oreo cookies in Vanilla ice cream.

Ingredients:

2 1/2 gallons	14 or 16% ice cream mix
4 1/2 ounces	Heavy cream*
2 1/2 ounces	Vanilla extract (two-fold)
3 pounds	Oreo cookies
	(broken into quarters)

*NOTE: If you want to beef up the butterfat of your ice cream mix, add 7 1/2 ounces heavy cream to a 14% mix or 4 1/2 ounces to a 16% ice cream mix.

Preparation:
Freeze the Oreo cookies prior to starting production. Pour the ice cream mix, heavy cream, and vanilla extract into batch freezer. Turn on the refrigeration and begin batch. At the end of the batch, pour in Oreo cookies. Extrude out the finished product.

Decorate top of the tubs with Oreo cookies.

Batch Time: 8-10 minutes

MINT CHIP ICE CREAM

Another terrific recipe from Denise's Ice Cream* of Somerville, Massachusuetts. "What Stan Zafran likes best about this flavor is that it does not taste like toothpaste!" A very subtle mint flavor made with organic peppermint leaves and semi-sweet chocolate flakes.

Ingredients:

2 1/2 gallons	14 or 16% ice cream mix
1 ounce	Organic peppermint leaves ground into powder
1 ounce	Pure peppermint extract
3 pounds	Semisweet chocolate flakes
2 1/2 ounces	Vanilla extract (two-fold)

Preparation:

Freeze the semisweet chocolate flakes. Ground down the peppermint leaves in a food processor. Pour the ice cream mix, peppermint leaf powder, peppermint extract, and vanilla extract into batch freezer.

Turn on the refrigeration and begin batch. At the end of batch, pour in chocolate flakes. Extrude out the finished product.

Decorate the top of the tubs with chocolate flakes.

Batch Time: 8-10 minutes

CREME CARAMEL ICE CREAM

Clearly the best seller of Longford's Ice Cream* of Port Chester, New York. I particularly love the succulent creamy mouth feel after each delicious bite.

Ingredients:

11 quarts	14 or 16% ice cream mix
12 ounces	Caramel base
1 1/2 quarts	Caramel fudge

Preparation:

Pour ice cream mix and caramel base into batch freezer. Turn on both dasher and refrigeration and begin batch. At the end of the batch, extrude out the finished product swirling the caramel fudge into the tubs with a pastry bag* slowly variegating the caramel throughout the tub as it fills up with ice cream.

Decorate top of tubs with swirls of caramel.

Batch time: 8-10 minutes

*Note: Longford's uses a pastry bag to swirl the caramel into the tubs. It gives an even controllable distribution of how much caramel to use.

LEMON CUSTARD ICE CREAM

If you follow this recipe to the "T", you will have produced the best lemon ice cream you could ever have imagined. Do you remember how good the lemon from a lemon meringue pie used to taste when it was made from scratch years ago? Well this recipe incorporates this idea because to make the flavor you will have to make a lemon curd.

Making the Lemon Curd:

This recipe for lemon curd comes from my good friend, David Talbot, who owned the Chelsea Ice Cream Company in New York during the early 1990's. It will produce enough curd for a number of batches of Lemon Custard Ice Cream. Whatever you don't use, freeze for later use.

16 ounces	Fresh lemon juice
6 3/4 pounds	Sugar, granulated
4 1/2 pounds	Butter, sweet
3 pounds	Eggs, whole
1/2 pound	Egg yolks
2 3/4 ounces	Gelatin

Heat lemon juice. Add sugar, gelatin, egg, and egg yolks. When hot add the butter. Cook until thick. Strain into container and cool. For use when cold, warm slightly in a double boiler and whip on the mixer.

Ingredients:

18 ounces	Lemon curd
3 gallons	14 or 16% ice cream mix
2 ounces	Two-fold vanilla extract
1 1/2 quart	Lemon curd (for variegating)

Preparation:

Pour all ice cream mix, vanilla extract and 18 ounces of lemon curd into batch freezer. Turn on dasher and refrigeration and begin batch. When batch is complete, turn off refrigeration and while you are extruding the finished product from batch freezer swirl in additional 1 1/2 quarts of lemon curd.

Batch time: 8-10 minutes

VARIATION

LEMON PIE ICE CREAM: Straight from Tucker's Ice Cream* of Alameda, California. Just one of the creative inventions of Kate Pryor and David Lee. Add 1/2 pound graham crackers to the batch when the batch is almost complete.

RICE PUDDING ICE CREAM

Simply put, I love rice pudding. For the book party for my book, ICE CREAM and Frozen Desserts, A Commercial Guide to Production and Marketing, I invented this flavor. It was a major success. The following year, at our ice cream seminar, we perfected it even more. I assume someday, someone like Ben & Jerry's, will produce this flavor and say they invented it. You will know better. Remember this date April 1998!

Making the Rice/Raisin Mixture:

Rice Mixture

2 pounds	Superfino Aborio rice- (Italian rice used for Risotto)
3 quarts	Water
3/4 pound	Sugar

Prepare rice using 3-1 ratio of 1 part rice to 3 parts water. Boil water. Once the water boils add rice and sugar. Turn to simmer and cook under "simmer" until rice is cooked. Let cooked rice sit with cover on for 1/2 hour.

Raisin Mixture

2 pounds	Golden raisins
2 1/4 pounds	Sugar
1 quart	Water
1 ounce	Cinnamon

Put all ingredients into pot and bring to boil. Cook for 15 minutes under "simmer." Drain off the water thoroughly and then add cooked rice to this mixture. Cool mixture for 2 hours.

Ingredients:

2 1/2 gallons	14 or 16% ice cream mix
4 ounces	Two-fold vanilla extract
6 pounds	Rice/raisin mixture
3 ounces	Cinnamon

Preparation:

Pour ice cream mix, vanilla extract, 1-ounce cinnamon, and 2 pounds of rice mixture into batch freezer. Turn on dasher. Set timer to 8 minutes, and then turn on refrigeration and begin batch.

When batch is almost complete, add remaining 4 pounds of rice mixture. Next, turn off refrigeration and extrude finished product sprinkling the tub with remaining cinnamon.

Batch Time: 8-10 minutes

DULCE De LECHE (Caramel) ICE CREAM

Originally introduced by Haagen-Dazs in South America, it is now their number one best selling flavor. The name in English means caramelized sweet milk.

Ingredients:

2 1/2 gallons	14 or 16% ice cream mix
3 ounces	Two-fold vanilla extract
2 1/4 pounds	Caramel Base 8951-Star Kay White
4 1/2 pounds	Caramel Kremia #1PE- Star Kay White

Preparation:
Pour ingredients except the Caramel Kremia into batch freezer. Turn on dasher and run for 1 minute. Next, set timer to 8 minutes. Turn on refrigeration and begin batch. When batch is complete, turn off refrigeration and as finished product is being extruded, variegate throughout the tubs the Caramel Kremia variegate. Decorate the top of the tubs with Caramel Kremia variegate.

Batch Time: 9-11 minutes

VARIATIONS

DULCE DE LECHE EXTRAVAGANZA: Add 1 pound each of chocolate chunks and pecan pralines at the end of the batch.
DULCE DE LECHE BANANA CHUNK ICE CREAM: Add 5 pounds peeled pureed bananas and 1 pound chocolate chunks to the batch.

FRESH GINGER ICE CREAM

A favorite flavor from Maraline Olson of Screamin Mimi's* of Sebastopal, California. Maraline says "I cannot keep it in stock." Need I say more?

Ingredients:

2 1/2 gallons	14 or 16% ice cream mix
2 pounds	Fresh gingerroot (yields 8 ounces juice)
2 ounces	Tahitian vanilla extract
2 1/2 pounds	Candied ginger pieces*

*Note: Royal Pacific Foods- 800-551-5284. Ask for dark sweet ginger cuts.

Preparation:
Juice the ginger with a fruit juicer. You may need more than 2 pounds to obtain the necessary 8 ounces of ginger juice. Pour all the ingredients into the batch freezer, turn on the dasher and blend for one minute. Next, turn on the refrigeration and begin batch. At the end of the batch, pour in candied ginger pieces and extrude out the finished product. Decorate the top of the tubs with candied ginger pieces.

Batch Time: 9-11 minutes

NUTTY VANILLA CHOCOLATE CHUNK ICE CREAM

After watching me experiment creating new flavors in our home, my Carole (as in Gordon-Stogo) said it was her turn. She loves almonds and her favorite gelato flavor is Stracciatella, so she came up with this incredible "chocolatey" chocolate chip flavor. Try it, you will go bananas over it!

Ingredients:

2 1/2 gallons	14 or 16% ice cream mix
4 ounces	Two-fold vanilla extract
1 pounds	Almonds, roasted and diced
1 pound	Chocolate Chunks
1pound	Stracciatella (Fabbri)

Preparation:

Using a double boiler, melt into liquid form 1 pound of Stracciatella. Pour ice cream mix and vanilla extract into the batch freezer. Turn on the dasher and refrigeration and begin batch. When the batch is almost complete, add the diced almonds and chocolate chunks and slowly pour in the liquid Stracciatella. Turn off refrigeration and extrude out the finished product. Decorate the top of the tubs with almonds, chocolate chunks, and liquid Stracciatella.

Batch time: 9-11 minutes

BISCOTTI ICE CREAM

I have to admit my clients, Tony and Marc Boccaccio of Fresco Desserts, East Northport, NY. spoil me. Every time I do a consultation for them, I arrive home with a box of their freshly made biscotti. Since I am in the ice cream business, the next thought is making an ice cream flavor with them.*

Ingredients:

2 1/2 gallons	14 or 16% ice cream mix
4 ounces	Two-fold vanilla extract
1 ounce	Almond or hazelnut flavor
3 pounds	Almond or hazelnut biscotti
2 pounds	Tempered chocolate disc

Preparation:

Melt chocolate in double boiler. Dip each Biscotti into the chocolate and put them in a refrigerator to harden. Once hardened, cut them into small pieces. Pour ice cream mix, vanilla extract, almond or hazelnut paste, and 1/2 of the chocolate covered Biscotti cookie pieces into the batch freezer. Turn on dasher and refrigeration and begin batch. When batch is complete, add remaining Biscotti cookies. Next, turn off refrigeration and extrude finished product.

Batch Time: 9-11 minutes

KULFI ICE CREAM

Kulfi is the traditional Indian ice cream and has a strongly cooked-milk flavor and dense icy texture. In India, Kulfi is served in cone-shaped lidded metal containers which are rubbed between the hands to warm and release the flavor of the ice cream. Can you imagine doing that here! The original way of preparing this flavor is time consuming and I am not sure it is suited to an American palate, but the overall taste is interesting and is a terrific dessert after an Indian curry meal. Make sure the pistachios are finely granulated to create a feel of nut flavor, but not actually to see or eat the pistachio nut itself.

Ingredients:

2 1/2 gallons	14 or 16% ice cream mix
7 ounces	Rosewater
2 ounces	Ground cardamom
2 pounds	Pistachios (finely granulated)

Preparation:
Pour all ingredients into batch freezer. Turn on dasher and refrigeration and begin batch. When batch is complete, extrude finished product. Garnish with pistachio pieces.

Batch Time: 8-10 minutes

CINNAMON BUN ICE CREAM

If you like to eat a cinnamon bun for breakfast, then you will surely like this ice cream flavor for dessert that has been developed by Star Kay White*.

Ingredients:

2 1/2 gallons	14 or 16% ice cream mix
2 ounces	Two-fold vanilla extract
1 1/4 pounds	SKW Cinnamon Base Emulsion*
2 1/2 pounds	SKW Caramel Cinnamon Variegate 994*
1 1/2 pounds	SKW Raisin Fruit*
1 pound	Dark roasted pecan pieces

*Note: Star Kay White can be contacted at 1-845-268-2600

Preparation:
Pour ice cream mix, vanilla extract, and cinnamon base emulsion into batch freezer. Turn on both dasher and refrigeration and begin batch. At the end of the batch, pour in the raisin fruit. Next, turn off the refrigeration and as the product is being extruded, swirl in the caramel cinnamon variegate. Decorate top of tubs with raisin fruit and caramel variegate.

Batch time: 8-10 minutes

WHITE GOLD

I found this flavor on the Internet from an ice cream company in the UK called G&D Ice Cream and Café*. They say that the idea came from the production crew who was bored making simple traditional flavors. Simply Vanilla ice cream with white chocolate chips, butterscotch and cookie dough.
The actual recipe is my interpretation. I know it will work, so try it out.

Ingredients
2 1/2 gallons	14 or 16% ice cream mix
3 ounces	Two fold vanilla extract
2 pounds	Cookie dough pieces
2 pounds	White chocolate chunks (soft)
2 quarts	Butterscotch topping

Preparation:
Pour ice cream mix and vanilla extract into batch freezer. Turn on both dasher and refrigeration and begin batch. Middle of the batch add the cookie dough pieces and white chocolate chunks. When batch is complete, turn off refrigeration and as the product is being extruded, swirl in the butterscotch topping. Decorate top of tubs with white chocolate chunks and butterscotch.
Batch time: 8-10 minutes

MINT PATTIE ICE CREAM

I have tasted mints from many USA companies, but nothing compares to the taste of Fabbri's mint paste.

Ingredients:
2 1/2 gallons	14 or 16% ice cream mix
4 ounces	Two-fold vanilla extract
24 ounces	Fabbri mint paste
2 pounds	Peppermint Mint Patties
1 pound	Soft dark chocolate chunks

Preparation:
Pour ice cream mix, vanilla extract and the mint paste into batch freezer. Turn on the dasher and let it run for a few minutes. Set timer to 8 minutes, turn on refrigeration and begin batch. When batch is almost complete, turn off refrigeration, add Peppermint Mint Patties and chocolate chunks, and then extrude out the finished product.

Decorate the top of the tub with a drizzle of Peppermint Mint Patties and chocolate chunks.
Batch Time: 8-10 minutes

ICE CREAM FRUIT FLAVORS

When it comes to fruit flavors, there is no end to one's imagination in developing something very unusual and different.

APPLE PIE ICE CREAM

From Ron Kotloff of Classic Creamery* of Aliso Viego, California comes this recipe that tastes like a Crumb Apple Pie.

Ingredients:

2 1/2 gallons	14 or 16% ice cream mix
2 ounces	Two-fold vanilla extract
1 #10 can	Apple pie filling- (Limpert Brothers)
1/2 teaspoon	Cinnamon flavor- (Limpert Brothers)
1/2 teaspoon	Apple pie flavoring- (Limpert Brothers)
3 tablespoons	Ground cinnamon
10	Graham crackers

Preparation:

Puree apple pie filling. Pour ice cream mix and rest of ingredients into the batch freezer. Turn on both dasher and refrigeration and begin batch. When the batch is complete, add the graham crackers (crumbled), turn off the refrigeration and extrude out the finished product.

Batch time: 8-10 minutes

STRAWBERRY ICE CREAM

Pete Schaffer of The Grateful Bean Café*, Oklahoma City, Oklahoma has told me they have twinked this flavor almost as much as their vanilla.

Ingredients:

2 1/2 gallons	14 or 16% ice cream mix
13 pounds	Frozen strawberries
3 1/4 pounds	Sugar
3 ounces	Tahitian vanilla extract
1/2 teaspoon	Irish cream extract

Preparation:

Combine the fruit and sugar and marinate the mixture for 8 hours. Next, pour all the ingredients except half the fruit into batch freezer. Turn on both dasher and refrigeration and begin batch. When batch is complete, add the remaining strawberries. Turn off refrigeration and extrude out the finished product.

Batch time: 8-10 minutes

STRAWBERRY CHEESECAKE ICE CREAM

Without a doubt, cheesecake is the number one selling restaurant dessert in the USA. What better idea is there than taking this great tasting dessert and making some incredible tasting variations in the form of ice cream.

To prove this point, in 1991 with the help of my associate Lisa Tanner, we won a 1st place prize for Penguin Frozen Yogurt for the best new foodservice dessert of the year for our creation- Raspberry Cheesecake Frozen Yogurt Cake. So let's get started with some great variations.

While this flavor is the same as the one listed on page 403 of my book, Ice Cream & Frozen Desserts, it is basically a hidden masterpiece. The reason being the cheesecake base that is used. Except for a few of my closest friends, no one knows the source of the cheesecake base. But here it is for you.

Ingredients:

2 1/2 gallons	14 or 16% ice cream mix
4 ounces	Two-fold vanilla extract
3 pounds	Cheesecake powder (Royal-Nabisco)*
2 quarts	Processed strawberries
1/2 pound	Graham crackers (broken)

*Note- Royal Cheesecake powder is a product of the Nabisco Company (800-852-9393). It can be purchased in a foodservice package from any foodservice distributor that handles Nabisco products.

Preparation:

Pour 1 gallon of ice cream mix into batch freezer and add the dry cheesecake powder and vanilla extract. Turn on the dasher and let it run for a few minutes.

Pour the balance of ice cream mix into the batch freezer. Set timer to 8 minutes, turn on refrigeration and begin batch. End of the batch, add the strawberries. When batch is complete, turn off refrigeration and extrude finished product.

Garnish top of tubs with strawberries and graham crackers.

Batch Time: 8-10 minutes

VARIATION

RASPBERRY CHEESECAKE ICE CREAM: Substitute 2 quarts of either raspberry topping or raspberry variegate for the strawberries. Swirl either into the batch as the product being extruded out into the tubs.

MANGO ICE CREAM

Mangos prepared in any form have now become my favorite fruit in ice cream, gelato, sorbet, and Italian ice.

Ingredients:

2 1/2 gallons	14 or 16% ice cream mix
2 ounces	Two-fold vanilla extract
8 pounds	Fresh or frozen mango puree
2 pounds	Sugar
1 ounce	Lemon juice
4 quarts	Water

Preparation:

Mix the mango puree with sugar. Separate out two pounds of the mango-sugar mixture and cut into small pieces. Puree the balance of the mangos.

Pour ice cream mix, vanilla extract, lemon juice, and mango puree into batch freezer. Turn on both dasher and refrigeration and begin batch.

When the batch is almost complete, pour in the mango pieces, turn off the refrigeration and extrude out the finished product.

Decorate top of tubs with mango pieces

Batch time: 8-10 minutes

VARIATIONS

MANGO GINGER ICE CREAM: At the end of the batch, add 1/2 pound sweet (crystallized) ginger pieces and 1 pound Ginger snap cookies.

MANGO HAZELNUT ICE CREAM: Beginning of the batch, add 2 ounces hazelnut extract or 12 ounces of a hazelnut liqueur. At the end of the batch, add 1 pound roasted hazelnut pieces.

APRICOT ICE CREAM

Fresh apricots are fine for eating, but their flavor can be too delicate for ice cream, so I recommend that you use dried apricots, from either California or Turkey, sulfured or unsulfured. They have an intense flavor that cuts through the cream.

Ingredients:

2 1/2 gallons	14 or 16% ice cream mix
2 ounces	Two-fold vanilla extract
12 pounds	Dried apricots
4 quarts	Water

Preparation:

In a heavy saucepan, cook 12 pounds of dried apricots with 4 quarts of water until water boils and apricots soften. Drain off the water and puree the mixture. Pour ice cream mix, vanilla extract, apricot puree into batch freezer. Turn on both dasher and refrigeration and begin batch.

Turn off the refrigeration and extrude out the finished product.

Decorate top of tubs with apricot slices.

Batch time: 8-10 minutes

VARIATIONS

PARISIAN APRICOT ICE CREAM: After the dried apricots have been softened and the water drained off, marinate the apricots with 16 ounces of brandy for at least two hours. Next, combine all the ingredients together and begin the batch.

APRICOT HAZELNUT ICE CREAM: At the end of the batch, pour in 1 1/2 pounds of chopped roasted hazelnut pieces.

DRUNKEN APRICOT ICE CREAM: At the end of the batch, pour in 26 ounces of dark rum, and begin extruding out the finished product.

PEACH ICE CREAM

If you ever had the experience of eating a peach from a farm stand in Georgia in June or July, you know what I mean when I say, "if you do it right, there is nothing better than freshly made peach ice cream." When made with processed peaches, there always seems to be an aftertaste of an artificial ingredient. The recipe I use takes time, but is certainly worth the effort.
The big secret to making this flavor is the use of very ripe fruit.

Ingredients:

26-28	Fresh ripe peaches- (yield 4 quarts puree)
3 1/2 pounds	Sugar
3 ounces	Natural peach extract
2 1/2 gallons	14 or 16% ice cream mix
3 ounces	Two-fold vanilla extract
1 ounce	Lemon juice

Preparation:

Blanch the peaches in boiling water for 30-45 seconds so that they peel easily. (You will quickly learn that the hardest part of this recipe is peeling the fruit.) Peel, then mix them with 3 1/2 pounds of sugar. Marinate mixture for at least 8 hours (preferably overnight) until ready to use. Puree 3/4 of this mixture, and cut remaining peaches into small pieces.

Pour pureed mixture into batch freezer along with remaining ingredients except small cut pieces of peaches. Turn on both dasher and refrigeration and begin batch. When batch is complete, pour in remaining small cut pieces of peaches, turn off refrigeration and extrude finished product. Decorate top of tubs with fresh peach slices.

Batch time: 8-10 minutes

VARIATIONS

PEACH AMARETTO ICE CREAM: Add 12 ounces of a peach liqueur and 1 pound diced roasted almonds to the above recipe just before you extrude out the finished product.

PEACH GINGER ICE CREAM: Add 1 pound of sweet ginger pieces to the batch just before you begin to extrude out the finished product.

PASSION FRUIT ICE CREAM

This exotic flavor is just the right flavor to offer as a special during the summer. While it does take some work to prepare the fruit for ice cream production, the effort is worth it.

Ingredients:

2 1/2 gallons	14 or 16% Ice cream mix
2 ounces	Two-fold vanilla extract
20 pounds	Passion fruit *- (strained yield is 6 3/4 quarts)
3 1/2 pound	Sugar
4 ounces	Lemon juice

Note: You can also purchase French passion fruit puree from numerous importers.

Preparation:

Cut passion fruit in half and scoop the pulp out into a strainer to extract as much juice as possible.

Discard seeds, but retain some pulp for body and texture.

Mix the passion fruit juice with sugar and marinate the mixture for eight hours.

Pour ice cream mix, vanilla extract, lemon juice, and passion fruit juice into batch freezer. Turn on both dasher and refrigeration and begin batch.

When the batch is almost complete, turn off the refrigeration and extrude out the finished product.

Batch time: 8-10 minutes

VARIATIONS

PASSION FRUIT RASPBERRY SWIRL ICE CREAM: When the batch is complete, turn off the refrigeration and swirl in 2 quarts of the raspberry variegate as the product is being extruded out.

PAPAYA & PASSION FRUIT ICE CREAM: Peel and remove the flesh from 8-9 papayas that should yield 3 quarts of papaya puree. Add 1 pound of sugar to this mixture and marinate for 8 hours. Next, add this mixture to the passion fruit mixture above, and begin the batch.

CANTALOUPE ICE CREAM

Procuring ripe melons is imperative to get the full flavor of this recipe.

Ingredients:

7-8	Ripe cantaloupes
2 ounces	Lemon juice
2 1/2 gallons	14 or 16% ice cream mix
3 ounces	Two-fold vanilla extract

Preparation:
Peel, cut, and remove seeds from cantaloupes. Puree enough cantaloupes to yield 4 quarts of puree. Add 3 pounds of sugar and 2 ounces of lemon juice to the puree. Marinate mixture for 8 hours. Pour all ingredients into batch freezer. Turn on both dasher and refrigeration and begin batch. At end of batch, turn off refrigeration and extrude finished product.
Batch time: 8-10 minutes

VARIATION

CANTALOUPE DRAMBUIE ICE CREAM: The addition of Drambuie helps bring out the full flavor of the Cantaloupe ice cream recipe. Add 12 ounces of Drambuie to the cantaloupe puree as it is being marinated.

PRUNE-ARMAGNAC ICE CREAM

A sophisticated recipe that's perfect for an upscale restaurant. Simply forget every image you have about prunes and proceed with the following recipe.

Ingredients:

3 pounds	Pitted prunes
3/4 pounds	Sugar
16 ounces	Armagnac (French brandy)
2 1/2 gallons	14 or 16% ice cream mix
3 ounces	Two-fold vanilla extract

Preparation:
Combine the prunes and sugar and marinate for 6 hours. Next, add the Armagnac and continue marinating for additional 2 hours and then puree the whole mixture. Pour pureed mixture into batch freezer, turn on both dasher and refrigeration and begin batch. When batch is complete, turn off refrigeration and extrude finished product. Decorate top of tubs with pieces of pitted prunes.
Batch time: 8-10 minutes

LAVENDER-FIG ICE CREAM

The evocative aroma of lavender is infusing desserts with distinctive flavor and a romantic flair.

Ingredients:

2 1/2 gallons	14 or 16% ice cream mix
4 ounces	Two-fold vanilla extract
1 1/2 pounds	Lavender honey
3 pounds	Dried figs, chopped

Preparation:

Heat (low heat) 1 quart of ice cream mix with the lavender honey until the honey is completely dissolved into the mix. Add the chopped dried figs and continue cooking for about five minutes. Remove and refrigerate this mixture.

Pour balance of ice cream mix and all the other ingredients into batch freezer. Turn on the dasher and refrigeration and begin batch. When batch is complete, turn off refrigeration and extrude out the finished product.

Decorate the top of the tub with a drizzle of lavender honey.

Batch Time: 8-10 minutes

PLUM PUDDING ICE CREAM

Ice cream lovers will welcome this nontraditional approach to an old English holiday favorite.

Ingredients:

2 1/2 gallons	14 or 16% ice cream mix
4 ounces	Two-fold vanilla extract
3/4 cup	Port wine
1 1/2 pounds	Golden raisins
48 ounces (canned)	Purple plums, drained and pitted
3 teaspoons	Ginger
1 pound	Chopped walnuts

Preparation:

Heat (low to medium heat) port wine adding raisins until 3/4ths of the port wine has evaporated. Puree the plums and combine the puree with the raisins.

Pour the balance of ice cream mix, and other ingredients into the batch freezer. Set timer to 8 minutes, turn on refrigeration and begin batch. When batch is complete, turn off refrigeration and extrude out the finished product.

Batch Time: 8-10 minutes

ENGLISH PLUM & CINNAMON ICE CREAM

Simply sensual!

Ingredients:

2 1/2 gallons	14 or 16% ice cream mix
4 ounces	Two-fold vanilla extract
3 quarts	Dessert plum puree-(32-36 plums, stones removed)
3/4 pound	Sugar
8 large	Cinnamon sticks
4 ounces	Lemon juice

Preparation:

Remove pits from the plums. Slowly cook the plums with sugar and cinnamon sticks until mixture reaches a slow boil. Immediately turn to simmer and cook for 30 minutes. Cool the mixture and add lemon juice. Remove the cinnamon sticks. Puree the mixture and then run it through a sieve. Marinate mixture for 8 hours. Pour ice cream mix, vanilla extract and fruit mixture into the batch freezer. Turn on dasher and refrigeration and begin batch. When batch is complete, turn off refrigeration and extrude finished product. Garnish top of tubs with plum slices and cinnamon.

Batch Time: 8-10 minutes

COCONUT ALMOND JOY

Absolutely, one of my most favorite flavors!

Ingredients:

2 1/2 gallons	14 or 16% ice cream mix
4 ounces	Two-fold vanilla extract
1 1/2 quarts	Coconut fruit base
1/2 pound	Chocolate chunks
1 1/2 quarts	Multi purpose fudge
1/4 pound	Shredded coconut
1 1/2 pounds	Sliced or chopped almonds

Preparation:

Pour ice cream mix, vanilla extract, and Coconut fruit base into the batch freezer. Turn on dasher and refrigeration and begin batch. When batch is almost complete, add chocolate chunks, shredded coconut, and almonds. Turn off refrigeration and swirl in the chocolate fudge into the tubs as the finished product is being extruded. Garnish top of tubs with fudge, chocolate chunks, shredded coconut, and almonds.

Batch Time: 8-10 minutes

SPUMONE DI TAORMINA ICE CREAM

This is the real McCoy- not your phony Tutti-Frutti, but the real Sicilian specialty accented with the flavor of blood oranges. (Adapted from a recipe in the book- The Great Cooks' Guide to Ice Cream & Other Frozen Desserts).

Ingredients:

2 1/2 gallons	14 or 16% ice cream mix
2 ounces	Two-fold vanilla extract
1 1/2 pounds	Toasted almonds (finely chopped)
1 1/2 pounds	Candied fruit (finely chopped)
	Grated rind of 4 oranges*
4 ounces	Orange liqueur

Note-Blood oranges are not always easy to find (available from November to May), so to strike the proper note of authenticity, substitute regular oranges and use several drops of red food coloring.

Preparation:

Pour ice cream mix, vanilla extract and grated orange rinds into the batch freezer. Turn on dasher. Set timer to 8 minutes, turn on refrigeration and begin batch. When batch is more than half-way done, add the toasted almonds, candied fruit and orange liqueur. Turn off refrigeration and extrude finished product. Decorate top of the tubs with toasted almonds and candied fruit.

Batch Time: 8-10 minutes

TUTTI-FRUTTI ICE CREAM (AMERICAN STYLE)

Another version of using candied fruits with certain kinds of nuts.

Ingredients:

2 1/2 gallons	14 or 16% ice cream mix
2 ounces	Two-fold vanilla extract
2 ounces	Almond extract
1 1/2 pounds	Mixture of chopped unsalted almonds, macadamias, pistachios, and cashew nuts
1 1/2 pounds	Candied fruit (finely chopped)

Preparation:

Pour ice cream mix, vanilla extract and almond extract into the batch freezer. Turn on dasher and refrigeration and begin batch. When batch is half way done, add the nut mixture and candied fruit. Turn off refrigeration and extrude finished product. Decorate top of the tubs with pieces of the nut mixture and candied fruit.

Batch Time: 8-10 minutes

162

ICE CREAM NUT FLAVORS

Pecans, walnuts, pistachios, hazelnuts, and almonds. The list goes on and on. When it comes to making ice cream, the world is your oyster. Any kind of nut will go great with any chocolate, coffee, or cookie ice cream flavor. Just make sure that regardless of the nut you might want to use that it is roasted with no salt added.

It's simply up to you to use your imagination to come up with your own creation. And don't be afraid to use more than one kind of nut in any particular flavor you might come up with.

The following are just a few for you to try out.

PRALINE CHILI ICE CREAM

The chili taste will knock your socks off!

Ingredients:

2 1/2 gallons	14 or 16% ice cream mix
4 ounces	Two-fold vanilla extract
1 ounce	Praline flavor
32 ounces	Caramel variegate

	Red-Pepper Pecan Praline Crunch
2 1/2 pounds	Large pecan pieces
3 ounces	Crushed red pepper flakes
2 pounds	Sugar
2 cups	Water

Combine sugar and water in a heavy saucepan over medium heat. Continue to cook until the sugar turns light amber. Immediately remove from heat and stir in the pecans and red pepper flakes. Stir vigorously to coat the nuts and then spread them out indivdually on a nonstick cookie sheet. When completely cool, use a heavy knife to chop the nuts into 1/4-1/3 inch pieces.

Preparation:

Pour ice cream mix, vanilla extract, and praline flavor into the batch freezer. Turn on dasher. Set timer to 8 minutes, turn on refrigeration and begin batch. End of the batch, add the pecan nut pieces. When batch is complete, turn off refrigeration and extrude finished product swirling into the tubs the caramel variegate. Garnish top of tubs with pecan nut pieces and caramel variegate.

Batch Time: 8-10 minutes

163

PISTACHIO ICE CREAM

This recipe is included to illustrate a simple fact. If you are going to produce an upscale product that is wholesaled to a restaurant, then the elimination of green food coloring is important. If you are simply selling it in a typical dip shop atmosphere this flavor might need the coloring to sell the product.

Ingredients:

2 1/2 gallons	14 or 16% ice cream mix
2 ounces	Two-fold vanilla extract
2 ounces	Pistachio extract flavoring or 30 ounces Fabbri pistachio paste
1 1/2 pounds	Pistachio pieces

Preparation:
Pour all ingredients except half of pistachios into batch freezer. Turn on dasher for 2 minutes to granulate the nuts. Turn on refrigeration and begin batch. At end of batch, add remaining nuts. When batch is complete, turn off refrigeration and extrude finished product. Decorate tops of tubs with pistachio pieces.

Batch time: 8-10 minutes

VARIATION

PISTACHIO HALVAH ICE CREAM: Add 1 1/2 pounds of cut-up halvah cubes to the above recipe. Halvah can be purchased from Joyva (718-497-0170).

AMARETTO ICE CREAM

Italian gelato pastes are not just for gelato. They are very versatile as seen by trying out this Amaretto ice cream flavor. Try it and you will have a real winner.

Ingredients:

2 1/2 gallons	16% ice cream mix
2 ounces	Two-fold vanilla extract
37 ounces	Amaretto paste- Fabbri
1 1/2 pounds	Sliced almonds (roasted)

Preparation:
Pour ice cream mix, vanilla extract, amaretto paste and 1/2 pound of sliced almonds into batch freezer. Turn on both dasher and refrigeration and begin batch. At the end of the batch, pour in the remaining sliced almonds. Turn off the refrigeration and extrude out the finished product. Decorate top of tubs with sliced almonds.

Batch time: 8-10 minutes

PRALINE ALMOND COFFEE ICE CREAM

Thinking up this flavor was a sheer delight. The addition of praline almonds and fudge to a traditional coffee flavor really works. I hope you enjoy making this as much as I have enjoyed licking it out of the batch freezer.

Ingredients:

5 ounces	Freeze-dried coffee
1/2 ounce	Cocoa (22-24% fat)
3 tablespoons	Hot water
2 1/2 gallons	16% ice cream mix
2 ounces	Two-fold vanilla extract
1 1/2 pounds	Praline almonds
3 pounds	Hot fudge

Preparation:

Mix freeze-dried coffee with as little hot water as possible and add cocoa. The resulting paste should be smooth with no dry coffee visible. Pour all ingredients except praline almonds and fudge into batch freezer. Turn on dasher and refrigeration and begin batch. Halfway into batch, add almonds. When batch is complete, turn off refrigeration, and swirl fudge into tubs as ice cream is being extruded from batch freezer. Decorate tops of tubs with almonds and fudge.

VARIATION

PECAN PRALINE CAFFE ICE CREAM: Instead of using praline almonds, add 1 1/2 pounds of pecan pralines at the end of the batch.

FRENCH ALMOND NOUGAT ICE CREAM

A very interesting ice cream flavor from France.

Ingredients:

2 1/2 gallons	14 or 16% ice cream mix
3 ounces	Two-fold vanilla extract
1 1/2 quarts	French Almond Crème (Blue Diamond)
1 1/2 pounds	French Nougat Chips, large (Blue Diamond)

Preparation:

Pour ingredients except the nougat chips into batch freezer. Turn on dasher and refrigeration and begin batch. When batch is almost complete, pour in the nougat chips. Turn off refrigeration and extrude the finished product. Decorate the top of the tubs with nougat chips.

Batch Time: 8-10 minutes

GIANDUJA ICE CREAM
(Chocolate and Hazelnut)

One of my favorite gelato flavors and now an ice cream flavor, why not? For the preparation of this flavor, we are substituting American ingredients for the traditional gelato flavoring produced in Italy. The same flavor at half the cost.

Ingredients:

2 1/2 gallons	16% ice cream mix
2 1/2 ounces	Two-fold vanilla extract
20 ounces	Cocoa
5 ounces	Hot water
22 ounces	Praline paste*
10 ounces	Chocolate chips
10 ounces	Chopped hazelnuts

Hazelnut pieces and chocolate chips for garnish

*Note: Praline Paste or hazelnut paste (sometimes called filbert paste) can be purchased from any bakery ingredient supply company. You can also use 32 ounces of Fabbri Gianduja paste to create the same flavor replacing the above cocoa, water and praline paste.

Preparation:

Mix cocoa with as little hot water as possible to create a smooth cocoa paste. This resulting paste should have no visible dry cocoa left.

Pour all ingredients into batch freezer. Turn on dasher and let it run for 3 minutes to blend cocoa and praline paste into mix. Turn on refrigeration and begin batch. When batch is just about complete, add chocolate chips and chopped hazelnuts, turn off refrigeration and extrude finished product.

Garnish with mixture of chocolate chips and hazelnut pieces.

Batch time: 8-10 minutes

VARIATION

GIANDUJA CARAMEL FUDGE SWIRL: As the finished product is being extruded, swirl in 1 1/2 quarts of caramel variegate throughout tubs.

ICE CREAM COFFEE FLAVORS

Very, very slowly, coffee ice cream flavors are becoming the third major category besides vanilla and chocolate. While there are many different coffee flavoring agents, I prefer freeze-dried instant coffee. I don't use brewed coffee regardless of the strength for two reasons: water used to brew coffee dilutes the ice cream mix and can cause ice to develop; and usually the strength of the coffee ends up weak even if you use a French roast or Italian espresso.

When using a freeze-dried coffee, only use a little amount of very hot water to create a smooth paste with no dry specks remaining. I also use cocoa to cut down on the bitterness of the coffee and to bring out a more pronounced clean coffee taste.

SLEEPLESS IN SEATTLE ICE CREAM

A great full-bodied coffee flavored ice cream. Not too strong in flavor. Simply smooth as silk. A great ice cream flavor from Liks Ice Cream*, Denver, Colorado.

Ingredients:

2 1/2 gallons	16% ice cream mix
10 ounces	Instant coffee
1 1/3 cups	Espresso coffee
40 ounces	Espresso supreme candies
1/2 ounce	Caramel color (darkens the flavor)

Preparation:

Create a paste with the instant coffee using very little hot water (1 or 2 ounces).

Pour the ice cream mix, coffee paste, espresso ground coffee and caramel color into batch freezer. Turn on the dasher for one minute.

Next, turn on the refrigeration and begin batch. At middle of batch, pour in 1/2 of the espresso candies. At the end of batch, pour in remaining espresso candies.

Turn off the refrigeration and extrude out the finished product.

Decorate the top of the tubs with Espresso candies.

Batch time: 8-10 minutes

COFFEE CHIP ICE CREAM

This ice cream recipe comes from the Sylvan Beach Café*, a non-profit mental health agency in Baltimore, Maryland that opened a wonderful dessert and espresso shop for young people learning to work in a retail environment. Rich coffee flavor with chocolate chunks makes this flavor a must for any store.

Ingredients:

2 1/2 gallons	14 or 16% ice cream mix
2 ounces	Vanilla extract (two fold)
6 ounces	Limperts Bavarian Base
24 ounces	Crema Caffe- coffee paste- (Intercontinental Imports)
1 1/2 quarts	Large dark soft chunks

Preparation:

Mix together for 2 minutes the Bavarian base, ice cream mix, vanilla extract, and coffee paste in the batch freezer. Set timer to 8 minutes, turn on refrigeration and begin batch. When the batch is complete, turn off refrigeration, pour in the chocolate chunks and extrude out the finished product. Decorate the top of the tubs with chocolate chunks.

Batch Time: 8-10 minutes

KAHLUA CHIP ICE CREAM

When Tom Arnold of Arnie's Place* in Concord, New Hampshire told me about this flavor, I smiled. There is something about the name Kahlua that intrigues people, especially those who love coffee.

Ingredients:

2 1/2 gallons	14 or 16% ice cream mix
8 ounces	Kahlua extract (Foss)
1 1/2 ounces	Instant coffee
1 teaspoon	Hot water
2 ounces	Two-fold vanilla extract
2 pounds	Callebaut chocolate chips

Preparation:

Prepare a coffee paste with a couple drops of very hot water. Next, pour in all the ingredients including 1 pound of the chips into the batch freezer. Turn on both dasher and refrigeration and begin batch. When batch is complete, pour in the remaining chocolate chips, turn off refrigeration and extrude out the finished product. Decorate top of tubs with chocolate chips.

Batch time: 8-10 minutes

CHOCOLATE ICE CREAM FLAVORS

There are many different forms of cocoa and chocolate that are used in the production of ice cream. Depending on its use, cocoa, especially, has many different functions. Not only does it add flavor to your ice cream mix, it adds body, especially a cocoa that is classified 22-24% fat. Almost all chocolate ice cream is produced using Dutch-process cocoa. It is a modified form of cocoa.

BLENDING COCOA WITH ICE CREAM MIX

To properly blend cocoa with ice cream mix, it's best to use hot water in equal weights to create a paste and to keep the solids of ice cream mixed stable. In other words, if your recipe calls for one pound of cocoa and eight ounces of sugar, you should use hot water at a weight of 24 ounces by weight, not fluid ounces. Using a large 10 quart mixer, hand mixer or spatula, add the water a little at a time until a chocolate paste appears with no dry cocoa specks showing.

Next, pour in one half of the required ice cream mix to the batch freezer, add the chocolate paste, turn on the dasher and let the mixture blend for 3-5 minutes. At this point add rest of the ingredients, turn on refrigeration and begin the batch.

BITTERSWEET CHOCOLATE

Besides Vanilla, the only other flavor that both your critics and customers will taste for quality is your basic Chocolate ice cream. Because I prefer a more bitter taste in my Chocolate ice cream, I use this recipe as the standard for all my chocolate recipes. It is very dark, heavy in weight, and not too sweet.

Ingredients:

2 pounds	Cocoa (22-24% fat)
3/4 pound	Sugar
2 3/4 pounds	hot water
2 1/2 gallons	14 or 16% ice cream mix
4 ounces	Two-fold vanilla extract

Preparation:

Thoroughly mix cocoa and sugar with 6-8 cups of extremely hot water, adding more water as needed, until a smooth creamy paste has been created.

Pour 1 gallon of mix into batch freezer and turn on dasher. Add cocoa paste and continue to let dasher run until smoothly blended. Pour in remaining ingredients, turn on refrigeration, and begin batch. When batch is complete, turn off refrigeration and extrude finished product.

Batch time: 8-10 minutes

BELGIAN CHOCOLATE CHUNK ICE CREAM

Only very recently have I become a fan of using imported Dutch process cocoa for producing any chocolate ice cream. To my amazement, I found this recipe in the New York Ice flavor recipe book from 1983.

Ingredients:

2 1/2 gallons	14 or 16% ice cream mix
2 pounds	Valrohona cocoa
1/2 pound	Sugar
2 1/2 pounds	Hot water
2 pounds	Belgian bittersweet chocolate (chopped or shaved)
4 ounces	Two-fold vanilla extract

Preparation:

Mix together the cocoa and sugar. Blend together with very hot water to create a smooth paste with no dry cocoa visible.

Chop or shave the Belgian chocolate into little pieces. Pour ice cream mix, vanilla extract, and cocoa paste into the batch freezer. Turn on dasher. Set timer to 8 minutes, turn on refrigeration and begin batch.

When batch is complete, turn off refrigeration, pour in the chopped pieces of Belgian chocolate and extrude finished product.

Garnish top of tubs with Belgian chocolate pieces.

Batch Time: 8-10 minutes

VARIATION

WHITE CHOCOLATE RASPBERRY TRUFFLE ICE CREAM: *This recipe comes from Chris Farell, one of our Ice Cream University instructors and owner of The Inside Scoop* of Trumbull, CT. The only difference is that I changed it to a White Chocolate ice cream rather than a dark chocolate. Either way, the raspberry paste from Fabbri makes this one great flavor to have on your ice cream flavor board. Add 1 1/2 pounds of Fabbri flavor paste to the batch.*

GHIRARADELLI CHOCOLATE ICE CREAM

Another wonderful flavor from Classic Creamery*, Aliseo, California. A very rich and very semi-sweet chocolate ice cream.

Ingredients:

2 1/2 gallons	10% ice cream mix
1 ounce	Two-fold vanilla extract
8 ounces	Bavarian Base #21- Limpert Brothers
64 ounces	Ghiraradelli Double Dutch Chocolate Syrup
16 ounces	Milk (regular)

Preparation:
Pour all the ingredients into the batch freezer. Turn on the dasher and mix them for about two minutes. Turn on the refrigeration and begin batch. When the batch is complete, turn off the refrigeration and extrude out the finished product.

Batch time: 8-10 minutes

WHITE CHOCOLATE ICE CREAM

At our seminar, Tom Arnold, of Arnie's Place*, Concord, New Hampshire mentioned this flavor to me. I laughed and immediately picked up my book-
ICE CREAM AND FROZEN DESSERTS to pages 405-406 and showed the recipe to him.

Ingredients:

2 1/2 gallons	14 or 16% ice cream mix
3 oz.	Single-fold vanilla extract
4 1/2 pounds	Van Leer White Breda Chunks

Preparation:
Using a double boiler, melt down 2 pounds of white chocolate. Cool down this chocolate slightly and set aside.

Pour the ice cream mix, vanilla extract, and melted down white chocolate into batch freezer. Turn on the dasher for one minute. Next, turn on the refrigeration and begin batch. At end of batch, pour in the remaining 2 1/2 pounds of white chocolate chunks and extrude out the finished product.

Decorate the top of the tubs with white chocolate chunks.

Batch time: 8-10 minutes

CHOCOLATE AMARETTO ICE CREAM

This Chocolate Amaretto ice cream flavor with an amaretto paste is outstanding. Add some roasted sliced almonds and you will have a real winner.

Ingredients:

2 1/2 gallons	14 or 16% ice cream mix
2 ounces	Two-fold vanilla extract
37 ounces	Fabbri amaretto paste
1 1/2 pounds	Sliced almonds (roasted)

Preparation:

Mix together the cocoa and sugar. Blend together with very hot water to create a smooth paste with no dry cocoa visible. First pour 1 gallon of ice cream mix and the cocoa paste into the batch freezer and mix for 2 minutes or so. Pour in the balance of the ice cream mix, vanilla extract, Fabbri amaretto paste and 1/2 pound of sliced almonds into batch freezer. Turn on both dasher and refrigeration and begin batch. At the end of the batch, pour in the remaining sliced almonds. Turn off the refrigeration and extrude out the finished product. Decorate top of tubs with sliced almonds.

Batch time: 8-10 minutes

CHOCOLATE PEANUT BUTTER FROZEN YOGURT

From Tom Arnold of Arnie's Place* of Concord, New Hampshire comes this wonderful frozen yogurt recipe. Very chocolate with a distinct peanut butter flavor. Tom simply has a difficult time keeping the flavor in stock.

Ingredients:

2 1/2 gallons	Low-fat vanilla frozen yogurt mix
3 ounces	Single-fold vanilla extract
1 1/4 pounds	Van Leer 22-24% cocoa
1 1/4 pounds	Sugar
40 ounces	Superior Nut Company (800-966-7688)- liquid peanut butter

Preparation:

Create a paste with the cocoa, sugar and 2 1/2 pounds of hot water. Pour the frozen yogurt mix, vanilla extract, cocoa paste into batch freezer. Turn on the dasher for two minutes. Next pour in 16 ounces of peanut butter and then turn on the refrigeration and begin batch. At end of batch, extrude out the finished product while swirling into the tubs the remaining 24 ounces of peanut butter.

Batch time: 8-10 minutes

GINGER CHOCOLATE ICE CREAM

Ginger and chocolate make one of the world's great food combinations- another of those marriages made in heaven.

Ingredients:

2 pounds	Cocoa (22-24%)
2 1/2 pounds	Hot water
1/2 pound	Sugar
2 1/2 gallons	14 or 16% ice cream mix
4 ounces	Two-fold vanilla extract
1 1/2 pounds	Sweet (crystallized) ginger pieces

Preparation:

Thoroughly mix cocoa, sugar with hot water, adding more hot water as needed until a smooth creamy paste has been created. Pour 2 gallons of mix into batch freezer and turn on dasher. Add cocoa paste and continue to let dasher run until smoothly blended. Pour in remaining ingredients. Turn on refrigeration, begin batch. When batch is complete, turn off refrigeration and extrude finished product. Decorate top of the tubs with sweet ginger pieces

Batch Time: 8-10 minutes

CHOCOLATE ORANGE ICE CREAM

Blending chocolate and orange together in ice cream is absolutely delicious.

Ingredients:

2 pounds	Cocoa (22-24%)
2 1/2 pounds	Hot water
1/2 pound	Sugar
2 1/2 gallons	14 or 16% ice cream mix
4 ounces	Two-fold vanilla extract- (Madagascar Bourbon)
2 quarts	Orange juice
8 ounces	Triple Sec
Zest of 4 oranges	

Preparation:

Thoroughly mix cocoa, sugar with hot water, adding more hot water as needed until a smooth creamy paste has been created. Pour ice cream mix into batch freezer and turn on dasher. Add cocoa paste and continue to let dasher run until smoothly blended. Pour in remaining ingredients. Turn on refrigeration, begin batch. When batch is complete, turn off refrigeration and extrude finished product. Decorate top of the tubs with orange zest.

Batch Time- 8-10 minutes

CHOCOLATE DULCE DE LECHE ICE CREAM

The original version of Dulce de Leche is great; this version is beyond great!

Ingredients:

2 pounds	Cocoa (22-24%)
2 1/2 pounds	Hot water
1/2 pound	Sugar
2 1/2 gallons	14 or 16% ice cream mix
4 ounces	Two-fold vanilla extract- (Madagascar Bourbon)
1 quart	Caramel Base 1PE-Star Kay White
2 quarts	Caramel Krema- 1PE- Star Kay White
1 pound	Pecan pieces
1 pound	Praline pecan pieces
1/2 pound	Chocolate chunks

Preparation:
Thoroughly mix cocoa, sugar with hot water until a smooth creamy paste has been created. Pour ice cream mix and cocoa paste into batch freezer and turn on dasher for two minutes. Pour in caramel base and vanilla extract. Turn on refrigeration, begin batch. When batch is almost complete, add pecan pieces, praline pecan pieces and chocolate chunks. Turn off refrigeration and swirl in the Krema Fudge as the product is being extruded. Decorate top of the tubs with pecan pieces, praline pecan pieces, chocolate chunks and Krema fudge.
Batch Time- 8-10 minutes

WHITE CHOCOLATE CHIP MACADAMIA NUT ICE CREAM

Incredibly upscale. What else can I say!

Ingredients:

2 1/2 gallons	14 or 16% ice cream mix
2 ounces	Two-fold vanilla extract
3 pounds	White chocolate
1 1/4 pounds	White Soft Chunks-Van Leer
1 1/4 pounds	Macadamia nuts

Preparation:
In a double boiler, melt the white chocolate with 1/2 gallon of ice cream mix. After mixture is melted, let it cool for one hour. Pour ice cream mix, white chocolate mixture and vanilla extract into the batch freezer, turn on dasher and refrigeration and begin batch. When batch is half-way done, add the chocolate chunks and macadamia nuts. Turn off refrigeration and extrude finished product. Decorate top of the tubs with chocolate chunks and macadamia nuts.
Batch Time: 8-10 minutes

KID'S ICE CREAM FLAVORS

There is nothing more exciting than seeing a young child get excited about eating a scoop of ice cream. It's called Kid's flavors, pure and simple.

For the most part, no effort is given to promoting kid's flavors in dipping stores outside of giving a flavor a funny name. Hopefully, what you read here will get you interested in experimenting with producing some of the kid's flavors featured below. Also, think about how you can promote the flavor. Simply put, how can I get kids to notice the new flavors? One way is with a mobile hanging down from the ceiling or giving out inexpensive kid's toys.

Research over the years has found that children beginning at age 10 take a very active role in determining what they eat. At this age, they also become more adventuresome in the products and flavors they like. Remember, they like mixed flavors, bright colors, and inclusions they can "relate to." Inclusions that are part of their world include gummy bears, cookie dough, cookie pieces, and chocolate, not fruit bits and pieces.

Most children identify their mother as the primary purchaser in the family, putting the parent in the role of both purchaser and "gatekeeper." Because of this, keep in mind that the marketing must also attract the parent as well. Since the months of January and February are the best time to experiment with new flavors, seriously take a look at the flavors featured below. If you do, you will be well rewarded in July when you see repeat sales being rung up in your cash registers. Below are numerous flavors that I believe can whet your appetite and that of your child customers.

BANANA COOKIE ICE CREAM

A great kid's flavor!

Ingredients:

2 1/2 gallons	14 or 16% ice cream mix
4 ounces	Two-fold vanilla extract
10 pounds	Bananas (8 pounds peeled)
2 1/2 pounds	Oreo cookies

Preparation:
Peel the bananas and puree them in a blender.

Pour ice cream mix, vanilla extract, and banana puree into the batch freezer. Turn on dasher. Set timer to 8 minutes, turn on refrigeration and begin batch. End of the batch, add the Oreo cookies. When batch is complete, turn off refrigeration and extrude finished product.

Garnish top of tubs with Oreo cookies and banana slices.

Batch Time: 8-10 minutes

FIRE & ICE CREAM

We are certainly on a "hot spicy" kick these days. So when I found this recipe, I couldn't resist letting all of you know about it.

Ingredients:

2 1/2 gallons	14 or 16% ice cream mix
4 ounces	Two-fold vanilla extract
2 cups	Milk
4 medium	Cinnamon sticks
16	Cloves
1 1/2 tablespoons	Tabasco Pepper Sauce
16 strips	Orange peel (from fresh orange)
16 strips	Orange peel*- (cut into very small pieces)
2 ounces	Cinnamon (ground)

NOTE: this means an additional 16 strips of orange peel.

Preparation:

In a saucepan over medium heat, heat milk, cinnamon sticks cloves, and orange peel to a boiling point. Continue simmering for an additional 10 minutes. Set mixture aside until it cools down. Strain mixture through a sieve. Pour ice cream mix, vanilla extract, Tabasco sauce and ground cinnamon into the batch freezer. Turn on dasher and refrigeration and begin batch. When batch is complete, pour in cut up pieces of orange peel, turn off refrigeration and extrude finished product. Garnish top of tubs with ground cinnamon and orange peel.

Batch Time: 8-10 minutes

ROCK-N-POP ICE CREAM

It's like getting a flavor burst of Alka Seltzer in your mouth. Red and blue popping candy in a vanilla ice cream base.

Ingredients:

2 1/2 gallons	14 or 16% ice cream mix
3 ounces	Two-fold vanilla extract
2 pounds	Rock-N-Pop candy
2 drops	Blue food color

Preparation:

Pour ice cream mix, vanilla extract and blue food color into batch freezer. Turn on both dasher and refrigeration and begin batch. When batch is almost complete, pour in Rock-N-Pop candy, turn off refrigeration and extrude finished product. Decorate top of tubs with Rock-N-Pop candy.

Batch time: 8-10 minutes

GUMMY BEAR ICE CREAM

Kids love them! They look great and taste terrific. Blended with Vanilla ice cream, the gummy bears slowly soften up in your mouth. It's a can't miss flavor.

Ingredients:
2 1/2 gallons	14 or 16% ice cream mix
3 ounces	Two-fold vanilla extract
2 pounds	Assorted gummy bear candy

Preparation:
Pour ice cream mix and vanilla extract into batch freezer. Turn on both dasher and refrigeration and begin batch. At middle of batch, pour in the gummy bear candy. When the batch is complete, turn off refrigeration and extrude finished product.

Decorate the top of the tubs with gummy bears.

Batch time: 8-10 minutes

ANIMAL CRACKERS ICE CREAM

Using Animal Crackers in the ice cream is "eye" appealing. Kids will love this flavor.

Ingredients:
2 1/2 gallons	14 or 16% ice cream mix
3 ounces	Two-fold vanilla extract
2 pounds	Animal Cracker cookies
10-12 ounces	Chocolate cone dip*

Preparation:
Melt the cone dip. Pour Animal Crackers into a bowl a few at a time. Pour chocolate into bowl barely covering the crackers. Toss both together until crackers are fully coated with chocolate.* Line a full size baking tray with aluminum foil. Place the coated cookies onto the tray and freeze them until you are ready to make the ice cream. Pour ice cream mix, vanilla extract, and 1/2 pound of the coated Animal Cracker cookies into batch freezer. Turn on both dasher and refrigeration and begin batch. At the end of the batch, pour in the remaining cookies. Turn off the refrigeration and extrude finished product.

Decorate top of the tubs with chocolate coated Animal Cracker cookies.

Batch time: 8-10 minutes

*Note: Coating the cookies with chocolate keeps them crisp and whole in the ice cream produced.

GRAPE NUTS® ICE CREAM

If they like the cereal, they'll surely like this ice cream flavor.

Ingredients:

2 1/2 gallons	14 or 16% ice cream mix
3 ounces	Two-fold vanilla extract
2 pounds	Post Grape Nuts® cereal
16 ounces	Butterscotch topping*

Note: Butterscotch topping can also be variegated into the finished product as it is extruded from the batch freezer instead of pouring it into batch at the beginning of the freezing process.

Preparation:

Pour ice cream mix, vanilla extract, butterscotch and 1/2 pound of the Grape Nuts cereal into batch freezer. Turn on both dasher and refrigeration and begin batch. At the end of the batch, pour in the Grape Nuts cereal. Turn off the refrigeration and extrude finished product.

Decorate top of tubs with Grape Nuts cereal.

Batch time: 8-10 minutes

TURTLES

Kids will love this flavor. The Turtles look so real that you almost feel they are going to pop out of the dipping case and jump into your arms.

Ingredients:

2 1/2 gallons	16% ice cream mix
3 ounces	Two-fold vanilla extract
4 ounces	Praline base
2 pounds	Caramel filled turtles -*(200579)
1 1/2 quarts	Caramel variegate

*Van Leer/Gertrude Hawk- 407-876-8673

Preparation:

Pour ice cream mix, vanilla extract and praline base into batch freezer. Turn on both dasher and refrigeration and begin batch. When batch is almost complete, pour in caramel filled Turtles, turn off refrigeration and as the product is being extruded, swirl in the caramel variegate. Decorate top of tubs with turtles and caramel variegate.

Batch time: 8-10 minutes

CONEHEADS

While the bright color of this flavor will grab the attention of any kid, it is the sight of these chocolate covered ice cream cones waiting to be snatched into a child's mouth that will make this flavor a real winner for you.

Ingredients:

2 1/2 gallons	16% ice cream mix
3 ounces	Two-fold vanilla extract
2 drops	Red food color
2 pounds	Mini ice cream cones *(200529)

*Van Leer/Gertrude Hawk- 407-876-8673

Preparation:
Pour ice cream mix, vanilla extract, and red food color into batch freezer. Turn on both dasher and refrigeration and begin batch. At end of batch, pour in the mini ice cream cones. When the batch is complete, turn off refrigeration and extrude finished product.
Decorate the top of the tubs with mini ice cream cones.
Batch time: 8-10 minutes

LITTLE BITY CRITTERS

Imagine Critter faces looking into your kid's eyes with each lick of this ice cream flavor. It's just too much!

Ingredients:

2 1/2 gallons	16% ice cream mix
3 ounces	Two fold vanilla extract
2 pounds	Milk caramel critters *(200512)
1 1/2 quarts	Caramel variegate *

*Van Leer/Gertrude Hawk- 407-876-8673

Preparation:
Pour ice cream mix and vanilla extract into batch freezer. Turn on both dasher and refrigeration and begin batch. At the end of the batch, pour in the milk caramel critters.
When batch is almost complete, pour in caramel filled Critters, turn off refrigeration and as the product is being extruded, swirl in the caramel variegate. Decorate top of tubs with Critters and caramel variegate.
Batch time: 8-10 minutes

FUNKY PRETZEL GOLDMINE

Kids love pretzels so much they will probably end up picking out the chocolate ones with their fingers.

Ingredients:

2 1/2 gallons	14 or 16% ice cream mix
3 ounces	Two-fold vanilla extract
2 pounds	Chocolate covered pretzels *
1 1/2 quarts	Caramel variegate

*Guernsey Bel- 800-621-0271 or Pecan Deluxe- 214-631-3669

Preparation:

Pour ice cream mix and vanilla extract into batch freezer. Turn on both dasher and refrigeration and begin batch. When batch is almost complete, pour in chocolate covered pretzels, turn off refrigeration and as the product is being extruded, swirl in the caramel variegate. Decorate top of tubs with chocolate covered pretzels and caramel variegate.

Batch time: 8-10 minutes

FRENCH FRIES & KETCHUP

It's like having your kid eat a messy meal at McDonald's!

Ingredients:

2 1/2 gallons	14 or 16% ice cream mix
3 ounces	Two-fold vanilla extract
2 pounds	Chocolate covered french fries *
1 1/2 quarts	Red fudge variegate *

*Pecan Deluxe- 214-631-3669

Preparation:

Pour ice cream mix and vanilla extract into batch freezer. Turn on both dasher and refrigeration and begin batch. When batch is almost complete, pour in chocolate covered french fries, turn off refrigeration and as the product is being extruded, swirl in the red fudge variegate. Decorate top of tubs with chocolate covered french fries and red fudge variegate.

Batch time: 8-10 minutes

VEGETABLE ICE CREAM FLAVORS

Ice cream makers have been making vegetable ice creams for years. Now, it's the rage in a lot of fancy restaurants. If you are in the wholesale ice cream business, you should make these flavors available "as special occasion flavors" to your customers.

AVOCADO ICE CREAM

I love avocados, so I figured, how could I go wrong!

Ingredients:

2 1/2 gallons	14 or 16% ice cream mix
4 ounces	Two-fold vanilla extract
40 ripe avocados*	or- 2 1/2 pounds avocado puree
3 ounces	Lime juice

Note: If you use avocados, they must be ripe. Peel avocados, remove meat from the pit and puree the mixture.

Preparation:

Pour ice cream mix, vanilla extract, avocado puree and lime juice into the batch freezer. Turn on dasher and refrigeration and begin batch. When batch is almost complete, turn off refrigeration and extrude finished product.

Batch Time: 8-10 minutes

JALAPENO ICE CREAM

Thanks to the wondering mind of Pete Schaffer of The Grateful Bean Café* in Oklahoma City comes this ice cream flavor. At our ice cream production seminar in 1997, Pete did a lot of research, and came up with the idea of using Triple Sec to smooth out the overall flavor. His idea worked!

Ingredients:

8 ounces	Jalapeno peppers
4 ounces	Triple Sec or any orange liqueur
2 1/2 gallons	14 or 16% ice cream mix
2 ounces	Two-fold vanilla extract

Preparation:

Puree the Jalapeno peppers. Pour all ingredients except the Triple Sec into batch freezer. Turn on dasher and refrigeration and begin batch. Halfway into batch, add Triple Sec. When batch is complete, turn off refrigeration and extrude the finished product from batch freezer. Decorate tops of the tubs with Jalapeno pepper pieces.

Batch time: 8-10 minutes

JAPANESE RED BEAN ICE CREAM

Another winner that came out of one of our Advanced Batch Freezer Production Seminars.

Ingredients:

2 1/2 gallons	14 or 16% ice cream mix
2 1/2 ounces	Two-fold vanilla extract
2 1/2 quarts	Prepared red beans (sweetened)*
15 ounces	Mirin (Japanese sweet rice wine)*
3 ounces	Lemon juice

Preparation:

Puree the red beans. Pour all ingredients into batch freezer. Turn on dasher and refrigeration and begin batch. When batch is complete, extrude finished product. Garnish with red beans.

Note: Sweetened red beans and Mirin can be purchased in any Japanese food shop.

Batch Time: 8-10 minutes

COCONUT-JALAPENO ICE CREAM

From faraway Margaret River, Australia, comes this wonderful coconut ice cream flavor that is spiked with Jalapeno peppers. The combination of the sweetness of the coconut and the spiciness of the pepper make this flavor very special in any upscale restaurant setting.

Ingredients:

2 1/2 gallons	14 or 16% ice cream mix
2 ounces	Two-fold vanilla extract
30-48 ounces	Coconut fruit base
1 pound	Shredded coconut
1 pound	Jalapeno peppers (cut into small pieces)

Preparation:

Pour ice cream mix, vanilla extract, and coconut fruit base into the batch freezer. Turn on dasher. Set timer to 8 minutes, and then turn on refrigeration and begin batch. When batch is almost complete, add shredded coconut and Jalapeno pepper pieces. Turn off refrigeration and extrude finished product.

Decorate top of the tubs with shredded coconut and Jalapeno pepper pieces.

Batch Time: 8-10 minutes

BRIE ICE CREAM
You'll have to try it to believe it!

Ingredients:

2 1/2 gallons	14 or 16% ice cream mix
4 ounces	Two-fold vanilla extract
10 pounds	Brie, rind removed
1 pound	Dried apricots
1/2 pound	Praline walnuts

Preparation:
Using a blender, blend the Brie cheese with 1/2 gallon of ice cream mix.

Pour the balance of ice cream mix, Brie mixture and other ingredients into the batch freezer. Set timer to 8 minutes, turn on refrigeration and begin batch. When batch is complete, turn off refrigeration and extrude out the finished product.

Batch Time: 8-10 minutes

PARMESAN ICE CREAM
This makes a wonderful ice cream to be served in a restaurant as a companion to crisp apples, pears, grapes or other fruits normally served with Parmesan cheese. Also, it's a great ice cream to serve over apple pie.

So if you are in the wholesale ice cream manufacturing business, offer this specialty ice cream flavor to your restaurant clients.

Ingredients:

2 1/2 gallons	14 or 16% ice cream mix
4 ounces	Two-fold vanilla extract
5 pounds	Fresh parmesan cheese, finely grated
3 ounces	Sweet paprika

Preparation:
Heat (low to medium heat) 1/2 gallon of ice cream mix with the parmesan cheese until the cheese dissolves into the ice cream mix.

Add the paprika to this mix.

Pour the balance of ice cream mix, and other ingredients into the batch freezer. Set timer to 8 minutes, turn on refrigeration and begin batch. When batch is complete, turn off refrigeration and extrude out the finished product.

Batch Time: 8-10 minutes

CHAPTER 12
<u>SORBETS</u>

It's here, it's hot, and it's getting bigger and bigger. If you are not producing sorbets, my question to you is "why not?" The most popular flavors are raspberry, lemon, strawberry, chocolate, and mango, followed by passion fruit, banana, strawberry-banana, peach, cantaloupe and watermelon. All it takes is fruit, sugar, water, and a stabilizer.

WHAT KIND OF FRUIT SHOULD YOU USE?

If there is one fallacy I have heard over the years it is the one about the cost of purchasing unpasteurized frozen fruit or purees. Mainly because of the lack of knowing, many operators in the past have purchased fruit purees from importers. While I don't question for a second the quality of these purees, they are quite expensive costing in many cases over $3.00 per pound.

Well let me tell you, there are many alternate suppliers that will give you the same result at a much cheaper per pound cost. They are as follows:

- **Trader Joe's-** Stores are located in California, Boston and New York. The price for their frozen mango cubes is approximately $1.00 per pound.
- **Global Fruit (800-849-9990)-** Based in South Carolina, they have many varieties of fruits from Mexico.
- **ITI (609-987-0550)-** Located in New Jersey, they are a great source for mango, etc.

Other sources of frozen fruit can be procured from either Alliant or Sisco, both very large food service distributors.

The best fruit to use is fresh (but it must be ripe, very ripe), especially in the summer. Why ripe? Because for the full flavor of the fruit to come out, the fruit must be sweet and that is characterized by the liquid juice of that fruit. For overall flavor, frozen fruit is terrific. Frozen fruit is uniform in flavor, especially if you purchase the fruit from the same manufacturer or distributor. Also, an added feature is that the juice of the fruit once you have defrosted the fruit prior to use, is free. So, make sure you use it!

Fresh Fruit

For the ultimate fruit flavor profile in a sorbet, there is no question fresh fruit is the best. But the fruit must be fully ripened to achieve the same taste sensation as if the consumer was eating the fruit by itself. This is only possible in the summer when ripened fruit is naturally more sweet than that purchased in the winter, regardless of where you get it from.

Below are some helpful hints on how to use some of the most popular fresh fruits:

Strawberries: The redder the berry, the sweeter it will be. If you see whiteness around the stem area, you can be fairly certain the fruit is not ripe or sweet. Cut the strawberries in half and follow the above marinating procedure. The blades of the dasher will break up the berries enabling you to retain the fiber so that the finished product has a textured instead of a pureed look.

Peaches: If the peach is hard, it is simply not ripe. Let it sit at room temperature until you see discoloring on the skin and/or you can feel the softness of the fruit by pinching it. Because peach is a very mellow flavor, whether you are making ice cream or sorbet, you will have to use a natural flavor extract to boost up the flavor (1 ounce per gallon).

Bananas: The more yellow they look, the riper they are. Frankly, when they look almost rotten is the best time to use them. Bananas do not even have to be cut, and/or pureed. The dasher blades will do the job.

Melons: You have to feel them by making an impression inwards with your fingers. If the melon seems soft you will notice it immediately. To be on the safe side, always give the melons an extra day to ripen even when you think they are ready. That extra day is worth the wait.

Raspberries: This fruit is seedy, so you have to make sure you strain the juice out with a sieve (strainer). Consumers do not like to eat the seed because it is hard and gets into the tooth cavity. Also, fruit flies attach themselves to the outer skin of the fruit.

Blueberries: When in production, do not over-process whether in sorbet or ice cream. Blueberries tend to absorb both cream and water leaving the finished product very grainy if the product is kept freezing too long in the batch freezer more than the allowable time. Because blueberries lack a definable flavor, you should consider using a natural flavor extract to boost up the flavor, usually 1-ounce per gallon of mix.

Watermelon: Don't be surprised by how little water is needed to make a sorbet with this fruit. Experiment with the amount needed depending on the ripeness and taste of the melons used.

Frozen Fruit

Frozen fruit is ideal for either sorbet or water ice production. For the most part you can expect frozen fruit to taste the same all year long because it is packed and frozen during the growing season and stored all year long. This is a big advantage over fresh, which depending on the time of the year, tastes differently. Most frozen fruit produced for commercial use has at least 10 per cent sugar added so it's naturally sweet to start out with. Always retain the juice from the fruit and use it as part of the mix. The juice has lots of flavor, and since it replaces some of the water needed to produce the flavor, I consider it to be "found money."

The only difference in preparation between fresh and frozen is that you must fully defrost frozen fruit before starting the marinating process. You do not have to wash the defrosted fruit with cold water. Once defrosted, follow the same sugar/stabilizer procedures used for fresh fruit.

Processed Fruit
Processed fruit is defined as fruit that has been pasteurized (cooked). The main reason to pasteurize is to remove all forms of bacteria that might be carried from the growing fields through to the end user. Pasteurized fruit is used by all major dairy manufacturers because of health concerns caused by bacteria in the fruit. Pasteurized fruit does not have the same fresh fruit taste characteristics that are pronounced in either fresh or frozen fruit.

Fruit Extracts
This is used mainly in water ice production because of cost concerns. In some instances, fruit extracts are used in sorbet production as an added flavor booster to improve the fruit flavor, especially when the fresh fruit being used is not fully ripened.

HOW TO USE THE FRUIT
The beauty of producing sorbets in the batch freezer is that for many fruits you don't have to puree all the fruit all the time. The batch freezer will do it for you. A good example is strawberry, especially when you use frozen whole strawberries. Simply pour the defrosted strawberry mixture (including sugar, stabilizer and water) into the hopper, turn on the dasher for 30 seconds, then the refrigeration and you are off and running. Bar none, this flavor when matched against one produced on a continuous freezer is far superior. The reason is that your sorbet will maintain the fiber texture of the berry while the one produced on the continuous freezer without exception is produced using a puree having no fiber texture at all. Other flavors like banana, pear, and pineapple will work just as well.

If you are using fresh fruit, wash the fruit thoroughly with cold water. Next, cut, peel, and/or hull the fruit. If you are using frozen fruit, defrost the fruit thoroughly leaving the juice in the container. Do not throw it away. At this point, mix together the dry sugar and stabilizer needed for the recipe. The reason for

186

combining the dry sugar and stabilizer is because otherwise there is a possibility the stabilizer might not immerse itself thoroughly with the fruit. Once they are mixed together, add the mixture to the fruit using a spatula to fully blend everything together. The fruit is now ready to begin the marinating process, which will take approximately 8 hours or preferably overnight. After the marinating process is complete, drain off all the juice and set apart. Take 25% of all the drained fruit and cut into small pieces. The remaining 75% should be poured back into the juice. Puree the juice portion and then pour this mixture into the batch freezer and begin the freezing process.

Using Sugar, and/or Corn Syrup Solids- 36 DE Corn

I never thought I would be a proponent of corn syrup solids for use in sorbets, but I am now, thanks to my associate, Bill Lambert, who has been pitching me this idea for a long time now. Corn syrup solids no longer have that taste of grain or corn. Thanks to an incredible improvement in food technology, either 36 DE or 42 DE corn syrup solids, have a clean sweet flavor that does not obstruct the true taste of fruit used in the production of sorbets, and in some cases actually helps bring out the flavor. DE stands for dextrose equivalent and indicates the percent of sweetness relative to dextrose, so they are about 36% or 42% as sweet as the sugar they replace.

Why is it Used?

To make the sorbet smoother and more scoopable. It will add body to the product by replacing some of the sugar on a 2 to 1 ratio, thereby increasing the total solids in the finished product.

How is it Used?

The big secret to using corn syrup is how much to use; too little is never a problem, but too much is. We recommend any brand of 36DE dry corn syrup. Replace one part of sugar with two parts of 36DE to a maximum ratio of no more than 50%-50% sugar to corn. In a recipe that calls for 6 pounds of sugar, replace 2 pounds of sugar with 4 pounds of 36DE. The resulting mixture is now 4 pounds of sugar and 4 pounds of 36DE, a 50%-50% ratio.

Simply sift in the dry corn with the sugar and follow the recipe of dissolving the sugar in hot water. It's as simple as that. To get the right ratio, start out slowly and build up the corn to what you think is a necessary level. That means starting out with a ratio of 75% sugar to 25% corn. The reason for this is that you can always add, but you can't subtract once you start a recipe.

Where to Purchase 36 DE Corn Syrup Solids

Both 36DE or 42 DE corn syrup solids can be purchased from most foodservice distributors like Dot Foods (800-366-6482, ext. 2740) or direct from the following manufacturers: Roquette America (800-553-7030) or Grain Processing Corporation (319-264-4265).

SO WHAT IS A STABILIZER?
Everyone thinks they know what a stabilizer is, but very few people know how to use one. It's the ingredient that is going to make your sorbet scoopable. All the recipes in this chapter use the stabilizer CC-917 from Continental Colloids. Call Continental Colloids at 631-231-8650 and ask for a sample of CC917, a cold water stabilizer that is simple to use. It's used at the rate of .50-1.00% by weight.

CC-917 Stabilizer-Ingredients
Sucrose, Guar Gum, Locust Bean Gum, Citric Acid, Sodium Bicarbonate.

How is the stabilizer used?
Usage level is approximately 1/2 of 1% (2 1/2-3 1/2 ounces per 3 gallon liquid sorbet batch) 917 stabilizer used based on the kind of fruit used. You simply mix the stabilizer with dry sugar and add to liquid portion with good agitation. You should allow a few minutes for the stabilizer to hydrate before freezing.

MAKING THE BATCH OF SORBET
The following tricks of the trade will help you prepare a terrific sorbet that in most cases will be far superior to that of your competition:
- When pureeing the fruit in the batch freezer, let the dasher run for at least five minutes.
- A batch of sorbet mix can be anywhere from 2 1/2 gallons to 3 1/2 gallons of mix per batch since the overrun of the sorbet product will not exceed 20%.
- Towards the end of the batch, pour the cut-up fruit pieces into the batch freezer and run for additional one minute. Turn off the refrigeration and extrude the finished product.
- Always extrude the finished sorbet product out of the batch freezer in a loose gravy state, not firm like ice cream. Otherwise you run the danger of producing an over processed un-scoopable product.
- The normal batch time for producing a batch of sorbet is 11-15 minutes, depending on amount of sugar used and liquid mix in the barrel. Where the amount of recommended batch time is longer then 13 minutes, the reason is usually that more sugar is being used in the recipe. The higher amount of sugar, the longer the batch time.

188

- When using fresh fruits, in most cases you will have to puree the fruit. Follow the chart below for the amount of fruit needed to yield 1 quart of pureed fruit.
- Always use <u>filtered water</u>. Regular tap water has cloride in it that will greatly effect the taste of the sorbet.

FRUIT WEIGHTS

FRUIT	WEIGHT OZ.	AMT. PD	LOSS %	AMT PD.
Peach	5	3	12	3 1/2
Banana	5 1/2	3	15	3 1/2
Apples	8	2	10	2 1/4
Orange	4	10 juice		
Grapefruit	2	10 juice		
Papaya	16	1	15	1 1/4
Pineapple	1	3 1/2	20	4 1/2
Cantaloupe	1	3	20	3 1/2
Kiwi	4	10 juice	10	5
Tangerine	4	10 juice		
Lime	5	10 juice		
Pear	5	3	15	4

Note

Weight: The weight of 1 piece of fruit
Amount/Pound: How many pieces to weigh 1 pound
Loss: The loss of weight after peeling/squeezing fruit
Amount Per Pound: Amount needed per pound after loss

SORBET IN LEMON SHELLS

A very popular dessert that is featured in many Italian restaurants. For the most part, this dessert is now imported directly from Italy, Spain or Greece. The following is a way you can make this yourself by hand.

Preparation:
Shave a thin slice off the bottom (pointed end of a lemon), so that the lemon will sit upright on a flat surface. Slice the top third from the lemon and discard. Holding the lemon over a strainer, scoop out the pulp with a grapefruit knife or spoon.

Cover the shells and place them in a freezer. Freeze for approximately one hour. Remove lemon shell from freezer, and scoop one large 4-5 ounce lemon sorbet portion into the lemon shell mounding it 1 to 2 inches over the top of the shells.

Cover and return the shells to the freezer.

Before serving the shells, place them in a refrigerator approximately 30 minutes before serving.

APPLE BRANDY SORBET

This is a perfect flavor for the fall season when apples are at their peak. This zesty flavor with a touch of apple brandy is just great!

Ingredients

10 1/2 pounds	Matsu or other eating apples- (4 quarts puree)
4 quarts	Unsweetened apple juice
1 1/2 ounces	Cinnamon
2 quarts	Hot water
7 3/4 pounds	Sugar
8 ounces	Apple brandy
5 ounces	Stabilizer- CC-917

Preparation:

Peel, core, and seed apples. Under good agitation (using a spatula), slowly sift the stabilizer into the apples. Allow the stabilizer to hydrate at least 30 minutes. Next, thoroughly mix sugar with 2 quarts of extremely hot water. Puree 75% of the apples with unsweetened apple juice. Add cinnamon to this mixture. Set aside the remaining 25% of the apples and cut into very small pieces. Pour apple puree and sugar-water solution into batch freezer. Turn on both dasher and refrigeration, and begin batch. Halfway into batch, as mixture begins to freeze, add apple brandy and the remaining 25% small apple pieces. As mixture starts to firm up and look fluffy (gravy), turn off refrigeration and extrude finished product.

Decorate tops of tubs with slices of apple and cinnamon.

Batch time: 13-15 minutes

APPLE CRANBERRY SORBET

This too is a perfect flavor for the fall season when apples are at their peak. This zesty flavor with a touch of apple brandy can also be merchandised as a winter holiday treat.

Ingredients

Marinate the Cranberries

4 1/2 pounds	Fresh or frozen cranberries
1 quart	Water
3 1/2 pounds	Sugar

Marinate the Apples

10 1/2 pounds	Matsu or other eating apples- (4 quarts puree)
1 1/2 ounces	Cinnamon
2 quarts	Hot water
7 3/4 pounds	Sugar
4 ounces	Stabilizer- CC-917

Preparation:

Marinate the cranberries, water, and sugar for three hours. Puree this mixture and strain thoroughly to yield approximately 3 quarts cranberry juice. Add this mixture to the batch recipe.

Peel, core, and seed apples. Under good agitation (using a spatula), slowly sift the stabilizer into the apples. Allow the stabilizer to hydrate at least 30 minutes or more. Next, thoroughly mix sugar with 2 quarts of extremely hot water. Puree 75% of the apples with unsweetened apple juice. Add cinnamon to this mixture. Set aside the remaining 25% of the apples and cut into very small pieces.

Pour apple puree and sugar-water solution into batch freezer. Turn on both dasher and refrigeration, and begin batch. Halfway into batch, as mixture begins to freeze, add apple brandy and the remaining 25% small apple pieces. As mixture starts to firm up and look fluffy (gravy), turn off refrigeration and extrude finished product.

Decorate tops of tubs with slices of apple, cinnamon and cranberries.

Batch time: 13-15 minutes

GREEN APPLE CANDIED GINGER SORBET

A wonderful fall promotion for your retail or wholesale customers. This Green Apple Sorbet is truly refreshing. A touch of ginger gives it that sweet kick to make this a flavor to remember. This recipe came to me (my adaptation) from an article about The Golden Door Restaurant of Escondido, California.

Ingredients:

4 quarts	Green apple puree
4 quarts	Unsweetened apple juice
4 ounces	Lime juice (fresh or frozen)
2 quarts	Water
7 1/2 pounds	Sugar
1 pound	Candied ginger pieces*
4 ounces	Stabilizer- CC-917

Sliced apples and candied ginger for garnish

*Note: Contact Royal Pacific Foods- 1-800-551-5284 for their dark sweet cuts of ginger. They also have ginger pulp and juice.

Preparation:

Peel, core, and seed apples. Puree apples with unsweetened apple juice. Thoroughly mix sugar and stabilizer with 2 quarts of extremely hot water. Under good agitation (using a spatula), slowly agitate the mixture for 1 minute. Allow mixture to stand for 30 minutes before adding it to the apple puree.

Pour apple puree, lime juice, candied ginger and sugar/stabilizer mixture into the batch freezer. Turn on both the dasher and refrigeration and begin the batch. When product begins to firm up again, turn off the refrigeration and begin extruding the finished product.

Decorate tops of tubs with apple slices and candied ginger pieces.

Batch time: 13-15 minutes

APRICOT SORBET

This recipe is a creation of my sorbet mentors, Shippen Lebzelter and Guido Magnaguagno, the owners of New York Ice. While no longer with us, when it came to creating ices and sorbets, these two guys had more talent than anyone I have ever met.

Ingredients:
To Prepare Apricot Puree
10 pounds	Dried apricots
2 quarts	Water

Other Ingredients Needed
6 quarts	Water
4 1/2 pounds	Sugar
3 1/2 ounces	Stabilizer- CC-917

Place sliced apricot slices on top of the container

Preparation:
Bring to a boil and then simmer for 30 minutes the dried apricots and 2 quarts water. Remove, cool and puree this mixture.

Mix the sugar and stabilizer together and combine this mixture with hot water and let it hydrate for 30 minutes.

Combine all ingredients, pour into batch freezer, and begin the batch. As mixture starts to firm up (gravy) and look slightly fluffy, turn off refrigeration and extrude finished product.
Batch time: 13-15 minutes

VARIATIONS
APRICOT COGNAC SORBET: The use of cognac adds a spike to this apricot sorbet. Add 12 ounces of cognac at the end of the above batch before extrusion.

APRICOT BANANA SORBET: Apricots and bananas, a very subtle sorbet. Peel and puree 6 pounds of bananas, and add them to the batch.

BANANA BLUEBERRY SORBET

A great summer sorbet! The taste of ripe fresh bananas with luscious summer blueberries are a great combination. Try it!

Ingredients:

18 pounds	Banana puree (from 22 pounds bananas)
6 quarts	Water
3 pounds	Sugar
4 quarts	Blueberries (fresh or frozen)
2 pounds	Sugar
4 tablespoons	Lemon juice
4 ounces	Stabilizer- CC-917

Banana slices and blueberries for garnish

Preparation:

Mix the blueberries and sugar together and marinate for 8 hours. Puree the bananas. Thoroughly mix sugar and stabilizer with 2 quarts of hot water. Under good agitation, slowly agitate the mixture for 1 minute. Allow mixture to stand for 30 minutes. Pour banana puree, lemon juice and sugar/stabilizer mixture into the batch freezer.

Turn on the dasher and refrigeration and begin the batch. When product begins to firm up again, add the blueberries.

Turn off the refrigeration and begin extruding the finished product.

Decorate the top of the tubs with banana slices, blueberries and raspberries

Batch time: 13-15 minutes

VARIATION

TROPICAL SUMMER DELIGHT SORBET: Add 2 quarts of raspberry puree and 2 more quarts of water to this batch before freezing.

BANANA COCONUT FUDGE SORBET

Bananas, coconut, and fudge, how can you go wrong!

Ingredients

16 1/2 pounds	Bananas
7 quarts	Water
3 pounds	Sugar
24 ounces	Coconut fruit base
19 ounces	Coco Lopez coconut base
2 1/2 ounces	Shredded coconut
2 quarts	Fudge variegate
5 ounces	Stabilizer- CC-917

Preparation:

Puree the bananas. Next, mix together the bananas with the coconut fruit base and Coco Lopez. Thoroughly mix the sugar and stabilizer together with 3 1/2 quarts of extremely hot water and allow the sugar/stabilizer mixture to hydrate for 30 minutes. Add to this mixture 3 1/2 quarts of cold water and the rest of the ingredients except the fudge and shredded coconut. Pour the mixture into the batch freezer, turn on both the dasher and refrigeration and begin batch. When the batch is almost complete, add the shredded coconut. Turn off the refrigeration. As the product is being extruded, using a pastry bag filled with the fudge variegate, squeeze the fudge into the semi-frozen mixture. Decorate tops of tubs with slices of bananas, shredded coconut, and fudge.

Batch time: 13-15 minutes

CLARET SORBET

This sorbet gives off the full flavor of the Bordeaux wine. Raspberries have an affinity for the red wine and also give the sorbet some body texture.

Ingredients:

6 - 26 oz. bottles	Red Bordeaux wine
2 1/2 quarts	Water
3 1/2 pounds	Sugar
3 pounds	Fresh or frozen red raspberries
3 ounces	Stabilizer- CC-917

Preparation:

Pour all ingredients into the batch freezer. Turn on both the dasher and refrigeration and begin the batch. When the batch is complete, turn off the refrigeration and begin extruding out the finished product. Decorate tops of tubs with raspberries.

Batch time: 13-15 minutes

CRANBERRY SORBET

This fall seasonal flavor sells very well around Thanksgiving and Christmas.

Ingredients

3 3/4 quarts	Water
14 1/4 pounds	Sugar
18 3/4 pounds	Fresh or frozen cranberries
	(above mixture yields 11 1/4 quarts juice)
10 ounces	Triple Sec liqueur
5 ounces	Stabilizer- CC-917

Preparation:

Mix together the water, sugar, and cranberries. Puree mixture and strain thoroughly to yield 11 1/4 quarts of cranberry juice. Under good agitation, slowly sift the stabilizer into the cranberry juice. Allow the stabilizer to hydrate at least 30 minutes. Pour cranberry juice and 3 3/4 more quarts of water into batch freezer. Turn on both dasher and refrigeration and begin batch. Halfway into batch, as sorbet begins to freeze, add Triple Sec. As mixture starts to firm up and look fluffy (gravy), turn off refrigeration and extrude finished product.

Batch time: 13-15 minutes

ESPRESSO SORBET

This sophisticated flavor is served in many Italian-style cafés and restaurants.

Ingredients:

3 gallons	Water
12 ounces	Espresso flavor-(Weber 21-85-1346 liquid coffee)
3/4 ounces	Cocoa (22-24% fat)
2 ounces	Hot water
4 1/2 pounds	Sugar
12 ounces	Kahlua liqueur
3 1/2 ounces	Stabilizer- CC-917

Preparation:

Mix the liquid espresso flavor and cocoa (create paste with 2 ounces extremely hot water). Thoroughly mix sugar with 1 gallon of extremely hot water, then add 2 gallons of cold water to this mixture. Under good agitation, slowly sift the stabilizer into the espresso mixture. Allow the stabilizer to hydrate at least 30 minutes. Pour coffee paste mixture into batch freezer. Turn on both dasher and refrigeration and begin batch. Halfway into batch, as sorbet begins to freeze, pour in Kahlua. As mixture starts to firm up and look gravy, turn off refrigeration and extrude finished product.

Batch time: 13-15 minutes

GRAPEFRUIT SORBET

If you use fresh grapefruit juice, you will have a real winner here.

Ingredients:

48	Grapefruits- (yields 8 quarts juice)*
4 quarts	Water
7 1/2 pounds	Sugar
4 ounces	Stabilizer- CC-917

Grapefruit slices for garnish

*Note: Do not discard pulp. It adds body and texture to the finished product.

Preparation:

Squeeze enough ripe grapefruits to obtain 8 quarts of juice. Strain juice and remove seeds. Save half of pulp and discard rest. (The pulp adds body and texture to the finished product.)

Thoroughly mix sugar with 2 1/2 quarts of hot water. Under good agitation (using a spatula), slowly sift the stabilizer into 1 1/2 quarts of cold water. Allow the stabilizer to hydrate at least 10 minutes or more.

Pour juice and pulp mixture into batch freezer. Turn on dasher and refrigeration and begin batch. As mixture starts to firm up and look fluffy (gravy), turn off refrigeration and extrude finished product.

Decorate top of tubs with fresh grapefruit slices.

Batch time: 11-13 minutes

VARIATIONS

GRAPEFRUIT CAMPARI SORBET: I love this flavor so much, it has been in every one of my books. I am quite sure your customers will love it as well. Add 26 ounces of Campari to the batch just prior to extruding the finished product.

MINTED GRAPEFRUIT SORBET: This easy-to-prepare, delicately flavored dessert is the perfect finale for a light lunch. A wonderful flavor to develop for wholesale restaurant accounts. Add 16 ounces of white crème de menthe to the batch just prior to extruding the finished product.

KIWI SORBET

Sometimes called "Chinese Gooseberry" because the fruit originated in eastern Asia. The fruit, which is the size of a large egg, has a thin skin, and is brown and hairy on the outside. Inside it is firm and sweet, with a slight acidity flavor. It is a very easy fruit to use in sorbet production. Simply peel off the skin and puree the fruit. To stop discoloring and bring out a better taste in the fruit, add lemon juice (1/2 lemon to every 15 kiwis used).

Ingredients:

38	Kiwi fruit- (yields 9 quarts juice)
3 quarts	Water
5 pounds	Sugar
5 ounces	Lemon or lime juice
3 1/2 ounces	Stabilizer- CC-917
Kiwi fruit slices for garnish	

Preparation:

Peel and puree the kiwi fruit. Thoroughly mix sugar and stabilizer with 1 quart of hot water using good agitation to allow mixture to hydrate. Next, add 2 quarts of cold water and either lemon or lime juice to this mixture.

Combine kiwi puree and sugar/stabilizer mixture, and pour into batch freezer. Turn on dasher and refrigeration and begin batch. As mixture starts to firm up (gravy) and look slightly fluffy, turn off refrigeration and extrude finished product.

Decorate tops of tubs with fresh kiwi and strawberry slices.

Batch time: 13-15 minutes

VARIATIONS

KIWI STRAWBERRY SORBET: The sweetness of the strawberries is a terrific contrast to the tartness of the kiwis. A winner! Add 4 quarts of strawberry puree to the batch before freezing.

KIWI LEMON SORBET: Add 16 ounces fresh lemon juice, 1 quart of water, and 1 pound of sugar to the above batch.

MANGO SORBET

Mango is my favorite sorbet. I like it more and more each year, and when you make it with either fresh or frozen mangos, you can't go wrong. I guarantee it.

Ingredients:

24	Mangos- (yield 9 quarts of puree)
4 1/2 quarts	Water
5 1/4 pounds	Sugar
4 ounces	Stabilizer- CC-917

Fresh mango slices for garnish

Preparation:

Peel, seed, and puree enough fully ripened mangos to yield 9 quarts of mango puree. Mix sugar thoroughly with 2 quarts of hot water, then add 2 1/2 quarts of cold water to this mixture. Under good agitation (using a spatula), slowly sift the stabilizer into the mango puree. Allow the stabilizer to hydrate at least 30 minutes or more.

Pour mango mixture and sugar-water solution into batch freezer, turn on both dasher and refrigeration, and begin batch. As mixture starts to firm up (gravy) and look slightly fluffy, turn off refrigeration and extrude finished product.

Decorate tops of tubs with fresh mango slices.

Batch time: 13-15 minutes

VARIATIONS

MANGO COCONUT SORBET: Two of my favorite flavors, so why not combine them? Add 16 ounces of Fabbri coconut paste or 1 quart of any commercial coconut fruit base to the mango liquid batch before freezing and 1/2 pound of shredded coconut poured into the batch at the end before extrusion.

NIEVE DE MANGO LIMON SORBET: For a truly refreshing Mexican sorbet, this mango lime flavor is one outstanding dessert. Add 16 ounces lime juice (fresh or frozen) to the batch before freezing.

200

PASSION FRUIT SORBET

This is an exotic fruit sorbet that adds excitement to any dinner table, especially in restaurants.

Ingredients:

20 pounds	Passion fruit
	(strained to yield 6 3/4 quarts of juice and pulp)
6 quarts	Water
3 1/2 pounds	Sugar
4 ounces	Fresh lemon juice and peel
3 1/2 ounces	Stabilizer- CC-917

Passion fruit pulp for garnish

Preparation:

Cut passion fruit in half and scoop the pulp out into a strainer over a bowl. Press pulp through strainer to extract as much juice as possible. Discard seeds, but retain some pulp for body and texture. Thoroughly mix sugar with 4 quarts of extremely hot water, then add 2 quarts of cold water and the lemon juice to this mixture. Under good agitation (using a spatula), slowly sift the stabilizer into the passion fruit puree. Allow the stabilizer to hydrate at least 30 minutes or more.

Pour juice, pulp, and sugar-water solution into batch freezer. Turn on both dasher and refrigeration and begin batch. As mixture starts to firm up and look gravy, turn off refrigeration and extrude finished product.

Decorate tops of tubs with passion fruit pulp.

Batch time: 13-15 minutes

VARIATION

PASSION MANGO SORBET: It's all about passion and your willingness to be creative! Reduce the passion fruit puree to 4 1/2 quarts of juice and pulp and add 3 quarts of mango puree to the batch before freezing.

ORANGE SORBET

Orange has always been a popular ice, and since oranges have a natural sweetness to them, producing Orange sorbet is not difficult. Use only fresh-squeezed orange juice and don't use too much sugar, as over sweetening will hide the natural flavor of the orange.

Ingredients:

96	Oranges- (yields 8 quarts juice)
4 quarts	Water
7 1/2 pounds	Sugar
4 ounces	Stabilizer- CC-917
Orange slices for garnish	

Preparation:
Using an orange juicer, squeeze enough ripe oranges to obtain 8 quarts of juice. Strain juice and remove seeds. Save half of pulp and discard rest. (The pulp adds body and texture to the finished product.) Thoroughly mix sugar with 2 1/2 quarts of hot water. Under good agitation, slowly sift the stabilizer into 1 1/2 quarts of cold water. Allow the stabilizer to hydrate at least 10 minutes. Pour juice and pulp mixture into batch freezer. Turn on dasher and refrigeration and begin batch. As mixture starts to firm up, turn off refrigeration and extrude finished product.
    Decorate tops of tubs with fresh orange slices.
Batch time: 13-15 minutes

VARIATIONS
TEQUILA SUNRISE SORBET: This recipe was the creation of two outstanding individuals, Shipen Lebzelter and Guido Magnaguagno, the owners of New York Ice. Add 1 quart of tequila (just before extrusion takes place) to the batch.

BLOOD ORANGE SORBET: Now that blood oranges are being grown in the United States, they are plentiful and reasonably priced. Just substitute blood oranges for regular oranges for the above recipe.

PEAR SORBET

Pears make a delicious tasting sorbet. They are a soft subtle fruit that has a terrific mouth feel taste.

Ingredients:

3 #10 cans	Pears in heavy syrup
2 quarts	Water
3 1/2 pounds	Sugar
1 quart	Pear nectar
2 ounces	Lemon juice
6 ounces	Stabilizer- CC-917
Sliced pears for garnish	

Preparation:

Drain and puree pears and retain heavy syrup. Thoroughly mix sugar with 1 quart of extremely hot water, then add 1 quart of cold water to this mixture. Under good agitation (using a spatula), slowly sift the stabilizer into the pear puree combined with the pear nectar and lemon juice. Allow the stabilizer to hydrate at least 30 minutes or more.

Pour the mixture into the batch freezer. Turn on both the dasher and refrigeration and begin the batch. When the batch is complete, turn off the refrigeration and begin extruding the finished product.

Decorate tops of tubs with pear slices.

Batch time: 13-15 minutes

PRICKLY PEAR SORBET

The prickly pear comes from any of the numerous cacti of the genus Opunita. They are native to the drier regions of Central America and the great deserts of the USA. Their fleshly, spiked leaves take the form of flattish disc or pads stacked one on another. The best types are the red Cardona and the yellow Amarilla. Eaten fresh, they are pleasantly sweet. Lime or lemon juice helps bring out the flavor of the fruit.

Ingredients:
8 quarts	Water
6.95 pounds	Sugar
2 ounces	Citric acid
.25 ounce	Pineapple extract
.25 ounce	Strawberry extract
60 ounces	Prickly Pear Puree- (Perfect Puree-800-556-3707)
3 ounces	Stabilizer- CC-917

Preparation:
Thoroughly mix sugar and stabilizer with 1 quart of extremely hot water, and then add 6 quarts of cold water to this mixture. Under good agitation (using a spatula), slowly agitate the mixture for 1 minute. Allow mixture to then stand for 30 minutes.

Combine the sugar-stabilizer mixture with the Prickly Pear puree, citric acid, strawberry and pineapple extract. Pour combined mixture into the batch freezer. Turn on both the dasher and refrigeration and begin the batch. When the batch is almost complete, turn off the refrigeration and begin extruding the finished product.

Batch time: 11-13 minutes

STRAWBERRY SORBET

The recipe for Strawberry Sorbet is one I have used for over ten years and it is featured here because I want you to fully understand how great your sorbet can be when made in your batch freezer. The real secret in this recipe is the use of frozen strawberries using all the juice from the package whether it is a number 10 can or 5-gallon pail.

Ingredients:

21 pounds	Frozen strawberries, thawed (with sugar)
3 1/2 quarts	Water
3 1/2 pounds	Sugar
4 ounces	Stabilizer- CC-917

Fresh strawberries for garnish

Preparation:
Defrost, and then puree strawberries in 2 1/2 quarts of water and combine with thawed frozen strawberries. Mix sugar thoroughly with 1 quart of hot water, then add 1 1/2 quarts of cold water to this mixture. Under good agitation (using a spatula), slowly sift the stabilizer into the strawberry puree. Allow the stabilizer to hydrate at least 30 minutes or more.

Pour strawberry mixture and sugar-water solution into batch freezer, turn on both dasher and refrigeration, and begin batch. As mixture starts to firm up and look fluffy, turn off refrigeration and extrude finished product.

Decorate tops of tubs with fresh strawberries.

Batch time: 13-15 minutes

VARIATIONS

STRAWBERRY BANANA SORBET: The addition of bananas is a can't miss winner! Add 4 pounds of very ripe bananas, pureed to the batch before freezing.

STRAWBERRY & CHAMPAGNE SORBET
A fabulous sorbet for any restaurant. Pour in 1 quart of Champagne to the batch just before the batch is finished freezing.

WINE PEACH SORBET

Just a great tasting dessert! Red-fleshed peaches are sometimes called "blood" peaches." If you find them hard to get, simply purchase the reddest looking skin peaches you can find.

Ingredients:

16 pounds	Red-flesh peaches
2 1/2 quarts	Water
2 1/2 quarts	Dry red wine
6 pounds	Sugar
16 ounces	Honey
8 ounces	Fresh lemon juice
4 ounces	Stabilizer- CC-917

Sliced peaches for garnish

Preparation:
Wash peaches thoroughly, cut them in half, remove stones and puree mixture. Thoroughly mix sugar and stabilizer with 1 quart of extremely hot water, then add 1 1/2 quarts of cold water to this mixture. Under good agitation (using a spatula), slowly agitate the mixture for 1 minute. Allow mixture to then stand for 30 minutes before adding it to the mixture.

Combine the sugar-stabilizer mixture with the pureed peaches, lemon juice and honey. Pour combined mixture into the batch freezer. Turn on both the dasher and refrigeration and begin the batch. When the batch is almost complete, but not before, add the dry red wine. When product begins to firm up again, turn off the refrigeration and begin extruding the finished product. Decorate tops of tubs with peach slices.

Batch time: 13-15 minutes

VARIATION
PEACH MANGO WINE SORBET: Adding a mango puree to this recipe adds additional body, sweetness, and flavor that goes real well with a dry red wine

CHOCOLATE SORBET

Creating quality in a specific product depends on the standards of the producer. I have always thought of my Chocolate sorbet as the finest sorbet flavor I have ever produced. The time spent creating that ultimate chocolate flavor in a sorbet was long and difficult.

I have tasted and eaten many different versions over the years, and most chocolate sorbets I have tried are weak in flavor. Part of this problem stems from the difficulty in processing dry cocoa with water and sugar to end up with a smooth, rich-tasting product. Most operators use too much water, which dilutes the flavor. This Chocolate sorbet recipe is smooth, rich in flavor, and quite scoopable. Without a doubt, the use of vanilla extract really helps bring out the full flavor of chocolate in the finished product.

Ingredients:

1 1/4 pound	Cocoa (22-24% fat)
4 pounds	Sugar
2 pounds	36DE corn syrup solids
2 ounces	Vanilla extract
2 gallons	Hot water
1 1/2 pounds	Fudge
3 1/2 ounces	Stabilizer- CC-917

Preparation:

Thoroughly mix 1 gallon of extremely hot water with cocoa, using a spatula or mixer so that the dry cocoa is completely dissolved. Pour sugar into the other gallon of hot water and mix until both are completely dissolved. Combine both mixtures. Under good agitation (using a spatula), slowly sift the stabilizer into the combined mixture. Allow the stabilizer to hydrate at least 10 minutes.

Pour cocoa mixture into batch freezer. Turn on dasher for 3 minutes, then turn on refrigeration to begin batch. Add fudge slowly to batch after 2 more minutes. As mixture starts to firm up and look fluffy, turn off refrigeration and extrude finished product.

Batch time: 13-15 minutes

VARIATIONS

CHOCOLATE COCONUT SORBET: Ever since I was a child, I loved chocolate coconut Easter eggs. Thanks to my friend Art Sherman who owned Zitners of Philadelphia (the very best ever), he kept me in supply with coconut Easter eggs year after year. It's just great! Add 2 quarts of coconut fruit base to the batch before freezing and 1/2 pound of shredded coconut at the end of the batch.

GIANDUJA SORBET: A new sorbet creation of chocolate and hazelnut that is absolutely wonderful! Add 20 ounces of Gianduja paste (Fabbri) and 1/2 pound of granulated hazelnuts to the batch before freezing.

CHOCOLATE STRAWBERRY SORBET: The more I get into thinking about unusual sorbet combinations, the easier it is to go crazy. Most of the time it works. This is one of those times. Add 2 quarts strawberry pieces- (frozen strawberries defrosted) to the batch when the sorbet is just beginning to firm up (half way into the batch).

CHOCOLATE RASPBERRY SORBET

Try it, you will be very pleased.

Ingredients:

4 1/2 pounds	Hershey's Chocolate Syrup
3 1/2 pounds	Red Raspberry Puree
	(Star Kay White's Seedless Raspberry Puree)
1.9 pounds	Sugar
2 pounds	36DE corn
1 3/4 gallons	Hot water
3 ounces	Stabilizer- CC-917

Swirl raspberry puree on top of the container

Preparation:
Blend the dry ingredients (sugar, 36DE corn, and stabilizer) together and add to one gallon of water with good agitation. After mixing, add enough water to make two gallons total (estimate of total water needed is 1 3/4 gallons).

Next, mix together 4 1/2 pounds of chocolate syrup and 3 1/2 pounds of raspberry puree. The amounts of both can be varied to provide a stronger flavor of each, but the total amount should be 8 pounds.

Combine all ingredients, pour into batch freezer, and begin the batch. As mixture starts to firm up (gravy) and look slightly fluffy, turn off refrigeration and extrude finished product.

Batch time: 13-15 minutes

CHOCOLATE BANANA COCONUT SORBET

You can't get more Caribbean than this!

Ingredients:

1/2 pound	Cocoa (22-24% fat)
6 pounds	Very ripe bananas- (5 pounds puree)
32 ounces	Coconut fruit base
1 pound	Shredded coconut
5 pounds	Sugar
2 ounces	Vanilla extract
2 gallons	Hot water
1 pound	Fudge
3 1/2 ounces	Stabilizer- CC-917

Banana slices and shredded coconut for garnish

Preparation:

Thoroughly mix 1 gallon of extremely hot water with cocoa, using a spatula or mixer so that the dry cocoa is completely dissolved. Pour sugar into the other gallon of hot water and mix until both are completely dissolved. Using a blender, blend bananas with just enough water so that no pieces remain. Under good agitation (using a spatula), slowly sift the stabilizer into the combined mixture. Allow the stabilizer to hydrate at least 10 minutes.

Pour cocoa mixture, bananas, and coconut fruit base into batch freezer. Turn on dasher for 3 minutes, then turn on refrigeration to begin batch. Add fudge and shredded coconut slowly to batch after 2 more minutes. As mixture starts to firm up (gravy) and look slightly fluffy, turn off refrigeration and extrude finished product.

Batch time: 13-15 minutes

MARGARITA SORBET

Can't get much more refreshing than this. Great for use in Mexican or any tropical theme restaurants.

Ingredients:

1 1/2 quarts	Fresh lime juice
6 quarts	Water
5 pounds	Sugar
2 pounds	36DE corn syrup
3 quarts	Tequila
1 1/2 quarts	Triple Sec
3 1/2 ounces	Stabilizer- CC-917

Key lime slices for garnish

Preparation:
Squeeze enough limes to obtain 1 1/2 quarts of juice. Strain fresh juice and retain half the pulp. (The pulp adds body and texture to the finished product.) Thoroughly mix sugar and 36DE corn syrup with 3 quarts of extremely hot water, then add 3 quarts of cold water to this mixture. Under good agitation (using a spatula), slowly sift the stabilizer into the lime juice. Allow the stabilizer to hydrate at least 30 minutes or more.

Pour juice and pulp into batch freezer. Turn on both dasher and refrigeration and begin batch. As mixture starts to firm up and look gravy, pour the Tequila and Triple Sec into the batch freezer. Next, turn off refrigeration and extrude finished product.

Decorate tops of tubs with fresh key lime slices.

Batch time: 13-15 minutes

VARIATIONS

MANGO MARGARITA SORBET: The mango puree adds wonderful body to this delicious sorbet. Add 2 quarts of mango puree to the batch before freezing.

RASPBERRY MARGARITA SORBET: Add 2 quarts of seedless raspberry puree to the above batch before freezing.

JALAPENO-LIME SORBET

A flavor that's both tart, sweet and ice cold.

Ingredients:

5 quarts	Water
2 1/2 pounds	Fructose sugar
3 quarts	Fresh squeezed lime juice
	(1 case of limes if they are juicy limes)
4	Jalapenos
2 cups	Lime zest
2 1/2 ounces	Stabilizer- CC-917

Preparation:

Juice and zest limes, preferably the same day you are making the sorbet, but never longer than 24 hours prior. Mix water, juice and fructose sugar. Put lime zest into a strainer and pour boiling water over it. This removes the real bitter taste and leaves a smooth lime taste to the zest. Allow to dry a bit and chop the zest. Meanwhile, seed and chop the jalapenos into tiny pieces. BE SURE TO WEAR GLOVES!

Add the tiny pieces of jalapenos to the lime juice mixture along with the lime zest. Again do not let this sit too long. The heat of the jalapenos intensifies as it sits. Stir in stabilizer and agitate slightly.

Pour combined mixture into the batch freezer. Turn on both the dasher and refrigeration and begin the batch. When the batch is almost complete, turn off the refrigeration and begin extruding the finished product.

Decorate top of the tubs with lime slices and 1/2 jalapeno. DO NOT MAKE ANY OTHER FLAVORS AFTER THIS and clean batch freezer thoroughly!

Batch time: 11-13 minutes

TOMATO & BASIL SORBET

The perfect appetizer or dessert for a sunny June day.

Ingredients:

24	Tomatoes (4 quarts tomato juice)
2 quart	Water
4 pounds	Sugar
1 teaspoon	Chives
1 ounce	Tabasco Sauce
1 teaspoon	Basil leaves
3 ounces	Lemon juice
2 ounces	Stabilizer- CC-917

Preparation:

Puree tomatoes with basil leaves, chives and lemon juice. Add a little salt and pepper for taste. Thoroughly mix sugar and stabilizer with 1 quart of hot water, then add remaining 1 quart of cold water to this mixture. Under good agitation, slowly agitate the mixture for 1 minute. Allow mixture to stand for 30 minutes before adding it to the tomato mixture. Pour combined mixture into the batch freezer. Turn on both the dasher and refrigeration and begin the batch. When product begins to firm up, turn off the refrigeration and begin extruding the finished product. Decorate tops of tubs with slices of tomatoes.

Batch time: 13-15 minutes

JAEGER TEA SORBET

Jaeger tea- hot tea with rum- is Austria's version of hot toddy.

Ingredients:

20 ounces	Lemon juice
8 quarts	Strong black tea (Ceylon tea)
5 pounds	Sugar
20 ounces	Rum
3 ounces	Stabilizer- CC-917

Preparation:

Thoroughly mix sugar and stabilizer with 2 quarts of hot water. Under good agitation, slowly agitate the mixture for 1 minute. Allow mixture to stand for 30 minutes. Brew enough tea leaves submerged in a pot. Add the sugar/stabilizer mixture to the tea. Set mixture aside to cool, then add the lemon juice. Pour the combined mixture into the batch freezer. Turn on both the dasher and refrigeration and begin the batch. When product begins to firm up again, add the rum. Turn off the refrigeration and begin extruding the finished product.

Batch time: 13-15 minutes

CHAPTER 13
ITALIAN WATER ICES

What's the difference between a great Italian water ice and an average one? "Clean smooth flavor and no chemical aftertastes," says March Boccaccio of Fresco's Famous Italian Water Ices,* East Northport , New York.

There is nothing more refreshing than digging into a cup of Italian water ice on a hot summer day. What New York and Philadelphia Italian ice manufacturers have known for many years is now sweeping the country. Producing Italian water ice is not difficult, it's an easy business to get into, and since the product costs are low, there's lots of money to be made in a short-selling season.

But the real key is not simply making a typical Italian water ice of flavor syrup, sugar and water. Anybody can do that. The difference between the success stories in this business and the entrepreneurs who get into this business for a simple killing is high quality flavor ingredients and customer satisfaction.

Customer satisfaction comes in two parts. If you are a manufacturer and sell to an Italian water ice store, that means delivering a consistent product on time when ordered during the short-selling season. If you are a retailer making the product and selling it directly to your customers, that means having a product that tastes so good, your customers will flock to you everyday during the summer for a lick.

While flavoring is important in creating a wonderful tasting water ice, equally important is the use of filtered water. Contact Grainger or even go the nearest Home Depot and purchase a charcoal filtering system. You will be amazed at what the difference filtered water will do to your finished water ice product.

All of the recipes in this chapter are produced in a 20 quart batch freezer. If you follow any of the below Italian Water Ice recipes, you will, without a doubt, be on the road to success. In other words, when you see the two words "trust me" when I describe a particular flavor, it means you can take it to the bank!

BASIC WATER ICE RECIPE

Ingredients:

3 1/2 Gallons	Water
6 pounds	Sugar
3 pounds	36 DE corn
3-4 ounces	Stabilizer- 917 (.5%-.75% by weight)
2-4 ounces	Fruit extract flavoring

(amount used depends on the manufacturer's recommended usage level)

Preparation:
Mix together all dry sweetener ingredients- sugar, 36DE corn, and stabilizer "thoroughly." Add 1 1/2 gallons hot water to above mixture, blend thoroughly. Pour this mixture and the rest of the ingredients into the batch freezer. Turn on the dasher for 2 minutes to stir the mixtures together. Set timer for 15 minutes. Turn on refrigeration and begin batch. As mixture firms up and looks wavy, turn off refrigeration and extrude finished product.

Batch Time: 15-18 minutes

OLD FASHIONED LEMON WATER ICE

It's as simple as this. Lemon is to water ice as vanilla is to ice cream. You will always be judged by the quality of your Lemon water ice.

Ingredients:

48 ounces	Lemon juice- (freshly squeezed, save pulp)
3 gallons	Water
6 1/2 pounds	Sugar
1 1/2 pounds	36 DE corn
3 ounces	Stabilizer-CC- 917

Preparation:
Combine sugar, 36 DE corn, and stabilizer together. Mix 1 gallon hot water with above dry sugar mixture until dry powders are completely dissolved and agitated. Pour lemon juice, liquefied sugar solution, and balance of water into the batch freezer. Turn on dasher to mix all ingredients together. Next, turn on refrigeration and begin batch. As mixture firms up and looks wavy, turn off refrigeration and extrude finished product.

Batch Time: 15-18 minutes

VANILLA ITALIAN WATER ICE

Using a Madagascar Bourbon vanilla will really make this an outstanding refreshing flavor.

Ingredients:

6 ounces	Pure vanilla extract (two-fold)
3 1/2 gallons	Water
6 pounds	Sugar
3 pounds	36 DE corn
1/4 ounce	Vanilla specks
3 ounces	Stabilizer- CC917

Preparation:
Combine sugar, 36 DE corn, and stabilizer together. Mix 1 gallon hot water with above dry sugar mixture until dry powders are completely dissolved and agitated. Pour vanilla extract, liquefied sugar solution, and balance of water into the batch freezer. Turn on dasher, mix all ingredients together, set timer to 15 minutes, turn on refrigeration and begin batch. As mixture firms up and looks wavy, turn off refrigeration and extrude finished product.

Batch Time: 15-18 minutes

VARIATIONS

VANILLA CHIP: Use only small chocolate chips or flakes, otherwise your customers could possibly have problems biting into this very popular Italian water ice flavor. As the batch begins to freeze, add 1 1/4 pounds of chocolate chips (mini).

VANILLA ALMOND: The bite of roasted diced or slivered almond works very well in this flavor. Add 2 ounces of almond extract and 1 1/4 pounds of roasted diced almonds to the batch before freezing.

BUBBLE GUM: Kids love this flavor, so make sure you make it. Add 3 ounces of bubble Gum flavor (I.Rice) to the batch before freezing and 2 1/2 pounds of bubble gum pieces as the batch begins to freeze. Reduce amount of vanilla extract used to 2 ounces.

BANANA WATER ICE

Not only will you taste the bananas, but you will also smell them as well in this very fresh water ice flavor.

Ingredients:

3 gallons	Water
6 pounds	Bananas- ripe (peeled)
2 1/2 pounds	Sugar
1 pound	36 DE corn
1 1/2 ounces	Citric acid (liquid)
2 ounces	Stabilizer- CC- 917

Preparation:

Puree the bananas. Combine sugar, 36 DE corn, and stabilizer together. Mix 2 gallons hot water with above dry sugar mixture until dry powders are completely dissolved and agitated. Pour banana puree, liquefied sugar, and balance of water into the batch freezer. Turn on dasher and refrigeration and begin batch. As mixture firms up, turn off refrigeration and extrude finished product.

Batch Time: 15-18 minutes

CHERRY WATER ICE

Cherry water ice has always been a popular flavor, as illustrated by this recipe.

Ingredients:

3 1/2 gallons	Water
3 ounces	DS Cherry flavor- I.Rice
2 pounds	IQF frozen diced cherries
6 1/2 pounds	Sugar
4 pounds	36 DE corn
2 ounces	Citric acid (liquid)
1 ounce	Stabilizer- CC-917

Preparation:

Defrost the cherries and chop them up into very small pieces. Mix together all dry sweetener ingredients: sugar, 36DE corn, and stabilizer. Add 1 1/2 gallons hot water to above mixture, blend thoroughly. Pour in diced cherries and DS cherry flavor. Pour this mixture and the rest of the ingredients into the batch freezer. Turn on the dasher for 2 minutes to stir the mixture together. Set timer for 18 minutes. Turn on refrigeration and begin batch. As mixture firms up and looks wavy, turn off refrigeration and extrude finished product.

Batch Time: 18-20 minutes

PEACH WATER ICE
This full bodied water ice is very close to being called a sorbet.

Ingredients:

3 gallons	Water
5 pounds	IQF peach slices- diced- (very small)
1 gallon	Peach base- I. Rice
2 1/2 pounds	Sugar
1 pound	36 DE corn
1 1/2 ounces	Citric acid (liquid)
2 ounces	Stabilizer- CC- 917

Preparation:
Combine sugar, 36 DE corn, and stabilizer together. Mix 2 gallons hot water with above dry sugar mixture until dry powders are completely dissolved and agitated. Pour peach base, peach cubes, liquefied sugar, and balance of water into the batch freezer. Turn on dasher and refrigeration and begin batch. As mixture firms up, turn off refrigeration and extrude finished product.

Batch Time: 15-18 minutes

COCONUT ALMOND JOY WATER ICE
It's not the candy bar nor the ice cream, it's simply a great Coconut water ice.

Ingredients:

1 1/2 pounds	Cocoa powder (22-24%)
3 gallons	Water
6 pounds	Sugar
3 pounds	36 DE corn
2 ounces	Vanilla extract (two-fold)
1 1/2 Quarts	Coconut fruit base
1 pound	Shredded coconut
1 1/2 pounds	Diced almonds
1 1/2 pounds	Hot fudge
4 ounces	Stabilizer- CC-917

Preparation:
Mix together all dry sweetener ingredients and stabilizer thoroughly. Add 1 1/2 gallons hot water to above mixture, blend thoroughly. Pour in 1 1/2 gallons water and balance of all ingredients into the batch freezer. Turn on the dasher and refrigeration and begin batch. As mixture firms up, turn off refrigeration and extrude finished product and swirl in the fudge throughout the tubs. Decorate top of the tubs with fudge, shredded coconut and diced almonds.

Batch Time: 15-18 minutes

STRAWBERRY WATER ICE

This Italian water ice is not cheap to make, but the results are outstanding.

Ingredients:
2 ounces	NFC Strawberry- Limpert (7058)
1/2 quart	Strawberry puree-Limpert (3120)
1 1/4 pounds	IQF frozen strawberries, (defrosted)
* 3 3/4 pounds	Sugar
* 2 3/4 pounds	36 DE corn
3/4 ounce	Citric acid (liquid)
2 1/4 gallons	Water
2 ounces	Stabilizer- CC-917

NOTE: If you don't use 36DE corn, use 5 pounds sugar

Preparation:
Combine sugar, 36DE corn and stabilizer together. Mix 1-gallon hot water with sugar solution until dry powders are completely dissolved and agitated.

Pour strawberry flavor, liquefied sugar solution, citric acid, and balance of water into the batch freezer. Turn on dasher to mix all ingredients together, set timer to 18 minutes, turn on refrigeration and begin batch. Towards middle of batch, as product begins to firm up, add IQF Strawberries. As mixture firms up and looks wavy, turn off refrigeration and extrude finished product.

Batch Time: 18-20 minutes

BLACK RASBERRY WATER ICE

Ingredients:
3 1/2 gallons	Water
36 ounces	Black raspberry base- I.Rice
6 pounds	Sugar
4 pounds	36 DE corn
1 ounces	Citric acid
3 ounces	Stabilizer- CC-917

Preparation:
Combine sugar, 36DE corn, and stabilizer together. Mix 2 gallons hot water with above dry sugar mixture until dry powders are completely dissolved and agitated. Pour black raspberry base, citric acid, liquefied sugar solution, and balance of water into the batch freezer.

Turn on dasher to mix all ingredients together, set timer to 15 minutes, turn on refrigeration and begin batch. As mixture firms up and looks wavy, turn off refrigeration and extrude finished product.

Batch Time: 15-18 minutes

CREAM ICES

What started out as a fad a few years ago has become the rage of the water ice business. So, what is a cream ice? It is a water ice product with approximately 2% butterfat as part of the basic formula. For the most part, many water ice manufacturers use either a 10 or 14% ice cream mix to create the cream ice flavor. Because of the butterfat content in the cream ice mix, the overrun of the finished product is higher (30%) than the overrun of the same flavor (15-20%) without the addition of butterfat.

Also, because butterfat is such an integral part of the cream ice formula, less stabilizer is needed in any cream ice recipe.

The most popular cream ice flavors are Vanilla Chip, Chocolate, and Cookie N' Crème, followed by Pistachio, Strawberry Cheesecake, and Creamsicle.

BASIC CREAM ICE RECIPE

Ingredients:

6 quarts	Water
3 1/4 pounds	Sugar
1 1/2 pounds	36 DE corn
1 1/2 quarts	Ice cream mix*
2 ounces	Stabilizer- CC-917
2-3 ounces	Flavoring

*Note: if you want a richer cream flavor, use 2-3 quarts of ice cream mix.

Preparation:

Mix together all dry sweetener ingredients- sugar, stabilizer, 36DE corn thoroughly. Add 3 quarts hot water to above mixture, blend thoroughly. Pour in 3 quarts water and balance of all ingredients. Pour the water/sugar mixture and ice cream mix into the batch freezer.

Turn on the dasher for 2 minutes to stir the mixtures together. Set timer for 15 minutes. Turn on refrigeration and begin batch

As mixture firms up and looks wavy, turn off refrigeration and extrude finished product.

Batch Time: 15-18 minutes

CREAMSICLE WATER ICE

One bite of this flavor is like biting into a Creamsicle Bar.

Ingredients:

1 1/2 gallons	Water
2 ounces	OJ- I.Rice, Flavor Chem, or Weber
6 1/2 pounds	Sugar
3 pound	36 DE corn
1 3/4 gallons	Fresh orange juice- including pulp and peel
3 quarts	Ice cream mix
1 1/2 ounces	Vanilla extract
1 ounce	Stabilizer- CC-917

Preparation:

Mix together all dry sweetener ingredients- sugar, 36DE corn, and stabilizer thoroughly. Add 1 1/2 gallons hot water to above mixture, blend thoroughly. Pour in another 1 1/2 gallons of water, orange juice, ice cream mix, and orange flavor into the batch freezer. Turn on the dasher for 2 minutes to stir the mixture together. Turn on refrigeration and begin batch. As mixture firms up and <u>looks wavy</u>, turn off refrigeration and extrude finished product.

Batch Time: 18-20 minutes

VANILLA CHIP CREAM ICE

Without a doubt, one of the most popular cream ices flavors produced.

Ingredients:

6 quarts	Water
3 1/4 pounds	Sugar
1 1/2 pounds	36 DE corn
1 1/2 quarts	Ice cream mix
2 ounces	Stabilizer- CC-917
2 ounces	Vanilla extract
2 pounds	Chocolate chips

Preparation:

Mix together all dry sweetener ingredients- sugar, stabilizer, 36DE corn thoroughly. Add 3 quarts hot water to above mixture, blend thoroughly. Pour in 3 quarts water and balance of all ingredients except the chocolate chips. Pour the water/sugar mixture and ice cream mix into the batch freezer. Turn on the dasher for 2 minutes to mix all the ingredients together. Turn on refrigeration and begin batch. End of batch add the chocolate chips. As mixture firms up and <u>looks wavy</u>, turn off refrigeration and extrude finished product.

Batch Time: 15-18 minutes

COCONUT ALMOND JOY CREAM ICE
I love this flavor and you will too!

Ingredients:

1 1/2 pounds	Cocoa
3/4 pounds	Sugar
6 quarts	Water
3 1/4 pounds	Sugar
1 1/2 pounds	36 DE corn
1 1/2 quarts	Ice cream mix
2 ounces	Stabilizer- CC-917
3 ounce	Vanilla extract
6 pounds	Fudge
1 1/2 pounds	Diced almonds
3 quarts	Coconut fruit base

Preparation:

Mix together all dry sweetener ingredients- cocoa, sugar, 36DE corn, and stabilizer thoroughly. Add 3 quarts hot water to above mixture, blend thoroughly. Pour in balance of all ingredients.

Pour the mixture into the batch freezer. Turn on the dasher for 2 minutes to stir the mixture together. Set timer for 18 minutes. Turn on refrigeration and begin batch.

As mixture firms up and <u>looks wavy</u>, turn off refrigeration and swirl in fudge when extruding finished product into the tub.

Batch Time: 18-20 minutes

VARIATIONS

BANANA COCONUT JOY: The addition of bananas only makes this flavor more interesting and enjoyable to eat as well. Add 3 pounds of peeled bananas, pureed to the batch before freezing.

PEANUT BUTTER COCONUT JOY: It's almost like eating a Peanut Butter Chocolate Easter egg. Replace the diced almonds with granulated peanuts and add 1 quart of peanut butter topping or base to the batch before freezing.

PISTACHIO CREAM ICE
Smooth as silk!

Ingredients:

6 quarts	Water
3 1/4 pounds	Sugar
1 1/2 pounds	36 DE corn
1 1/2 quarts	Ice cream mix
2 ounces	Stabilizer- CC-917
2 ounces	Vanilla extract
33 ounces	Pistachio flavor (Fabbri)
1 pound	Pistachios

Preparation:

Mix together all dry sweetener ingredients- sugar, stabilizer, 36DE corn thoroughly.

Add 3 quarts hot water to above mixture, blend thoroughly. Pour in 3 quarts cold water and balance of all ingredients. Pour the water/sugar mixture and ice cream mix into the batch freezer.

Turn on the dasher for 2 minutes to stir the mixtures together. Set timer for 15 minutes. Turn on refrigeration and begin batch.

As mixture firms up and looks wavy, turn off refrigeration and extrude finished product.

Decorate the top of the tubs with pistachios.

Batch Time: 15-18 minutes

VARIATION

PISTACHIO CHIP CREAM ICE: Let's face it, the Pistachio Cream Ice recipe is great all by itself. The addition of chocolate chunks justs makes it even better. Trust me! At the end of the batch, pour in 1 pound of chocolate chips, and begin extruding out the finished product.

PISTACHIO KULFI CREAM ICE: Pistachio Kulfi is a classic dessert in India. Converting it into a cream ice will open up many wholesale restaurant customers for you. Add 6 ounces of Rosewater and 1 ounce ground cardamon to the batch. At the end of the batch, pour in 1 pound of chocolate chunks, and begin extruding out the finished product.

PEANUT BUTTER CREAM ICE

When the cream ice business just started to take off a few years ago, my buddy, Tony Lana of A. Panza & Sons told me that adding peanut butter to a water ice with ice cream mix would work very well. He was right. Peanut Butter Cream Ice is now considered one of the top four cream ice flavors produced today.

Ingredients:

3 gallons	Water
6 1/2 pounds	Sugar
3 pounds	36 DE corn
3 quarts	Ice cream mix
4 ounces	Stabilizer- CC-917
3 ounces	Vanilla extract
2 quarts	Peanut butter topping
	(A. Panza- 800-ICE CREAM)
1 pound	Granulated peanuts

Preparation:

Thoroughly mix the peanut butter topping so the oil in the topping is evenly disbursed. Mix together all dry sweetener ingredients- sugar, 36DE corn, stabilizer thoroughly. Add 1 gallon hot water to above mixture, blend thoroughly. Pour peanut butter topping, granulated peanuts and balance of all ingredients into the batch freezer.

Turn on the dasher for 2 minutes to stir the mixtures together. Set timer for 15 minutes. Turn on refrigeration and begin batch.

As mixture firms up and looks wavy, turn off refrigeration and extrude finished product.

Batch Time: 15-18 minutes

VARIATIONS

CHOCOLATE PEANUT BUTTER CREAM ICE: Chocolate and peanut butter have always been a perfect match when produced as an ice cream flavor, so why not do the same here. Combine 1/2 pound each of cocoa and sugar with 1 pound of very hot water to create a smooth creamy paste. Add this mixture to the above batch before freezing.

PEANUT BUTTER CUP CREAM ICE: Believe me when I tell you, this is an outrageous flavor. At the end of the batch pour into the batch freezer 1 pound of crumbled Reese's Peanut Butter Cups before extruding out the finished product.

CREAM-A-LATTA WATER ICE

The origin of cream ices started many years ago with this old-fashioned water ice flavor called Cream-A-Latta.

Ingredients:

3 gallons	Water
5 1/2 pounds	Sugar
3 pounds	36DE corn
1/2 gallon	Ice cream mix
2 ounces	Rum extract or 16 ounces rum
2 ounces	Cinnamon
1 pound	Diced almonds
3 ounces	Stabilizer- CC-917

Preparation:
Mix together all dry sweetener ingredients- sugar, stabilizer, 36DE corn thoroughly. Add 1 1/2 gallons hot water to above mixture, blend thoroughly. Pour in balance of all ingredients. Pour the water/sugar mixture, ice cream mix, rum, cinnamon, and diced almonds into the batch freezer. Turn on the dasher for 2 minutes to stir the mixtures together. Turn on refrigeration and begin batch. As mixture firms up and looks wavy, turn off refrigeration and extrude finished product.

Batch Time: 15-18 minutes

BANANA CREAM ICE

Tastes just like eating a frozen banana.

Ingredients:

6 quarts	Water
3 1/4 pounds	Sugar
1 1/2 pounds	36 DE corn
1 1/2 quarts	Ice cream mix
2 ounces	Stabilizer- CC-917
2 ounces	Vanilla extract
14 pounds	Bananas (very ripe-peeled)

Preparation:
Puree the bananas. Mix together all dry sweetener ingredients thoroughly. Add 1 1/2 gallons hot water to above mixture, blend thoroughly. Pour in 1 1/2 gallons cold water and balance of all ingredients into the batch freezer. Turn on the dasher and refrigeration and begin batch. As mixture firms up and looks wavy, turn off refrigeration and extrude finished product.

Batch Time: 15-18 minutes

LEMON CREAM ICE
If you are in the Italian Ice business, you must try making this flavor.

Ingredients

17 ounces	Fabbri Lemon powder
3 quarts	Ice cream mix
2 1/2 gallons	Water
7 1/2 pounds	Sugar
1/4 ounce	Faffrisoft stabilizer

Preparation:

Thoroughly mix the sugar and stabilizer with 1 gallon of extremely hot water. Add the lemon powder to this mixture along with the remaining 1 1/2 gallons of cold water. Mix all ingredients thoroughly. Pour the lemon mixture and ice cream mix into the batch freezer. Turn on both the dasher and refrigeration and begin batch. When the batch is complete, turn off the refrigeration and begin extruding the finished product. Decorate tops of tubs with lemon slices.

Batch Time: 15-18 minutes

STRAWBERRY CHEESECAKE CREAM ICE
A bite of this flavor is like eating a reduced fat slice of "great" cheesecake.

Ingredients:

6 quarts	Water
3 1/4 pounds	Sugar
1 1/2 pounds	36 DE corn
1 1/2 quarts	Ice cream mix
2 ounces	Stabilizer- CC-917
2 ounces	Vanilla extract
2 pounds	Commercial cheesecake powder
2 quarts	Processed strawberries
1/2 pound	Graham cracker (broken)

Preparation:

Mix together all dry sweetener ingredients- sugar, stabilizer, 36DE corn thoroughly. Add 3 quarts hot water to above mixture, blend thoroughly. Pour in 3 quarts cold water and balance of all ingredients. Pour the water/sugar mixture and ice cream mix into the batch freezer. Turn on the dasher for 2 minutes to stir the mixtures together. Set timer for 15 minutes. Turn on refrigeration and begin batch. As mixture firms up and looks wavy, turn off refrigeration and extrude finished product.

Batch Time: 15-18 minutes

PINA COLADA CREAM ICE

On a hot day, there is no better flavor than a Pina Colada, whether it is a drink, ice cream flavor, or now a cream ice.

Ingredients:

6 quarts	Water
3 1/4 pounds	Sugar
1 1/2 pounds	36 DE corn
1 1/2 quarts	Ice cream mix
2 ounces	Stabilizer- CC-917
1 quart	Coconut fruit base
1 1/2 quarts	Pineapple puree
2 pounds	Shredded coconut
2 ounces	Vanilla extract

Preparation:
Mix together all dry sweetener ingredients- sugar, stabilizer, 36DE corn thoroughly. Add 3 quarts hot water to above mixture, blend thoroughly. Pour in 3 quarts water and balance of all ingredients. Pour the water/sugar mixture and ice cream mix into the batch freezer.

Turn on the dasher for 2 minutes to stir the mixtures together. Set timer for 15 minutes. Turn on refrigeration and begin batch. As mixture firms up and looks wavy, turn off refrigeration and extrude finished product.
Batch Time: 15-18 minutes

VARIATIONS

PINA BANANA COLADA CREAM ICE: To really enjoy this flavor, you should be on a beach under an umbrella reading a juicy novel. I love to dream! Add 5 pounds of peeled bananas pureed to the above batch before freezing.

CHA CHA CHA BERRIES COLADA: Taking this flavor a step further, chop up frozen strawberries before they are defrosted into very small pieces. Once defrosted, add the mixture to the Pina Colada Cream Ice recipe before freezing.

CHOCOLATE MOUSSE CREAM ICE

One might think biting into this flavor is like eating ice cream. That's how good this flavor is with 1/6 the butterfat of regular ice cream.

Ingredients:

1 1/2 pounds	Cocoa powder (22-24%)
1/2 pound	Sugar
6 quarts	Water
3 1/4 pounds	Sugar
1 1/2 pounds	36 DE corn
1 3/4 quarts	Ice cream mix
2 ounces	Stabilizer- CC-917
2 ounces	Vanilla extract
20 ounces	Pasteurized egg yolks- (or 36 ounces egg base)
1 1/2 pounds	Hot fudge

Preparation:

Mix together all dry sweetener ingredients- sugar, stabilizer, 36DE corn thoroughly. Add 3 quarts hot water to above mixture, blend thoroughly. Pour in 3 quarts water and balance of all ingredients.

Pour the water/sugar mixture and ice cream mix into the batch freezer. Turn on the dasher for 2 minutes to stir the mixtures together. Set timer for 15 minutes. Turn on refrigeration and begin batch.

As mixture firms up and <u>looks wavy</u>, turn off refrigeration and extrude finished product.

Batch Time: 15-18 minutes

VARIATIONS

CHOCOLATE CHOCOLATE CHIP CREAM ICE: Anybody who loves chocolate will go nuts over this outrageous lowfat (seriously) crème ice flavor. Add one pound of mini chocolate chips at the end of the batch, or better yet, pour in 1 quart of liquid chocolate just before the product is being extruded.

CHOCOLATE ALMOND CREAM ICE: Roasted diced almonds are a wonderful complement to anything chocolate, so "trust me," this flavor will sell. Add one pound of diced roasted almonds at the end of the batch just before the product is being extruded.

COOKIES & CREME CREAM ICE

Twenty years ago, when Cookies & Crème ice cream was first introduced, it became the number three best-selling ice cream flavor. Today, the same is true with Cookies & Crème Ice.

Ingredients:

6 quarts	Water
3 1/4 pounds	Sugar
1 1/2 pounds	36 DE corn
1 1/2 quarts	Ice cream mix
2 ounces	Stabilizer- CC-917
2 ounces	Vanilla extract
2 pounds	Oreo cookies
	(1/2 crushed and 1/2 broken pieces)

Preparation:

Mix together all dry sweetener ingredients- sugar, stabilizer, 36DE corn thoroughly. Add 3 quarts hot water to above mixture, blend thoroughly. Pour in 3 quarts cold water and balance of all ingredients.

Pour the water/sugar mixture, ice cream mix, and 1/2 of the crushed Oreos into the batch freezer. Turn on the dasher for 2 minutes to stir the mixtures together. Set timer for 15 minutes. Turn on refrigeration, and begin batch.

As mixture firms up and <u>looks wavy</u>, add broken Oreo pieces, turn off refrigeration and extrude finished product.

Batch Time: 15-18 minutes

VARIATION

MINT COOKIES & CRÈME ICE: It's like eating a snack of Girl Scout cookies for dessert. Add 2 ounces of any natural mint extract to the batch before freezing.

DULCE DE LECHE CREAM CHIP ICE

Every once in a while a flavor a new flavor really takes off and is not just a fad. Dulce de Leche fits into that category, first as an ice cream flavor and now as a cream ice flavor. This is one of my "trust me" flavors.

Ingredients:

6 quarts	Water
3 1/4 pounds	Sugar
1 1/2 pounds	36 DE corn
1 1/2 quarts	Ice cream mix
2 ounces	Stabilizer- CC-917
2 ounces	Vanilla extract
1 1/2 pounds	Caramel Base 8951-Star Kay White
3 pounds	Caramel Kremia #1PE- Star Kay White
1/2 pound	Chocolate chunks
1/2 pound	Pecan pieces (dark roasted)
1/2 pound	Pecan Pralines

Preparation:

Mix together all dry sweetener ingredients- sugar, stabilizer, 36DE corn thoroughly. Add 3 quarts hot water to above mixture, blend thoroughly. Pour in 3 quarts cold water and balance of all ingredients.

Pour the water/sugar mixture and ice cream mix into the batch freezer. Turn on the dasher for 2 minutes to stir the mixtures together. Set timer for 15 minutes. Turn on refrigeration and begin batch.

As mixture firms up and looks wavy, pour in the nuts and chocolate chunks. Turn off refrigeration and extrude finished product as you swirl in the Caramel Krema variegate.

Batch Time: 15-18 minutes

CHAPTER 14
ITALIAN GELATO

The secret to making any great frozen dessert product is the ingredients used and the effort and care of the person making the product.

Italian gelato is the perfect restaurant frozen dairy dessert because of its freshness, flavor, and foreign mystique, and the way it is served- soft. When made in Italy, gelato typically contains 5.7% butterfat and is produced at 20-30% overrun. In the United States, consumers prefer a creamier flavor with the gelato having an approximate 10% butterfat produced at 30-35% overrun.

Preparing a gelato flavor is like venturing into fantasyland. Because gelato is really a European-based product, our knowledge of most of the flavor ingredients used in Europe is foreign to us. That's what I really like: venturing into the unknown.

Whether you use a Coldelite, Emery Thompson or Taylor batch freezer, you must operate the freezer on a "low speed."

The basic ingredients remain the same: milk, fresh cream, sugar, and egg-yolk solids.

While there are a number of reputable Italian gelato ingredient manufacturers selling flavor ingredients in the United States, we have chosen Fabbri (North American importers, Des Choix Specialty Foods, Woodside, New York) of Bologna, Italy. The use of Fabbri ingredients will give you a leg up on your competition. It's up to you to produce the flavor and freeze it properly. The following recipes are each on their own "outstanding flavors." A general rule of thumb for using Fabbri flavor ingredients for gelato production is 13 ounces of flavor for each gallon of gelato mix (5 or 10% with eggs) used. A 2 1/2 gallon batch needs approximately 28-32 ounces of flavor when using Fabbri flavor ingredients.

If you want to use these flavors to produce an ice cream flavor with either 14% or 16% butterfat, increase the usage level by 15%. (additional 3-5 ounces per each 2 1/2 gallon batch- 37-39 ounces of flavor used)

MAKING A GELATO MIX FROM SCRATCH

I have been asked many times over the years exactly what is Italian gelato. Why is it so incredibly great and popular in Italy and not nearly so here in the States? Part of the answer lies in our different cultures. In Italy, almost anyone you meet that makes and sells gelato considers his/her craft a true "passion." Can we say that?

They are willing to go to any length to make a great product and that means getting up at 5:00 A.M. to make the gelato mix for that day. That's right, what is made that day is sold that day. No blast freezing or leftovers. Every day is a new day. What is left over is reprocessed the next day.

The results of all this is a fresh soft creamy product presented at 11:00 A.M., every morning fresh when their gelateria opens for business.

Is it possible to make a fresh mix yourself? Yes, it is. But only for product prepared and sold that day. Here's how you can do it.

BASIC GELATO MIX RECIPE

A gelato mix is quite low in solids so it is important when actually producing flavors with the mix that the flavoring agent used be intense. This will help keep the product smooth and creamy when served to your customers. Half & half is used because this product is already homogenized, while most cream is not.

Ingredients:

4 quarts	Half & Half cream*
21 ounces	Sugar
6 ounces	Pasteurized egg yolks

Preparation:
Mix the sugar and egg yolks together and then add this mixture to the cream. Refrigerate mixture for approximately one hour before beginning the freezing process.
NOTE: You can substitute 3 quarts of whole milk and 1 quart of cream for the half & half.

VANIGLIA GELATO
(Vanilla)

A very unique intense flavor. When comparing Vanilla gelato to an American Vanilla, the difference is remarkable. The resulting finished product is very smooth, textured and has a show of little black flecks of vanilla.

Ingredients:

2 1/2 gallons	5-10% gelato mix
18 ounces	Vanilla flavor (Fabbri)

Preparation:

Pour all ingredients into batch freezer. Turn on dasher and refrigeration and begin batch. When batch is complete, turn off refrigeration and extrude finished product.

Batch time: 8-10 minutes

CROCCANTINO GELATO
(Almond Crunch & Rum)

Very intense, very unique. A great Italian restaurant flavor for that after dinner smash dessert.

Ingredients:

2 1/2 gallons	5-10% gelato mix
26 ounces	Croccantino flavor
1/2 pound	sliced or diced almonds

Preparation:

Pour all ingredients except the sliced almonds into the batch freezer. Turn on dasher and refrigeration and begin batch. Just before the batch is complete, pour in the sliced almonds, turn off the refrigeration and begin extruding the finished product.

Decorate top of the gelato pans or tubs with sliced or diced almonds.

Batch time: 8-10 minutes

APRICOT GELATO
(Albicocca)
A very unique subtle flavor. You will love it!

Ingredients:

2 1/2 gallons	5-10% gelato mix
30 ounces	Apricot flavor

Preparation:
Pour all ingredients into the batch freezer. Turn on dasher and refrigeration and begin batch. Just before the batch is complete, turn off the refrigeration and begin extruding the finished product. Decorate top of the gelato pans or tubs with dried apricot pieces.

Batch time: 8-10 minutes

VARIATIONS
APRICOT CHOCOLATE GELATO: White chocolate chunks are just as subtle as apricots. Put the two together, and you have a great flavor. Add 1 1/2 pounds of white chocolate chunks just before the batch is complete, and extrude out the finished product.

GINGERED APRICOT GELATO: The accent of the ginger with the tenderness of the apricots makes for a wonderful sensual eating dessert. Simply another way to be creative with ginger. Add 1 pound of candied ginger pieces just before the batch is complete, and extrude out the finished product.

FRUTTA DI BOSCO GELATO
(Wild Berries)
If you like a fruity gelato flavor, then you can't miss with this one. Frutta di Bosco contains raspberries, blueberries, strawberries, and wild cherries.

Ingredients:

2 1/2 gallons	5 or 10% gelato mix
2 ounces	Two-fold vanilla extract
33 ounces	Frutta di Bosco paste

Preparation:
Pour all ingredients into the batch freezer. Turn on the dasher and let it run for one minute. Set timer to 8 minutes, turn on refrigeration and begin batch. When batch is complete, turn off refrigeration and extrude out the finished product.
Decorate top of the gelato pans or tubs with pieces of the above fruit.

Batch Time: 8-10 minutes

MANDARINO GELATO
(Orange)

This very refreshing orange gelato flavor is a delight to eat. Try it, it's very different than anything you ever made.

Ingredients:

2 1/2 gallons	5 or 10% gelato mix
2 ounces	Two-fold vanilla extract
33 ounces	Mandarino paste
2 ounces	Orange liqueur

Preparation:
Pour all ingredients except the orange liqueur into the batch freezer. Turn on the dasher and let it run for one minute. Set timer to 8 minutes, turn-on refrigeration and begin batch. When batch is almost complete, pour in the orange liqueur, turn off refrigeration and extrude out the finished product.
Batch Time: 8-10 minutes

ORANGE & CARDAMOM GELATO

I have really gone way overboard with this recipe using cardamom, but don't worry, the effect is fabulous. Always use green cardamom pods. The larger black cardamom pods are also good, but they have a slightly coarse flavor.

Ingredients:

2 1/2 gallons	5 or 10% gelato mix
2 ounces	Two fold vanilla extract
2 quarts	Fresh orange juice
8 ounces	Triple Sec liqueur
	Zest of 4 oranges
6 tablespoons	Green cardamom pods

Preparation:
Place the cardamom pods in a mortar and pestle, mash until all the pods have opened, then remove the green pods and mash the black seeds further. Place the orange zest, cardamom pods, and one quart of the gelato mix in a double boiler and simmer the mixture for 30 minutes. Strain the mixture in a sieve and cool. Next, pour the gelato mix and all the other ingredients into batch freezer. Turn on both dasher and refrigeration and begin batch. When the batch is complete, turn off the refrigeration and extrude out the finished product. Decorate the top of gelato pans with orange zest.
Batch Time: 8-10 minutes

WHITE CHOCOLATE MACADAMIA NUT GELATO

Both white chocolate and macadamia nuts are considered sensual subtle ingredients. As a pair, they work well together. Try this recipe, I am sure you will like it!

Ingredients:

2 1/2 gallons	5 or 10% gelato mix
2 ounces	Two-fold vanilla extract
3 pounds	White chocolate chunks
1 1/2 pounds	Macadamia nuts

Preparation:

In a double boiler, melt down 1 1/2 pounds white chocolate with 1/2 gallon of gelato mix. Set mixture aside to cool down for 30 minutes.

Pour gelato mix, vanilla extract, white chocolate-gelato mix mixture into batch freezer. Turn on both dasher and refrigeration and begin batch. Halfway through the batch, add half of the macadamia nuts. End of the batch, add the rest of the macadamia nuts and white chocolate chunks. When the batch is complete, turn off the refrigeration and extrude out the finished product.

Decorate top of tubs with white chocolate chunks and macadamia nuts.

Batch Time: 8-10 minutes

MELONE GELATO
(Melon)

When you take one lick of this Melon gelato you will feel like you are eating the real thing.

Ingredients:

2 1/2 gallons	5-10% gelato mix
32 ounces	Melon flavor
2 pounds	Cantaloupe pieces
1/2 pound	Sugar

Preparation:

Combine 1/2 pound sugar with the cantaloupe pieces and marinate this mixture for 8 hours. Pour all ingredients except the cantaloupe pieces into batch freezer. Turn on dasher and refrigeration and begin batch. When the batch is almost complete, turn off the refrigeration and pour in cantaloupe pieces and then begin extruding the finished product.

Decorate the top of the gelato pans or tubs with cantaloupe pieces.

Batch time: 8-10 minutes

NOCCIOLA GELATO
(Hazelnut)

There is no gelato flavor that is more traditional than Nocciola. In any retail gelato operation, it will probably become one of the best sellers offered. This dense hazelnut flavor has a fabulous sensual feel to it. Everyone I know who has been to Italy at one time or another has always mentioned Nocciola when describing how great the gelato they tasted was.

I highly recommend you offer this flavor to your customers.

Ingredients:

2 1/2 gallons	5-10% gelato mix
2 ounces	Two-fold pure vanilla extract
32 ounces	Nocciola paste
1 1/2 pounds	Hazelnut (chopped) pieces

Preparation:

Pour the gelato mix, vanilla extract, Nocciola paste, and 1/2 pound of the chopped hazelnut pieces into the batch freezer. Turn on dasher and refrigeration and begin batch. Just before the batch is complete, pour in the remaining hazelnut pieces. Turn off the refrigeration and begin extruding the finished product chunks.

Batch Time: 8-10 minutes

VARIATIONS

RUM & HAZELNUT GELATO: Can't get any more unusual than the following recipe. The hazelnut flavor is greatly reduced to allow the rum flavor to come out. Reduce hazelnut paste to 20 ounces, add 16 ounces of dark rum at the end of the batch, and then extrude out the finished product.

WHITE CHOCOLATE HAZELNUT GELATO: The combination of hazelnut and white chocolate works real well together. A dense smooth flavor that your customers will have no problem getting used to. At the beginning of the batch, reduce hazelnut paste to 18 ounces. At the end of the batch, add 1 1/2 pounds of soft white chocolate chunks and 1/2 pound of roasted chopped hazelnut pieces.

WHITE CHOCOLATE CHUNK GIANDUJA GELATO: Substitute 32 ounces of Gianduja paste for the hazelnut paste and add 1 pound of soft white chocolate chunks at the end of the batch.

MALAGA GELATO
(Rum Raisin)
Very similar to the flavor of Rum Raisin ice cream. The major difference is the intensity of the rum flavor when produced on a low overrun batch freezer.

Ingredients:

2 1/2 gallons	5-10% gelato mix
18 ounces	Malaga flavor
1/2 pound	Golden raisins

Preparation:
Pour all ingredients except the raisins into the batch freezer. Turn on dasher and refrigeration and begin batch. Just before the batch is complete, pour in the raisins, turn off the refrigeration and begin extruding the finished product. Decorate the top of the gelato pans or tubs with raisins.
Batch time: 8-10 minutes

CHOCOLATE APRICOT CHIP GELATO
(Cioccolato Albicocca)
Can't get any more creative than this creamy and delightful flavor.

Ingredients:

2 1/2 gallons	5 or 10% gelato mix
2 ounces	Two fold vanilla extract
1 1/2 pounds	Cocoa 22-24%
1/3 pound	Sugar
32 ounces	Hot water
1 pound	Dried apricots
1/4 pound	Sugar
1 pound	Mixture of soft white and dark chunks

Preparation:
Cut dried apricots into very tiny small pieces. Mix with 1/4 pound sugar and let marinate for 4 hours. Blend thoroughly together dried cocoa and sugar. Pour hot water into this mixture and create a paste (make sure no dried cocoa specks are left). Pour gelato mix, vanilla extract, and cocoa paste into the batch freezer. Turn on dasher. Set timer to 8 minutes, turn on refrigeration and begin batch. Halfway into the batch, add the apricots and chocolate chunks. End of the batch, add the dark rum. When batch is complete, turn off refrigeration and extrude finished product. Decorate top of gelato pans with white and dark chocolate chunks and apricot pieces.
Batch Time: 8-10 minutes

LAURETTA GELATO
(Cherries with Cream)
Lauretta in Italian means cream with cherries. It is the perfect dessert in an Italian restaurant where presentation is the "ultimate."

Ingredients:

2 1/2 gallons	5-10% gelato mix
2 ounces	Two-fold pure vanilla extract
32 ounces	Fabbri's Amarena wild cherries

Preparation:
Pour the gelato mix, vanilla extract and 16 ounces of the Amarena wild cherries into the batch freezer. Turn on dasher and refrigeration and begin batch. Just before the batch is complete, pour in the remaining Amarena wild cherries. Turn off the refrigeration and begin extruding the finished product.
Decorate the top of the gelato pans or tubs with Amarena wild cherries.
Batch time: 8-10 minutes

VARIATION
CHOCOLATE LAURETTA GELATO: A chocolate version of Lauretta gelato that is just luscious. You will love it! Mix together and add to the above recipe before freezing- 1 1/2 pounds of cocoa, 1/2 pound sugar, and 2 pounds of very hot water to create a smooth paste with no dry cocoa visible.

GELATO DI MIRTILLI GELATO
(Blueberry)
The flavor is so fresh that you will want more!

Ingredients:

2 1/2 gallons	5-10% gelato mix
2 ounces	Two-fold vanilla extract
30 ounces	Delipaste Fruitta Blueberry
1 pound	Blueberries (fresh or frozen)
4 ounces	Sugar

Preparation:
Marinate the blueberries with sugar for 8 hours. After the marinating process is over, using a chopping knife, mash up the blueberries. Pour all ingredients into batch freezer. Turn on dasher and refrigeration and begin batch. When the batch is complete, turn off the refrigeration and begin extruding the finished product. Decorate the top of the tubs or pans with fresh or frozen blueberries.
Batch time: 8-10 minutes

GIANDUJA BISCOTTI AMORE GELATO
(Chocolate & Hazelnut with Cookies)
A perfect match. A chocolate and hazelnut flavor side by side with the crunch of a Biscotti cookie.

Ingredients:

2 1/2 gallons	5 or 10% gelato mix
2 ounces	Two-fold vanilla extract
26 ounces	Gianduja paste
1 pound	Chocolate chunks
1/2 pound	Granulated hazelnut pieces
1 pound	Biscotti cookies (small broken pieces)

Preparation:
Pour gelato mix, vanilla extract, and Gianduja paste into the batch freezer. Turn on dasher. Set timer to 8 minutes, turn on refrigeration and begin batch. Halfway into the batch, add the chocolate chunks and hazelnuts. End of the batch, add the small broken up biscotti pieces. When batch is complete, turn off refrigeration and extrude finished product. Decorate top of gelato pans or tubs with chocolate chunks and hazelnut and biscotti pieces.
Batch Time: 8-10 minutes

LEMONGRASS GELATO
Lemongrass is one of the herbs typically used in Thai and Vietnamese cooking, and is sold in most Asian shops. Though it does have the taste of lemon, there is really no substitute for its elusive flavor.

Ingredients:

2 1/2 gallons	5 or 10% gelato mix
2 ounces	Two-fold vanilla extract
18 stalks	Lemongrass
8 ounces	Fresh lemon juice

Preparation:
Cut the lemongrass in half lengthways and bruise it with a rolling pin. Place lemongrass and one quart of the gelato mix in a double boiler and heat the mixture just below the boiling point. Set mixture aside for 15 minutes. Strain the mixture in a sieve and cool the mixture. Pour gelato mix, vanilla extract, lemon juice and lemongrass mixture into batch freezer. Turn on both dasher and refrigeration and begin batch. When the batch is complete, turn off the refrigeration and extrude out the finished product.
Batch Time: 8-10 minutes

PISTACHIO GELATO
(Pistacchio)

We make this flavor at every one of our seminars, mainly because my associate Bill Lambert likes it so much. It is simply luscious and nutty, and the flavor of pistachio really stands out. It does have a green color.

Ingredients:

2 1/2 gallons	5-10% gelato mix
2 ounces	Two-fold pure vanilla extract
32 ounces	Pistachio paste
1 1/2 pounds	Pistachio (chopped) pieces

Preparation:

Pour the gelato mix, vanilla extract, pistachio paste, and 1/2 pound of the chopped pistachio pieces into the batch freezer. Turn on dasher and refrigeration and begin batch. Just before the batch is complete, pour in the remaining pistachio pieces. Turn off the refrigeration and begin extruding the finished product. Decorate top of the gelato pans with pistachio pieces.

Batch time: 8-10 minutes

VARIATION

PISTACHIO CHIP GELATO: Adding chocolate chips or liquid Stracciatella to the pistachio makes for an interesting variation of the pistachio flavor. At the end of the batch, pour in 1 3/4 quarts of Stracciatella liquid chip.

COCONUT GELATO
(Cocco)

Luscious, that's all I can say!

Ingredients:

2 1/2 gallons	5 or 10% gelato mix
2 ounces	Two-fold vanilla extract
32 ounces	Coconut paste
1/4 pound	Shredded coconut

Preparation:

Pour all ingredients except the shredded coconut into the batch freezer. Turn on the dasher and let it run for one minute. Set timer to 8 minutes, turn-on refrigeration and begin batch. When batch is almost complete, pour in the shredded coconut, turn off refrigeration and extrude out the finished product.

Batch Time: 8-10 minutes

STRACCIATELLA GELATO
(Chocolate Chip)

The traditional way of making this Italian Vanilla Chocolate Chip flavor is with the use of a liquid chocolate chip called Stracciatella. It has an excellent flavor profile.

Ingredients:

2 1/2 gallons	5-10% gelato mix
3 ounces	Two-fold pure vanilla extract
1 3/4 quarts	Stracciatella liquid chip

Preparation:

In a double boiler, heat the can Stracciatella liquid chip up to 95 degrees F. Using a spatula, mix thoroughly and then pour out 1 3/4 quarts of the liquid chip into a measuring container.

Pour the gelato mix and vanilla extract, into the batch freezer. Turn on the dasher and refrigeration and begin batch. As the product firms up just prior to its extrusion, start pouring in the liquid Stracciatella. (The liquid chocolate reacts with the semi-frozen gelato by solidifying into very thin strings of chocolate.)

Turn off the refrigeration and begin extruding out the finished product.

Decorate the top of the gelato pans or tubs with a little swirl of the liquid Stracciatella.

Batch time: 8-10 minutes

VARIATIONS

MINT STRACCIATELLA GELATO (MINT CHOCOLATE CHIP): The combination of the mint and the liquid chocolate chip makes this flavor stand out. Pour in 8 ounces of Fabbri mint flavor at the beginning of the batch before freezing.

STRACCIATELLA PISTACHIO GELATO: The subtle smooth taste of the granulated pistachios with chocolate is simply delicious. Add one pound granulated pistachios at the beginning of the batch before freezing.

COOKIES & CRÈME GELATO: This is a great children's gelato flavor. Add two pounds of Oreo cookies (broken) at the end of the batch right before you pour in the Stracciatella liquid chip.

241

MARRON GLACES GELATO
(Chestnut)
What else can we call this but a "Roasted Chestnut Gelato!"

Ingredients:

2 1/2 gallons	5 or 10% gelato mix
2 ounces	Two-fold vanilla extract
33 ounces	Marron Glaces Crème

Preparation:
Pour ice cream mix, vanilla extract, and Marron Glaces Crème into the batch freezer. Turn on dasher and refrigeration and begin batch. When batch is complete, turn off refrigeration and extrude finished product.
Batch Time: 8-10 minutes

VARIATION
CHESTNUT GELATO: A different version of Marron Glace Gelato. This very rich gelato flavor is the perfect winter dessert. Tell your customers to take it home and enjoy this dessert with a snifter of brandy and roasted chestnuts, fresh from the fire. At the end of the batch, add 2 ounces of dry sherry and 1 ounce of brandy rum just before the product is extruded.

ZABAGLIONE w/ STRAWBERRIES GELATO
(Marsala Wine)
The touch of strawberries dispersed into this flavor makes it a wonderful sensual dessert for almost any upscale Italian restaurant to serve.

Ingredients:

2 1/2 gallons	5 or 10% gelato mix
2 ounces	Two-fold vanilla extract
33 ounces	Zabaglione flavor
2 pounds	Sliced strawberries
8 ounces	Sugar

Preparation:
Combine strawberries and sugar and marinate mixture for eight hours. Strain off the juice from this mixture. Pour ice cream mix, vanilla extract, and zabaglione flavor into the batch freezer. Turn on dasher. Set timer to 8 minutes, and then turn on refrigeration and begin batch. When batch is almost complete, pour in the sliced strawberries, turn off refrigeration and extrude finished product. Garnish top of gelato pans or tubs with sliced strawberries.
Batch Time: 8-10 minutes

MANGO BANANA GELATO

By combining mango with banana, you will end up with a very different but fabulous fruit gelato. As a summertime featured flavor, it can't miss being a winner.

Ingredients:

2 1/2 gallons	5-10% gelato mix
2 ounces	Two-fold vanilla extract
15 ounces	Mango paste
6-8 pounds	Bananas (peeled)

Preparation:
Puree the bananas. Pour all ingredients into batch freezer. Turn on dasher and refrigeration and begin batch. When the batch is complete, turn off the refrigeration and begin extruding the finished product.

Decorate the top of the tub or gelato pans with fresh banana and mango slices.

Batch time: 8-10 minutes

MANGO COCONUT GELATO

What a combination!

Ingredients:

2 1/2 gallons	5-10% gelato mix
2 ounces	Two-fold vanilla extract
24 ounces	Delipaste Fruitta Mango (Fabbri)
24 ounces	Coconut fruit base
1/2 pound	Shredded coconut

Preparation:
Pour all ingredients into batch freezer except the shredded coconut. Turn on dasher and refrigeration and begin batch. When the batch is almost complete, pour in the shredded coconut, turn off the refrigeration and begin extruding the finished product.

Decorate the top of the tubs or gelato pans with mango slices and shredded coconut.

Batch time: 8-10 minutes

CHAPTER 15
ICE CREAM CAKES & PIES

If you really want to aggressively pursue growing your business, then having an active ice cream cake business is a must. In many cases, the first choice for a birthday party is an ice cream cake. It's a very special treat, and it's the perfect **TAKE-OUT** dessert. But you must remember one thing, the average consumer has just so much discretionary money to spend for meals, drinks, desserts, etc. You must establish your niche to motivate consumers to spend their "dessert dollars" with you. Ice cream cakes are a good motivator that brings customers into your establishment.

ICE CREAM CAKES

The most popular size ice cream cake for a birthday or anniversary is an eight or nine inch round that serves 8 to 12 people. During graduation times, sheet cakes, either full or half, sell very well. When it comes to Valentine's Day, there is nothing better than a Chocolate Heart ice cream cake. Clearly, two holidays-Mother's Day and Father's Day are huge days for cake sales with a three day sales span from Friday and climaxing on Sunday. On average the price of an eight inch round (hard ice cream) goes for about $14.50-$20.00. Average price for an eight inch round (soft ice cream) goes for about $12.95-$14.95, costing approximately $3.00 to produce (including packaging).

PRICING AN ICE CREAM CAKE

On average, if you use a 3.5 factor times cost, you will have a very fair mark-up. The cost used in the 3.5 times factor includes product, packaging and labor. Product cost includes the ice cream, bakery base, decorating materials such as flowers, whipped cream etc. Material costs include cake circles, cake

244

boxes etc. Labor includes the time taken to prepare, manufacture, empty cake molds, decorate and box the cakes. Below is an example of what an ice cream cake really costs you and how the 3.5 factor cost figures into your selling price of an ice cream cake.

Eight Inch Round Hard Ice Cream Cake

Ice cream mix- $6.50 per gallon	
39 ounces, 4.5 cents per ounce, ice cream mix	1.76 per cake
Crunch- .12 per ounce	
5 ounces per cake, cake crunch	.60
Manufacturing Cost-	.33
Labor-	.17
Decorating-	.67
Misc.-	.20
Cake Box-	.45
Circle-	.05
Total	$4.23 per cake

Total Cost- $4.23 x 3.5 cost factor- Selling Price- $14.80

- *Mfg. Cost*- 3 batches per hour, 2 employees, 60 cakes per hour ($20 per hour) equals 33 cents per cake.
- *Preparation*- Includes cake mold cleaning, sanitizing, removal of cake from mold, putting on circles, etc., 60 cakes per hour, $10 per hour, 1 employee.
- *Decorating*- varies from 15 to 30 cakes per hour depending on size of cake. Includes time for boxing, icing, whipped cream for trim, 1 employee, $10 per hour.
- *Misc.*- Includes flowers, leaves, etc and labels on box.

MAKING SURE THE CAKE IS SERVED WELL

Make sure every cake customer is given information about how to serve and store the ice cream cake. This is very important, because everyone in general has problems cutting an ice cream cake, mainly because no one takes the time at home to temper it properly before serving it. The card emphasizes what must be done to serve it well. Using your batch freezer or soft serve machine, you are in a perfect position to produce a lot of cakes at any given time. What this means is that you can produce them in quantity and store them for an instant sale by a customer at any time.

Our book, **ICE CREAM CAKES** really explains how to make an ice cream cake (and I highly recommend you getting this book). Reading the book will inspire you to be creative. The book has many recipes for ice cream cakes and pies, with specific instructions on how to decorate cakes and what other ingredients you need to get to be really successful in this business.

So let's get started. **RIGHT NOW!**

THE BASIC BIRTHDAY CAKE

This cake should be a main "staple" in your display case and you should keep a backstock available at all times, but "price" the cake to sell. If Stan Somekh, of our 1st Ice Cream Seminar can make an ice cream cake, so can you!

Ingredients:

1	8" Chocolate or white cake layer, frozen (3/4" to 1" high/approx.-6.5 oz.)
4-6 ounces	Chocolate fudge, caramel topping, or variegate of your choice (optional)
25 ounces	Ice cream of your choice
9 ounces	Non-dairy whipped topping, divided

Preparation:

Place cake layer in bottom of 8" cake pan. If desired, spread chocolate fudge or other topping evenly over cake using small offset spatula. Pour ice cream into pan. Spread ice cream into an even layer, making sure you eliminate any air pockets. Smooth surface with offset spatula. Freeze cake approximately 8 hours. Remove cake from pan. Place a small spoonful of non-dairy topping in center of 10" round cake board. Place cake on board. Crumb coat sides of cake, if necessary. Freeze cake briefly to set ice cream. Frost cake with 6 oz. non-dairy whipped topping. If time permits, freeze cake briefly before decorating to allow frosting to set. Put 3 oz. non-dairy topping into a pastry bag. Using tip #2-E, pipe a reverse shell border around top edge of cake and a regular shell border around base of cake. Decorate the cake as desired.

Makes (1) 8" cake- Approx. 45 oz.-Serves 10

OREO BOMB ICE CREAM CAKE

The original idea for this cake came from Longford's Ice Cream* of Port Chester, NY. Our version is slightly different from theirs, but both are terrific sellers.

Remember, if your cake does not look terrific, it won't matter how wonderful it tastes. First impressions are extremely important and it will become the difference in making that first sale or not.

If you like Oreo ice cream you'll love this eight-inch cake. This cake is simply all ice cream.

Ingredients:

25 ounces	Oreo ice cream
9 ounces	Non-dairy whipped topping
1 ounce	Oreo dry crumbs (Nabisco)
12	Oreo cookies

Preparation:

After ice cream comes out of the batch freezer, pour Oreo ice cream into a 9" cake pan.

After the cake pan is filled up, using an offset spatula, smooth surface of the ice cream into a flat even layer. Cover with wax paper and blast freeze the cake for 6-8 hours.

Remove cake from pan. Place a spoonful of non-dairy topping in center of a 9" cake board. Freeze briefly to set the ice cream on the board. Coat sides of the cake with Oreo cookie crumbs. Spread non-dairy whipped topping on surface of cake. At this point, you can keep the top surface of the cake clean or you can create a rosette (13) pattern (tip 2-E). Next, place the 12 Oreo cookies all the way around the top of the cake, and slightly sprinkle Oreo crumbs on top of the rosettes.

Makes (1) 8" cake- Approximately 48 oz.- Serves 6-8

247

VALENTINE'S DAY CHOCOLATE HEART

This heart shaped ice cream cake looks and tastes just great. Be creative and give this cake a try. After all, Valentine's Day is one special day, isn't it!

Ingredients:

1 nine inch	Round Sponge cake
2 1/4 pounds	Chocolate ice cream
3/4 cup	Belgian dark chocolate or bar coating
8 ounces	Dark chocolate bar- to make chocolate leaves

Preparing the Chocolate Leaves

Take a few bay leaves. Disinfect them by soaking for 5 minutes in 1/1000 solution of cold water, then another 5 minutes in a 1/100 solution of white vinegar and cold water. Drain and wipe dry. Using a brush, spread a thin layer of chocolate over the surface of the leaf. Leave to crystallize, then un-stick.

Preparation:

Using a heart shaped cake pan, cut out a heart with the sponge cake. Place the cut-out sponge cake inside the heart pan. Pour the ice cream into the pan. Freeze filled pan for 6 hours. Remove cake from freezer and place it on top of wire rack.

Place a pan beneath wire rack. Melt down 3/4 cup of Belgian dark chocolate and ladle it into a measuring cup. Set aside to cool to 70 degrees F. Slowly pour Belgian chocolate on cake. When cake is covered with chocolate, return the cake to freezer to harden. Before chocolate hardens, place chocolate leaves on top of the cake. Place the cake in the freezer to harden.

Makes (1) 8" cake- Approximately 48 ounces- Serves 6-8

CHOCOLATE CHIP ROLL CAKE

This recipe will make the following: 3 roll cakes, each 8" long, 2 roll cakes, 12" long, or 1 very long 24" cake for that special holiday or birthday celebration.

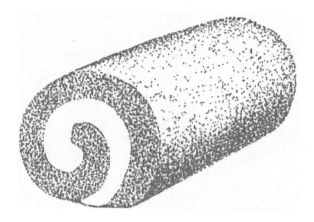

Ingredients:

1 full sheet	Chocolate layer cake, approx. 1/2" thick
96 ounces	Vanilla Chip Ice Cream
2 quarts	Fudge
18 ounces	Chocolate non-dairy whipped topping
12 ounces	Chocolate chips or chunks

Preparation:

Place the chocolate cake on a bakers tray with the waxed paper side of the cake on the bottom of the tray. Using an offset spatula, spread 3 quarts of ice cream evenly throughout the sheet cake (like buttering a piece of bread). Allow 3/4" space exposed at either end of the sheet cake. Standing in front of the pan, use your fingers to lift cake up and forward towards you, slowly peeling the loose wax paper from the cake until you have reached a form of a "C." Using very gentle pressure, keep peeling the wax paper away from the cake. Roll the cake towards you until you have reached the shape of a cylinder. Place roll cake securely down on the pan with the seam side down. Cover the cylinder with wax paper and freeze the roll cake for eight hours or overnight.

Remove wax paper from the roll cake. Using a knife, cut a thin slice off each end of the cake (approx. 1/3"). Next, cut the cake either in half or thirds. Spread a 1" wide strip of fudge down the length of a 6 x 9 inch cake board and secure the seam side of the cake to the fudge. Place the cake on a turntable. Spread the entire top of the roll cake with fudge. Pour chocolate chunks over the fudge, pressing slightly into the fudge. Fill pastry bag with non-dairy chocolate whipped creme topping and using tip #4SR, pipe shells all around the base of the cake.

TARTUFO

An Italian chocolate covered frozen dessert served at most Italian restaurants. Each is the size of a large ice cream ball (4 ounces) with an Italian Amarena cherry placed in the bottom of the ball. The ice cream can be either Vanilla, Vanilla and Chocolate combination, or Gianduja. Once you get the technique down pat, they are a cinch to make. For anyone in the wholesale ice cream business selling to restaurants, this dessert is a great revenue source for you. Package them 36 to a box. You can sell them for about $1.25-1.50 each.

Ingredients- To Make One Tartufo

6 ounces	Ice cream
1	Italian Amarena Cherry*
	Chocolate bar coating

Note: Amarena Cherries by Fabbri can be purchased through De Choix Specialty Foods. Call 800-332-4649.

Preparation:

Place sheet of aluminum foil on bakers tray. Take a tub of ice cream out of the freezer, tempered so you can scoop out balls. Using a No. 10 ice cream scoop, scoop out a ball of ice cream, turn scoop upside down and place one Amarena cherry inside the ball. Release the scoop onto the tray. Fill up the tray (24 balls, 8 to a line, 3 rows.) Place the tray back into the blast freezer for at least 6 hours.

Heat up chocolate bar coating to 95 degrees F. Pour bar coating into a large bowl (5-6 inches deep), large enough to enable fork to be placed into the bowl.

Remove the ice cream balls from the blast freezer. Place ball on fork, then dip it into the chocolate until completely covered. Remove ball from the bowl and place ball on bakers tray. Before placing balls back inside the blast freezer, dip the fork into the chocolate and then wave the fork over the balls to give them a decorative chocolate look.

Keep the balls inside the blast freezer for at least one hour. Remove from the blast freezer, pack each one individually with senior wax deli paper, and place the Tartufos back inside a box (36 to a box).

ICE CREAM PIES

The perfect take-out dessert for any ice cream store operation that <u>does not</u> <u>make its own ice cream</u>. Using your soft serve machine, it's an easy procedure that can only bring you success and revenue.

The Crust:
Pies are usually about 8" or 9" in diameter. Frozen ready-to-fill pie crusts can be purchased in graham cracker, chocolate and even vanilla crumb. These pre-made pie crusts give you the opportunity to make pies very quickly, especially from ice cream freshly produced from your soft serve machine.

The Filling:
Almost any ice cream, frozen yogurt, or sorbet you produce in your shop will make an excellent pie filling. Just look at these combos:

- Frozen yogurt can team up with a "healthier" pie crust like granola or oatmeal cookie crumb.

- Sorbets can be swirled with creamy vanilla ice cream or frozen yogurt for a refreshing pie. Try decorating this combination with slices of glazed fruit, whipped topping and nuts.

Just how much soft serve ice cream does it take to fill a pie? This depends on the size of the pie crust, and how big and mounded you want the pie to be. Big, bountiful ice cream pies are the restaurant craze now and can really attract a lot of attention. Of course, the bigger the pie, the more expensive it will be to produce.

Recommended Filling Weights
8" or 9" Pie Crusts
24 ounces for a slightly mounded pie
32 ounces for a medium-size pie
36-40 ounces for a large domed pie

If you plan on layering a topping (example: fudge) or mixing in cookies or another ingredient into the filling, subtract that weight from the total ice cream weight.

The Decoration:
Now is the time to get creative and have some fun. There are many delicious ways to finish a pie. Most pies call for a border of whipped topping, but a "zigzag" border of fudge looks luscious and tastes wonderful, too! Try using chocolate non-dairy whipped topping for a change of pace. Or, cover the entire pie with a "meringue" of fluffy white whipped topping swirls, garnished with drizzles of chocolate, caramel, or nuts. Don't be afraid to experiment and try new ideas.

Tips of the Trade:

- If the ice cream filling is appetizing and colorful, don't cover it up completely. Be sure to show it off in your finished dessert.
- Use garnishes that relate to the flavor of the ice cream or crust. (Example: Cookies' N Cream ice cream garnished with chocolate cookie crumbs or whole chocolate creme-filled Oreo cookies.
- Give your finished pie fun names to make them more exciting! ("Hot Fudge Sundae Splurge" or "Peanut Butter Passion.")
- Make special holiday pies by featuring flavors that are popular that time of year. Decorate them lavishly with the spirit of the season.
- Try decorating a pie with colored sprinkles or edible confetti candies. These pies look particularly festive and appeal to children.
- Use 1, 2, and even 3 different flavors of ice cream in a pie. Different flavors can be swirled together or layered. If layering, let each flavor freeze before adding the next one.
- Keep a variety of pies in stock. If you sell them competitively priced and usually below that of a cake, you will sell pies all year 'round, and not have to wait for a "holiday occasion."
- If you plan on layering a topping (example: fudge) or mixing in cookies or another ingredient into the filling, subtract that weight from the total ice cream weight.

BASIC ICE CREAM PIE FORMULA

Below is a very good example of what you can do decorating a simple ice cream pie. Use your imagination, and create to your heart's content.

Ingredients:

1	9" Pie crust, frozen (approx. 6 ounces)
24 ounces	Ice cream
4 ounces	Non-dairy whipped topping
1-2 ounces	Decoration (drizzles, nuts, chocolate shavings, etc.)

Preparation:

Weigh ice cream filling. Using a white rubber spatula, carefully mound ice cream into pie crust, mounding most of the filling in the center.

Place pie on a turntable. Using a small offset spatula, spread ice cream into crust, making sure there are no air pockets. Form ice cream into a slightly mounded dome shape, with highest point in center of pie, and filling sloped downwards to edges of crust. Top edges of crust should be visible. Smooth surface with offset spatula, making sure the dome shape is uniform all around the pie. Freeze pie until firm, several hours or overnight.

Place frozen pie on a turntable. Using an 18" pastry bag and large star tip, make rosettes around edge of pie with whipped topping.

Garnish pie as desired.

Makes (1) 9" pie - Approximately 36 ounces - Serves 8

MISSISSIPPI MUD PIE

A Mississippi Mud Pie (that is really a cake) is a simply rich, stylish ice cream cake bursting with flavor.

Ingredients:

8 ounces	Basic Cookie Crumb Crust
	6.5 oz. Chocolate cookie crumbs-(Oreo or Hydrox)
	1.5 oz. margarine
10 ounces	Chocolate fudge, divided
4 ounces	Graham crackers (crumbled)
13 ounces	Chocolate ice cream
13 ounces	Coffee ice cream
1/2 ounce	Chocolate cookie crumbs (dry), for side crumb

Preparation:

Melt margarine. Blend chocolate cookie crumbs with margarine until thoroughly combined. Press crumb mixture evenly into bottom of 9" cake pan. Freeze crust briefly to harden crumb. Spread 5 ounces chocolate fudge on top of crust in an even layer. Pour Coffee ice cream into pan on top of fudge layer. Using offset spatula, smooth surface of ice cream into a flat even layer. Freeze cake until filling is frozen solid. Spread 5 oz. chocolate fudge over the Coffee ice cream on surface of cake. Next place crumbled graham crackers on top of the fudge. Freeze at least 1/2 hour, or until topping has hardened slightly.

Pour Chocolate ice cream over the fudge layer. Freeze cake approximately 1 hour, and then spread chocolate fudge over the top surface of the cake. Freeze ice cream 4-6 hours or overnight. Remove cake from pan and immediately coat sides of cake with chocolate cookie crumbs.

Makes (1) 9" cake - Approximately 50 ounces- Serves 12

APPENDIX

SOURCES OF SUPPLIES AND INFORMATION

SUPPLIERS

Equipment

Continuous Freezing and Filling Equipment

APV Ice Cream
9525 W. Bryn Mawr Ave.
Rosemont, IL 60018
888-278-9087
Continuous freezing equipment

Autoprod
5355 115th Ave North
Clearwater, FL 34620
813-572-7753
Ice cream filling equipment

Cherry-Burrell/Waukesha
611 Sugar Creek Road
Delavan, WI 53115
414-728-1900
Continuous freezing equipment

Frigomat
Via 1 Maggio
20070 Guardamiglio (MI)
Milan, Italy
0377-451170
Gelato pasteurizing equipment

Gram Equipment of America
1212 N. 39th St., Suite 438
Tampa, FL 33605
813-248-1978
Ice cream continuous freezing and filling equipment

Northfield Freezing Systems
719 Cannon Road
Norhtfield, MN 55057
507-645-9546
Ice cream freezing systems

Promag, Via Romagna 12
20098 S. Giulano Milanese
Milan, Italy
02-98296-1
Gelato continuous freezing equipment

Processing Machinery & Supply
WCB Waulkesa- Cherry Burrell
625 State Street
New Lisbon, WI 53950
800-252-5200
New & re-conditioned ice cream continuous freezing equipment

Separators, Inc.
747 East Sumner Avenue
Indianapolis, IN 46227
800-233-9022
Separators

Silverson Machines
PO Box 589
East Longmeadow, MA 01028
413-525-4825
Batch and shear mixers

Tetra Laval Food (Hoyer)
753 Geneva Parkway
Lake Geneva, WI
262-249-7410
  Ice cream continuous freezing
  and filling equipment

Tindall Packaging
1150 East U Street
Vicksburg, MI 49097
616-649-1163
  Ice cream filling and packaging
  equipment

Walker Stainless Equipment Company
625 State Street
New Lisbon, WI 53950
608-562-3151
  Processing tanks

T.D. Sawvel Co. Inc.
5775 Highway 12
Maple Plan, MN 55359
612-479-4322
  Ice cream filling equipment

Tri-Clover, Inc.
9201 Wilmont Road
Kenosha, WI 53141
262-694-5511
  Batch mixers

Batch Freezing Equipment
Carpigiani
Via Emilia 45
Anzola Emilia
Bologna, Italy
051-6505111
  Gelato batch freezers and soft
  serve equipment

Sunrise Refrigeration
3040 Simmons St #103
North Las Vegas, NV 89109
702-796-1600
  Cattibriga Italian Gelato batch
  freezers, display showcases

Electro-Freeze
2116 8th Ave.
East Moline, IL 61244
800-755-4545
  Soft-serve freezers, batch
  freezers, blend-in machines

Emery Thompson Company
15350 Flight Path Road
Brooksville, FL 34604
718-588-7300
  Batch freezers

Ross's Manufacturing
3707-19th Ave.
Escanaba, MI 49829
906-786-4894
  Frozen custard machines

Taylor Company
88 Executive Avenue
Edison, New Jersey 08817
732-225-4620
  Soft-serve freezers, batch
  freezers, frozen drink machines

Refrigeration
Beverage Air
P.O. Box 5932
Spartansburg, South Carolina 29304
800-845-9800
  Refrigerators and freezers

Big Apple Equipment Company
Industrial Park
PO Box 408
Yonkers, New York 10705
914-376-9300
  Refrigeration distributors for
  Master-Bilt & Beverage Air

Delfield
PO Box 470
Mt. Pleasant, MI 48804
517-773-7981
  Refrigeration and freezing
  equipment

Detecto
PO Box 151
Webb City, MO 64870
800-641--2008
　Portion control scales

Excellence Commercial Products
PO Box 770127
Coral Springs, FL 33077
800-441-4014
　Freezer dipping cabinets and
　merchandising equipment

Fun Food Depot
2910 N.W. Commerce Park Drive
Boynton Beach, FL 33426
561-533-0001
　All kinds of refrigeration
　equipment

Hussmann Corporation
Convenience and Specialty Store
Group
Gloversville, New York 12078
518-725-0644
　Dipping cabinets

Glabo Group - Oscartielle
33300 Central Ave.
Union City, CA 94587
800-672-2784
　Orion Gelato dipping cabinets

Kelvinator Commercial Products
707 Robins St.
Conway, AR 72032
501-327-8945
　Dipping cabinets, storage
　refrigerators and freezers, ice
　cream cake display cases

Silver King Company
1600 Xenium Lane North
Minneapolis Industrial Park
Minneapolis, Minnesota 55441
763-553-1881
　Refrigerators and freezers

McCray Refrigerator
Grant Avenue and Blue Grass Road
Philadelphia, Pennsylvania 19114
215-464-6800
　Dipping cabinets, storage
　refrigerators and freezers

Master-Bilt
Highway 15N
New Albany, Mississippi 38652
800-647-1284
　Dipping cabinets, storage freezers
　and refrigerators, ice cream cake
　display cases

C. Nelson Manufacturing Co.
265 No. Lake Winds Parkway
Oak Harbor, Ohio 43449
800-922-7331
　Ice cream storage chests and
　hardening chests

Trucks & Mobile Vending Carts
All Star Carts
1565D Fifth Industrial Court
Bayshore, New York 11706
631-666-5252
　Mobile vending carts

Custom Sales and Service
11th Street and Second Road
Hammonton, New Jersey 08037
609-561-6900
　Ice cream vans

David Cummings USA, Inc.
PMB #204, 2332 Fortune Road
Kissimmee, FL 34744
407-30-4435
　Ice cream vending trucks

Hackney Brothers Inc.
P.O. Box 2728
Wilson, North Carolina 27894-2728
919-237-8171
　Mobile carts

257

Johnson Truck Bodies
215 E. Allen Street
Rice Lake, WI 54868
800-922-8360
   Refrigerated and freezer truck
   bodies

Workman Trading Corporation
94-15 100th St.
Ozone Park, NY 11416
718-322-2000
   Mobile vending carts

Sanitation Equipment & Supplies
Haynes Manufacturing Company
24142 Detroit Rd.
Westlake, OH 44145
800-992-2166
   Food grade lubricants

McGlaughlin Oil Company
3750 East Livingston Avenue
Columbus, Ohio 43277
614-231-2518
   Lubricating oil (Petro Gel) for
   processing equipment

Nelson-Jameson
2400 E. 5th St.
Marshfield, WI 54449
800-826-8302
   Sanitation and lab supplies

Purdy Products
379 Hollow Hill Drive
Wauconda, IL 60084
800-726-4849
   Sanitation supplies

Refrigiwear, Inc.
Breakstone Drive
PO Box 39
Dahlonega, Georgia 30533
706-864-5457
   Refrigerator and freezer plant
   clothing

Weber Scientific
2732 Kuser Road
Hamilton, NJ 08691
800-328-8378
   Lab equipment and supplies

Misc. Equipment
American Soda Fountain
455 N. Oakley Blvd.
Chicago, IL 60612
312-733-5000
   Old fashioned ice cream equipment

Blendec
1206 S. 1680 W
Orem, Utah 84058
800-253-6383
   Smoothie blenders

The Buddy System
3495 Winton Place
#290, Rochester, NY 14623
888--280-7031
   Cone dispensers and holders

CRC
3218 Nebraska Ave.
Council Bluffs, Iowa 51501
712-323-9477
   Mix-in shake machines

Cal-Mil Plastic Products
4079 Calle Platino
Oceanside, Ca 92056
760-630-5100
   Cone holders

Diamond Brands
1660 South Highway 100, Suite 590
Minneapolis, MN 55416
612-541-1500
   Ice cream novelty sticks

Flavor Burst Company
499 Commerce Drive
Danville, IN 46122, 800-264-3528
   Soft serve machine flavor injector

Frozen Dessert Machine Cleaning
PO Box 554, Jericho, NY 11753
516-731-8617
  Soft serve cleaning maintenance

Echo Industries
61 R.W. Moore Ave.
Orange, MA 01364
978-544-7000
  Metal cans

Geltecnica Machine
Salita Al Molinello, 32
Rapallo, Italy
0185-230339
  Italian novelty bar machines

Gruenwald Mfg. Co., Inc
100 Ferncroft Rd.
Danvers, MA 01923
800-229-9447
  Whipped cream machines

Hamilton Beach Commercial
4421 Waterfront Drive
Glen Allen, VA 23060
800-572-3331
  Milk shake blenders and scoops

Innovative Marketing
9909 South Shore Drive
Plymouth, MN 55441
612-525-8686
  Five gallon pail opener

ISI North America, Inc.
30 Chapin Rd.
Pine Brook, NJ 07058
973-227-2426
  Whip Cream Dispensers

Lloyd Disher Company
5 Powers Lane Place
Decatur, IL 62522
217-423-2611
  Ice cream scoops

Negus Container Company
110 North Bedford Street
Madison, Wisconsin 53703
608-251-2533
  Plastic containers

Novelty Baskets
1132 Heather Lane
Carrillton, TX 75007
972-492-4738
  Wire trays to hold novelties

Pelouze Scale Company
7560 W. 100th Place
Bridgeview, IL 60455
800-654-8330
  Weight scales

Ropak Corporation
20024 87th Avenue South
Kent, Washington 98031
800-426-9040
  Plastic containers

Server Products
P.O. Box 249
Menomonee Falls, Wisconsin 53051
800-558-8722
  Hot fudge machines

Solon Manufacturing Company
PO Box 285
Solon, ME 04979
207-643-2210
  Ice cream novelty sticks

Swirl Freeze Corporation
2474 Directors Row
Salt Lake City, UT 84104
801-972-0109
  Blend-in machines

T.J.'s Racks
1141 W. Swain Road, #132
Stockton, CA 95207
800-532-3917
  Ice cream can collars

The Zeroll Company
PO Box 999
Fort Pierce, FL 34954
800-872-5000
 Ice cream scoops

Flavoring Ingredients
Chocolates
ADM Cocoa
12500 W. Carmen Ave.
Milwaukee, Wisconsin 53225
800-558-9958
 Cocoa, chocolate chips, & coatings,

Barry Callebaut
1500 Suckle Highway
Pennsauken, NJ
800-836-2626
 Cocoa and chocolates bar coatings

Forbes Chocolate
PO Box 214
Terrace Park, OH 451-74-0214
513-576-6660
 Cocoa and chocolate chips

Gertrude Hawk Chocolates
5117 Pine Top Place
Orlando, FL 32819
407-876-8673
 Chocolate inclusions for ice cream

Guittard
10 Guittard Road
Burlingham CA 94010
800-468-2462
 Cocoa and chocolate chunks

Henry & Henry, Inc.
3765 Walden Ave.
Lancaster, NY 14986
800-828-7130
 Fudge toppings and variegates

The Masterson Company
P.O. Box 691
Milwaukee, Wisconsin 53201
414-647-1132
 Cocoa, fudges, chocolate chips, etc.

Kalva Corporation
3940 Porett Drive
Gurnee, IL 60031
800-525-8220
 Ice cream cone dip coatings

W.L.W. Bensdorp Co.
1800 Westpark Drive #305
Westborough, MA 01581
508-366-9910
 Cocoa

Fruit (Processed)
Bunge Foods
885 No. Kinzie Ave.
Bradley, IL 60915
800-828-0800
 Ice cream flavor ingredients

Chiquita Brands
250 East Fifth Street
Cincinnati, OH 45202
800-438-0015
 Banana ingredients and shapes

Coco Lopez
180 E. Broad Street
Columbus, OH 43215
800-341-2242
 Coconut cream

Extreme Smoothies
963 Worcester Road
Framingham, MA 01701
508-435-9058
 Sells smoothies pucks & equipment

Fantasy Flavors/Blanke Bear, Inc.
611 N. 10th Street
St. Louis, MO 63101, 800-886-3476
 Ice cream production ingredients

Flavor Chem Corp.
1525 Brook Drive
Downers Grove, IL 60139
630-355-3013
Flavor extracts

Lyons-Magnus
1636 South Second Street
Fresno, CA 93702
800-344-7130
Ice cream flavor ingredients

Limpert Brothers, Inc.
P.O. Box 520
Vineland, New Jersey 08360
800-691-1353
Ice cream production ingredients etc.

Milne Fruit Products
PO Box 111
Prosser, WA 99350
509-786-2611
Fruit purees

Ramsey/Sias
6850 Southpointe Parkway
Brecksville, OH 44141
800-477-3788
Fruit preps and purees

I. Rice & Company
11500 D. Roosevelt Blvd.
Philadelphia, PA 19116
800-232-6022
Ice cream & Italian ice flavorings

SBI Systems
8 Neshaminy Interplex, Suite 213
Trevose, PA 19053
215-638-7801
Ice cream flavorings and purees

Star Kay White
85 Brenner Drive
Congers, NY 10920
914-268-2600
Ice cream bases, fruits, nuts, etc.

Fruit (Frozen)
Clermont Fruit Packers
503-648-8544
Fruit purees

Global Trading Company
PO Box 26809
Greenville, SC 29616
800-849-9990
Fruits from all over USA and Mexico

ITI Inc.
3371 Route 1
Lawrenceville, NJ 08648
609-987-0550
Fruit ingredients

Oregon Cherry Growers
PO Box 7357
Salem, OR 97303
800-367-2536
Cherries, various kinds and sizes

Prima Foods International
1604 Esex Avenue
Deland, FL 32724
904-736-9138
Fruit purees

Ravifruit- French Food Exports
100 Manhattan Ave.
Union City, NJ 07087
201-867-2151
Fruit purees from France

Wawona Frozen Fruit
100 W. Alluvial, Clovis, CA 93612
209-299-2901
Frozen fruits

Nuts
Ace Pecan Company
900 Morse Village
Elk Grove Village, Illinois 60007
312-364-3250
Nuts

Boyer Brothers, Inc.
821 17th Street
Altoona, Pennsylvania 16603
814-944-9401
   Peanut butter pastes and variegates

Peanut Corporation of America
P.O. Box 10037
Lynchburg, Virginia 24506
800-446-0998
   Peanuts: all sizes and varieties

Pecan Deluxe Candy Company
2570 Lone Star Drive
Dallas, Texas 75212
214-631-3669
   Candy-coated nuts

Superior Nut Company
225 Monsignor O'Brien Highway
Cambridge, MA 02141
800-966-7688
   Peanut butter variegate

Tracy-Luckey
110 N. Hicks Street
Harlem, Georgia 30814
800-476-4796
   Pecan nuts

SNA Nut Company
1348-54 West Grand Ave
Chicago, IL 60622
800-544-NUTS
   Pecan nuts

Young Pecan Shelling Company
1200 Pecan Street
Florence, SC 29501
800-829-6864
   Pecan nuts

Westcott Nut Products
93-97 Colt St.
Irvington, NJ 07111
201-373-1866
   Variety of nuts

Flavor Extracts
Beck Flavors
411 E. Gano
St. Louis, MO 63147
800-851-8100
   Flavor extracts and vanilla

David Michael & Company
10801 Decatur Road
Philadelphia, Pennsylvania 19154
215-632-3100
   Extracts and fruit flavors

Edgar A. Weber & Company
549 Palwaukee Drive
Whelling, IL 60090
800-558-9078
   Vanilla and coffee flavor ingredients

Lochhead Vanillas
3100 Gravois Ave.
St Louis, MO 63118
888-776-2088
   Natural vanilla extracts

Nielsen-Massey Vanillas
1550 Shields Drive
Waukegan, IL 60085
800-525-7873
   Natural vanilla extracts

OSF
PO Box 591
Windsor, CT 06095
800-466-6015
   Fruit flavor extracts

Virginia Dare Extract Company, Inc.
882 Third Avenue
Brooklyn, New York 11232
800-847-4500
   Extracts and flavors

Overall Flavor Ingredient Companies

Carmi Flavor & Fragrance Company
6030 Scott Way
Commerce, CA 90040
323--888-9240
Flavor extracts

CTL
514 Main Street
P.O. Box 526
Colfax, Wisconsin 54730
800-962-5227
Malt powder, serving merchandisers

Guernsey-Bell, Inc.
4300 South Morgan Street
Chicago, Illinois 60609
800-621--0271
Fruits, coated nuts, fudges, etc.

Hershey Foodservice
14 East Chocolate Street
Hershey, Pennsylvania 17033
717-534-6397
Chocolate candies for ice cream production and toppings

Instantwhip Foods
2200 Cardigan Ave.
Columbus, OH 43215
800-544-9447
Whip cream and toppings

Kraus & Company/Battle Creek
Flavors
32140 Old Farm Lane
Walled Lake, MI 48237
800-662-5871
Ice cream ingredient flavorings

Precision Foods
11457 Olde Cabin Road
St. Louis, MO 63141
800-442-5242
Distributes ice cream production ingredients

Leaf Inc.
500 N. Field Drive
Lake Forest, IL 60045
708-735-7500
Candy ingredients

M&M/Mars
Division of Mars, Incorporated
High Street
Hackettstown, New Jersey 07840
908-852-1000
Candies

Nabisco Brands, Inc.
7 Campus Drive
Parsippany, NJ 07054
800-828-0398
Oreo cookies & candy ingredients for ice cream production

Nestle Foodservice
800 N. Bland Blvd.
Glendale, CA 91203
800-288-8682
Candy ingredients and toppings for ice cream production

Oringer
10 Minuteman Way
Brockton, MA 02301
508-580-1700
Ice cream production ingredients

A. Panza & Sons, Ltd.
60 Parkway Place
Raritan Center
Edison, New Jersey 08837
800-ICE CREAM
Distributor of ice cream production, cake and serving ingredients

Parker Brothers
2737 Tillar Street
P.O. Box 9335
Fort Worth, Texas 76107
817-336-7441
Ice cream ingredients

The Perfect Puree
975 Vintage Avenue, Suite B
St. Helena, CA 94574
800-556-3707
  Fruit purees

Sethness-Greenleaf
1826 North Lorel Avenue
Chicago, Illinois 60639
773-889-1400
  Ice cream fruits, nuts, and extracts

Torani
233 E. Harris Avenue
So. San Francisco, CA 94080
800-775-1925
  Syrups for espresso

Yohay Baking Company
75 Grand Ave.
Brooklyn, NY 11205
800-255-9642
  Cookies for espresso bars

Gelato Flavor Ingredients
Elenka- Howard Gordy
871 Shepard Ave
Brooklyn, NY 11208
  Elenka flavorings

PreGel USA
8700 Red Oak Blvd. #A
Charlotte, NC 28217
704-333--6804
  Gelato flavorings

Belizio Fine Foods- Fabbri
57-01 49th Place
Maspeth, NY 11378
718-764-8311
  Gelato flavorings

Inter-Continental Imports
149 Louis Street
Newington, CT 06111
800-424-4221
  Gelato flavorings

Stabilizers
Continental Custom Ingredients
246 West Roosevelt Road
West Chicago, IL 60185
800-323-9489
  Stabilizers

Germantown USA
200 Lawrence Drive
West Chester, PA 19380
800-345-8509
  Stabilizers

Hercules Inc.
500 Hercules Road
Wilmington, DE 19808
302-594-4578/
  Stabilizers

Ice Cream Cake Production
Bakery Crafts
9300 Allen Road
West Chester, OH 45069
800-543-1673
  Ice cream cake supplies

Inline Plastics
42 Canal Street
Shelton, CT 06484
800-826-5567
  Ice cream cake packaging

Kopycake Enterprises
3701 W. 240th Street
Torrance, CA 90505
800-999-5253
  Cake decorating equipment

Cold Molds
985 Carrington Rd.
Cutchogue, NY 11935
631-614—3648
  Cake pans, novelty molds

Lucks Food Decorating Company
3003 S. Pine Street
Tacoma, WA 98409
800-426-9778
  Cake decorating equipment & Edible
  Images

Wilton Industries
2240 West 75th Street
Woodridge, IL 60517
708-963-7100
  Ice cream cake equipment and
  supplies

Parrish's
225 W. 146th St.
Gardenia, CA 90248
800-736-8443
  Ice cream cake-making supplies

Rich's
1150 Niagara Street
Buffalo, NY 14213
800-45-RICHS
  Non-dairy whipped cream for ice
  cream cakes

Ice Cream Cones
CoBatCo Inc.
1327 NE Adams Street
Peoria, Illinois 61603
309-676-2663
  Waffle cone batter and machines

Cream Cone
P.O. Box 1819
Columbus, Ohio 43216
614-294-4931
  Waffle, sugar, and wafer cones: all
sizes and varieties

Derby Cone Company, Inc.
2208 Plantside Drive
Louisville, KY 40206
502-491-1220
  Ice cream cones

Keebler Foodservice
One Hollow Tree Lane
Elmhurst, Illinois 60126
897-511-5777
  Waffle, sugar, and wafer cones: all
  sizes and varieties

Matt's Supreme Cones
125 Byrd St.
Orange, VA 22960
800-888-2377
  Ice cream cones

Novelty Cone Company
807 Sherman Avenue
Pennsauken, New Jersey 08110
609-665-9525
  Wafer and cake cones

PDI Cone Company
69 Leddy St.
Buffalo, NY 14210
716-825-8750
  Ice cream cones and sprinkles

The Cone Guys
PO Box 17614
Philadelphia, PA 19135
888-266-3489
  Flavored ice cream cones

Mixes: Ice Cream, Frozen Yogurt, Soft-Serve, and Nondairy
AE Farms
2420 E. University Avenue
Des Moines, Iowa 50317
800-234-6455
  Ice cream mixes

Ice Cream Club
1580 High Ridge Rd
Boynton Beach, Fl 33426
800-535-7711
  Ice cream mix

Bison Foods
196 Scott Street
Buffalo, New York 14204
716-854-8400
  Soft-serve ice cream mixes

Colombo/General Mills
800-343-8240
  Soft-serve frozen yogurt mix

Fresco Famous Italian Ices
1337-1 Lincoln Road
Holbrook, NY 11741
  Italian ices, gelato, and ice cream

Greenwood Farms
Atlanta, GA
800-678-6166
  Ice cream mixes

Gise Creme Glace
6064 Corte Del Cedro
Carlsbad, CA 92009
800-448-4473
  Non-dairy frozen dessert shop

Kohler Mix Specialties
4041 Hwy. 61
White Bear Lake, MN 55110
800-231-1167
  Ice cream mixes

Welsh Farm
55 Fairview Avenue
Long Valley, New Jersey 07853
908-876-3131
  Hard ice cream mix

Packaging

Airlite Plastics
914 North 18th Street
Omaha, NE 68102
402-341-7300
  Plastic cups, all sizes and varieties

Anderson Packaging
PO Box 510
Oak Ridge, New Jersey 07438
201-697-8888
  Cup and aluminum seal packaging

Cardinal Packaging
1275 Ethan Ave.
Streetsboro, OH 44241
800-544-9573
  Plastic cup packaging

Douglas Stephans Plastics
22-36 Green Street
Paterson, NJ 07509
201-523-3030
  Plastic lids

Gelato Supply.Com
1025 Virginia Ave, NE
Atlanta, GA 30306
404-392-5115

Spartech/Gen Pak Canada
260 Rexdale Boulevard
Rexdale, Ontario M9W 1R2
Canada
800-387-7452
  Plastic containers

Plastican, Inc.
196 Industrial Rd.
Leominister, MA 01453
978-537-4911
  Ice cream 2 1/2 gallon plastic tubs

Polar Plastics
7132 Daniels Drive
Allentown, PA 18106
215-398-7400
  Plastic cups and spoons

Sealright Company
9201 Packaging Drive
Desoto, KS 66018
800-255-4243
  Paper cups, all sizes and varieties

Sweetheart Packaging
10100 Reisertown Road
Owings Mill, Maryland 21117
410-363-1111
  Paper and plastic cups and lids

Menu Boards
Colafranseco Associates
3408 N. Chase
Williamsburg, VA 23185
757-565-5076
  Menu boards, POP signage

Cow Tunes For Kids
PO Box 2445
Brentwood, TN 37024
877-269-8273
  Promotional ice cream CD's

WWW.IMAGEdeLIGHT.COM
847-288-9366
  Food photography

Mainstreet Menu Systems
1375 North Barker Road
Brookfield, Wisconsin 53005
800-782-6222
  Menu boards

Packaging and Storage Containers
Polar Tech Industries
415 E. Railroad Ave.
Genoa, IL 60135
800-423-2749
  Insulated boxes for shipping

Polyfoam Packers
2320 Foster Avenue
Wheeling, IL 60090
800-323-7442
  Insulated boxes for shipping

Buckhorn
55 West Techcenter Drive
Milford, OH 45150
800-543-4454
  Storage handling containers

ASSOCIATIONS
American Dairy Association
Dairy Management Inc.
10255 W. Higgins Rd.
Suite 900
Rosemont, IL 60018
847-803-2000

Dairy and Food Industries Supply
Assoc.
1451 Dolley Madison Blvd.
McClean, VA 22101
703-761-2600

Hazelnut Marketing Board
PO Box 23126
Portland, OR 97281
503-639-3118

Ice Cream University
12 Riverpointe Road
Hastings-On-Hudson, NY 10706
914-478-0610
  Annual Gelato Tour of Italy, books,
  seminars, and newsletters on batch
  freezer and ice cream cake
  production and retailing

International Ice Cream Association
1250 H Street NW Suite 900
Washington, D.C. 20005
202-737-4332
  Annual source book- The Latest
  Scoop

National Ice Cream & Yogurt Retailers
Association (NICRA)
1028 West Devon Ave
Elk Grove Village, IL 60007
800-847-8522

National Pecan Marketing Council
Knapp Hall
Louisiana State University
Baton Rouge, LA 70803
504-388-2222

267

National Soft Serve and Fast Food
Association
9614 Tomstown Road
Wayneboro, PA 17268
800-535-7748

New England Ice Cream Association
Po box 1677
Merrimack, NH 03054-1677
603-424-1410

Underwriters Laboratories
333 Pfingsten Road
Northbrook, IL 60062
847-272-8800
 UL approval for equipment

PRINTED INFORMATION
Batch Freezer News (Newsletter)
12 Riverpointe Road
Hastings-On-Hudson, NY 10706
914-478-0610

Ice Cream Cakes
12 Riverpointe Road
Hastings-On-Hudson, NY 10706
914-478-0610

Ice Cream and Frozen Desserts- A
Commercial Guide to Production and
Marketing
12 Riverpointe Road
Hastings-On-Hudson, NY 10706
914-478-0610

Ice Cream, Fifth Edition
Chapman & Hall
115 Fifth Avenue
New York, New York 10003
212-254-3232

Ice Cream Store News (Newsletter)
12 Riverpointe Road
Hastings-On-Hudson, NY 10706
914-478-0610

Dairy Field Magazine
Stagnito Publishing Company
1935 Shermer Road, Suite 100
Northbrook, IL 60062
708-205-5660

Dairy Foods Magazine
Cahners Publishing Company
200 Clearwater Drive
Oak Brook, IL 60523
303-470-4445

Food Production Management
2619 Maryland Ave.
Baltimore, MD 21218
410-467-3338

The National Dipper
1028 West Devon Ave
Elk Grove Village, IL 60007
800-847-8522

Correspondence Course 102: Ice
Cream Manufacture
The Pennsylvania State University
Department of Independent Living
128 AG-Mitchell Building
University Park, Pennsylvania 16802
814-865-7371
Frozen Desserts Magazine
45 West 34th Street, #600
New York, NY 10001
212-239-0855

Pastry Art & Design Magazine
45 West 34th Street, #600
New York, NY 10001
212-239-0855

Scandinavian Dairy Magazine
Frederiks Alle 22
DK-8000 Arhus C
Denmark
45-86-13-26-93

FLAVOR RECIPES

ICE CREAM

Amaretto, 164
Animal Crackers, 177
Apple Pie, 153
Apricot, 156
Apricot, Drunken, 156
Apricot Hazelnut, 156
Apricot Parisian, 156
Avocado, 181

Biscotti, 150
Banana Cookie, 175
Brie, 183

Cantaloupe, 159
Cantaloupe Drambuie, 159
Chocolate Amaretto, 172
Chocolate, Bittersweet, 169
Chocolate, Belgian, 170
Chocolate, Dulce de Leche, 174
Chocolate, Ginger, 173
Chocolate, Orange, 173
Chocolate Peanut Butter, 172
Chocolate, White, 171
Chocolate, White Macadamia, 174
Chocolate, White Rasp. Truffle, 170
Chocolate, Ghiradelli, 171
Cinnamon Bun, 151
Coconut Almond Joy, 161
Coffee Chip, 168
Coneheads, 179
Crème Caramel, 146

Dulce de Leche, 149
Dulce de Leche Extravaganza, 149
Dulce de Leche Banana Chunk, 149

Fire & Ice, 176

French Almond Nougat, 165
French Fries & Ketchup, 180
Fresh Ginger, 149

Funky Pretzel, 180

Gianduja, 166
Gianduja Caramel Fudge, 166
Grape Nut, 178
Gummy Bear, 177

Japanese Red Bean, 182
Jalapeno, 181
Jalapeno, Coconut, 182

Kulfi, 151
Kahlua Chip, 168

Lavender Fig, 160
Lemon Custard, 147
Lemon Pie, 147
Little Bity Critters, 179

Mango, 155
Mango Ginger, 155
Mango Hazelnut, 155
Mint Chip, 146
Mint Pattie, 152

Nutty Vanilla Chocolate Chip, 150

Oreo Cookie, 145

Papaya & Passion Fruit, 158
Parmesan, 183
Passion Fruit, 158
Passion Fruit Raspberry, 158
Peach, 157
Peach Amaretto, 157
Peach Ginger, 157
Pistachio, 164
Pistachio Halvah, 164
Plum Pudding, 160
Plum & Cinnamon, English, 161
Praline Almond, 165
Praline Chili, 163

Praline Caffe, 165
Prune Armagnac, 159

Raspberry Cheesecake, 154
Rock-N-Pop, 176
Rice Pudding, 148
Sleepless In Seattle, 167
Spumone Di Taormina, 162
Strawberry, 153
Strawberry Cheesecake, 154

Tutti-Fruitti, 162
Turtles, 178

Vanilla, 145
Vanilla, French, 144

White Gold, 152

SORBETS

Apple, Green Candied Ginger, 193
Apple Brandy, 191
Apple Cranberry, 192
Apricot, 194
Apricot Banana, 194
Apricot Cognac, 194

Banana Blueberry, 195
Banana Coconut Fudge, 196
Banana Raspberry (Tropical), 195

Chocolate, 207
Chocolate Banana, 209
Chocolate Coconut, 208
Chocolate Raspberry, 208
Chocolate Strawberry, 208
Claret, 196
Cranberry, 197

Espresso, 197
Grapefruit, 198
Grapefruit Campari, 198
Grapefruit, Mint, 198
Gianduja, 208
Jaeger Tea, 212
Jalapeno-Lime, 211

Kiwi, 199
Kiwi Strawberry, 199
Kiwi Lemon, 199

Mango, 200
Mango Coconut, 200
Mango Limon (Nieve De), 200
Margarita, 210
Margarita Mango, 210
Margarita Raspberry, 210

Orange, 202
Orange (Tequila Sunrise), 202
Orange, Blood, 202

Passion Fruit, 201
Passion Mango, 201
Pear, 203
Peach, Wine, 206
Peach, Wine Mango, 206
Prickly Pear, 204

Sorbet in Lemon Shells, 190
Strawberry, 205
Strawberry Banana, 205
Strawberry & Champagne, 205

Tomato & Basil, 212

ITALIAN WATER ICE

Basic Water Ice Recipe, 214
Banana, 216
Black Raspberry, 218
Bubble Gum, 215

Cherry, 216
Coconut Almond Joy, 217

Lemon, Old Fashioned, 214

Peach, 217
Strawberry, 218
Vanilla, 215
Vanilla Chip, 215
Vanilla Almond, 215

ITALIAN CREAM ICES

Basic Cream Ice Recipe, 219
Banana Cream Ice, 224
Banana Coconut Cream Ice, 221

Cha Cha Berries Cream Ice, 226
Chocolate Chocolate Cream, 227
Chocolate Almond Cream Ice, 227
Chocolate Mousse Cream Ice, 227
Coconut Almond Joy Cream Ice, 221
Cookies & Crème Cream Ice, 228
Cookies & Cream (Mint) Ice, 228
Cream-A-Lotta, 224
Creamsicle Cream Ice, 220

Dulce de Leche Cream Ice, 229

Lemon Cream Ice, 225

Peanut Butter Cream Ice, 223
Peanut Chocolate Cream Ice, 223
Peanut Coconut Joy Cream Ice, 221
Peanut Butter Cup Cream Ice, 223
Pina Colada Cream Ice, 226
Pina Banana Colada Cream Ice, 226
Pistachio Cream Ice, 222
Pistachio Chip Cream Ice, 222
Pistachio Kulfi Cream Ice, 222

Strawberry Cheesecake Cream, 225
Vanilla Chip Cream Ice, 220

ITALIAN GELATO

Apricot, 233
Apricot Chocolate, 233
Apricot Gingered, 233
Basic Gelato Mix Recipe, 231

Chocolate Apricot Chip, 237
Chocolate Lauretta, 247
Coconut, 249
Cookies & Crème, 241
Croccantino, 241

Di Mirtilli, 238
Fruitta Di Bosco, 233

Gianduja Biscotti Amore, 239

Lauretta, 238
Lemongrass, 239

Mandarino, 234
Malaga, 237
Mango Banana, 243
Mango Coconut, 243
Marron Glaces, 242
Marron Glaces (Chestnut), 242
Melone, 235

Nocciola, 236
Nocciola & Rum, 236
Nocciola, White Chocolate, 236

Ornage & Cardamon, 234

Pistachio, 240
Pistachio Chip, 240

Stracciatella, 241
Stracciatella (Mint), 241
Stracciatella Pistachio, 241

Vaniglia, 232
White Chocolate Gianduja, 236
White Chocolate Macadamia, 235
Zabaglione w/Strawberries, 242

ICE CREAM CAKES & PIES

Chocolate Chip Roll Cake, 249
Oreo Bomb Cake, 247
Tartufo, 250
The Basic Birthday Cake, 246
Valentine's Day Heart, 248
Basic Ice Cream Pie, 253
Mississippi Mud Pie, 254

DESSERT & BEVERAGE RECIPES

Sugar Free Monkey, 132
Sugar free Truffle, 132
Strawberry Blondie Float, 129

SMOOTHIES
FRUIT BASED
Singing The Blues On Blueberry Hill, 138

SORBET BASED
Blueberry Passion, 139
Mango Orange Passion, 138
Mocha Frappe, 139
Panama Slush, 139
Passion Fruit, 138
Peach Smash, 138
Pineapple Crush, 139
Smooth Chocolate Freeze, 138
Strawberry Banana Paradise, 138

ICE CREAM BASED
Apple Hummer, 139
Chocolate Cappuccino Supremo, 140
Derby Day, 140
Hawaii Fizz, 140
Mixed Oreo Berry, 140
Ra-Ma-Tazz, 139
Red Necktie, 140
Strawberry Paradise, 139

FROZEN YOGURT BASED
Blueberry Passion, 141
Cappuccino Quencher, 141
Capricorn Delight, 142
Chocolate Mousse, 141
Mango Mania Cream, 141
Peach, 141
Pineapple Delight, 141
Strawberry Rush, 142

BREAKFAST
Breakfast Blast, 142
Pear Yogurt Ginger, 142

EXOTIC HEALTH
All American, 142
Rose Garden, 142

SUBJECT INDEX

GREAT ICE CREAM PEOPLE

A SPECIAL THANK YOU TO THE FOLLOWING FOR SHARING
THEIR KNOWLEDGE OF ICE CREAM IN THIS BOOK

ARNIE'S PLACE
TOM ARNOLD
164 LOUDON ROAD
CONCORD, NH 03301
603-228-3225
Kahlua Chip, 168
Chocolate Peanut Butter Yogurt, 172

BAKED TO PERFECTION
ROBERT ELLENGER
91 MAIN STREET
PORT WASHINGTON, NY 11050
516-944-5642

DURANGO CREAMERY
MIKE AND ERIN SHINDELL
600 MAIN STREET
DURANGO, CO 81301
970-382-9278

G & D ICE CREAM
DARTINGTON HOUSE
55 LITTLE CLARNDON STREET
OXFORD, OX1 2HS, UK
01865-516652
White Gold, 152

HAAGEN-DAZS ICE CREAM SHOP
JERRY SIEGEL
8108 HAMPSON STREET
NEW ORLEANS, LA
504-861-2500

MOOTIME CREAMERY
DAVID SPATAFORE
1025 ORANGE AVENUE
CORONADO, CA 92118
619-522-6890
NIFTY FIFTIES

BOB MATEI
7060 GREEN HILL ROAD
PHILADELPHIA, PA 19151
215-477-1950

BILL LAMBERT
3940 43RD STREET
DES MOINES, IOWA 50310
515-279-7245

SCREAMIN MIMI'S
MARALINE OLSON
6902 SEBASTOPOL AVE
SEBASTOPOL, CALIFORNIA 95472
707-823-5902
Fresh Ginger Ice Cream, 149
Jalapeno-Lime Sorbet, 211

THE GRATEFUL BEAN CAFÉ
PETE SCHAFFER
1039 N. WALKER
OKLAHOMA CITY, OK 73102
405-236-3503
Vanilla Ice Cream, 145
Strawberry Ice Cream, 153

THE MALT SHOP
2516 LYNDALE AVE. SOUTH
MINNEAPOLIS, MN
612-872-1326

LEMON QUENCH
GARY HUNTER
400-B CLINTON ROAD
CHARLOTTE, NC 28217
704-525-8927

DO 80206

le Ice Cream, 167
bet, 204

ICE CREAM
:ST
IS AVE.
ESTER, NY 10573
9469
Caramel Ice Cream, 146
Bomb Ice Cream Cake, 247

AN'S
OAN KAMENSTEIN
12 CLEMATIS STREET
WEST PALM BEACH, FL 33401
561-833-3335

SYLVAN BEACH CAFÉ
7 WEST PRESTON STREET
BALTIMORE, MARYLAND 21201
410-685-5752
Coconut Almond Chip Ice Cream, 161
Coffee Chip Ice Cream, 168

CLASSIC CREAMERY
RON KOTLOFF
22912 PACIFIC PARK DRIVE
ALISO VIEJO, CALIFORNIA 92656
949-831-2672
Apple Pie Ice Cream, 153
Ghiraradelli Double Dutch, 171

WHITEY'S
JEFF & JON TUNBERG
2525 41ST STREET
MOLINE, IL 61265
309-762-2175

THE PIAZZA
NORM AND PAT LAPALME
149 MAIN STREET
KEENE, NEW HAMPSHIRE
603-352-5133

TUCKER'S ICE CREAM
KATE PRYOR & DAVID LEE
1349 PARK STREET
ALAMEDA, CALIFORNIA 94501
510-522-4960
Lemon Pie Ice Cream, 147

DENISE'S HOMEMADE ICE CREAM
STAN ZAFRAN
4 A COLLEGE AVENUE
SOMMERVILLE, MA 02144
617-628-2764.
Oreo Cookie Ice Cream, 145
Mint Chip Ice Cream, 146

FRESCO FAMOUS ITALIAN ICES
MARC & TONY BOCCACCIO
502 LARKFIELD ROAD
EAST NORTHPORT, NY 11731
631-368-4730
Old Fashioned Lemon Ice, 214
Vanilla Italian Water Ice, 215
Vanilla Chip Italian Water Ice, 215
Vanilla Almond Water Ice, 215

THE INSIDE SCOOP
CHRIS FARREL
926 WHITE PLAINS ROAD
TRUMBULL, CT 06611
203-459-4780
Chocolate Raspberry Ice Cream, 170
Pistachio Ice Cream, 164

G.G. GELATI
JOHN GAROFALO
705 CORYDON AVENUE
WINNEPEG, MB R3M OW4
CANADA
453-5710